Beyond Photoshop

Advanced Techniques Integrating Photoshop with Illustrator, Poser, Painter, Cinema 4D, and ZBrush

Cover model photo: *Vincent Lions*
Cover model: *Josie Lee*
Hair and makeup: *Angela Veel*
Author photo: *Vincent Lions*

Beyond Photoshop

Advanced Techniques Integrating Photoshop with Illustrator, Poser, Painter, Cinema 4D, and ZBrush

Derek Lea

AMSTERDAM • BOSTON • HEIDELBERG • LONDON • NEW YORK • OXFORD • PARIS
SAN DIEGO • SAN FRANCISCO • SINGAPORE • SYDNEY • TOKYO
Focal press is an imprint of Elsevier

Focal Press is an imprint of Elsevier
30 Corporate Drive, Suite 400, Burlington, MA 01803, USA
Linacre House, Jordan Hill, Oxford OX2 8DP, UK

Library of Congress Cataloging-in-Publication Data
Application submitted

British Library Cataloguing-in-Publication Data
A catalogue record for this book is available from the British Library.

ISBN: 978-0-240-81190-1

For information on all Focal Press publications
visit our website at www.elsevierdirect.com

Typeset by MPS Limited, a Macmillan Company, Chennai, India
www.macmillansolutions.com

10 11 12 13 14   5 4 3 2 1

Printed in the United States of America

For my wife, Janet. I would be absolutely lost without you.

Contents

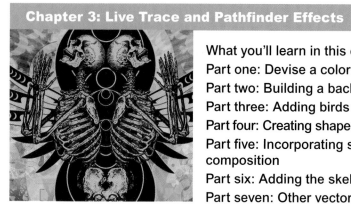

Chapter 7: Sculpting Raw Materials — 299

Foreword

Foreword by Issac Stolzenbach, former Managing Editor, *Photoshop User* magazine; current Managing Editor of *Layers*: The How-to Magazine For Everything Adobe.

The quintessential amalgamation of inspirational and instructional

This ambitious book you hold in your hands is exactly the book that you or I would've written had we the talent, training, time—and fewer excuses—as Professor Derek Lea. Thankfully, Derek didn't take the excuse-laden path of least resistance. Instead, he undertook the arduous challenge of mastering the hottest software in the creative market. He studied the interoperability of these programs, plucking out the most useful bits of each experience, and incorporated them into his own workflow, which resulted in a bounty of stunning artwork. He kept notes along the way and vetted the resulting techniques by sharing them with the creative communities behind such award-winning publications as *Photoshop User*, *Computer Arts* and *Computer Arts Projects*, *Digital Camera*, *.net*, *Advanced Photoshop*, and *Digital Creative Arts* magazines.

Sounds good, right? But is this book for *you*. Go ahead and flip through the pages and see if the artwork speaks to you, then come on back here and I'll tell you why this book is probably for you, and why it's an essential next step in Derek's oeuvre.

Welcome back! That's some killer artwork, right? This guy's got an eye for aesthetics—and he knows how to communicate that vision too—you'll actually *learn* how to do that stuff. What? Yeah, sure thing, go head up to the checkout counter, we'll chat more when you get this home.

Derek has been a professional digital artist for more than a decade and he learned how to use creative software the same way most of us do (for the most part): we poke around in Photoshop, exploring the tools and menu items, then, once we're overwhelmed from being unable to reach our artistic vision due to the technical complexity of the software, we head up to the bookstore or library and seek out work from someone who is both inspired and inspiring—an all too rare combination. We may or may not grab the book based on the images we see within or perhaps the random, gonzoesque wordfreak blathering in the foreword persuades us to make the purchase. Either way, if we do end up taking the book home, when we get it home and take a closer look, we find that the author is either a talented artist or a gifted teacher—it's the rarest Pokémon to find both powers in the same creature—and we find this time and time again.

The techniques are awesome, but the artist doesn't aptly communicate everything they're doing, so the book gets chucked into the "inspirational" pile. Or the techniques are written in a way that resonates in our heads and our brains sop up the information like a biscuit on that last splash of Sunday gravy: we finally learn those shortcuts; we discover where to go to make our own shortcuts; and—after gaining a little dexterity in our fingers—we realize that using them is indeed a faster way to work. That sort of book does teach us something, but our artwork will still suck because the author was an educator, not an artist. The book's images were picked up from a stock photography agency and the end results are meekly presented as being "…for demonstration purposes only."

I've edited Derek's work for a number of years. It's been a pleasure because the guy really gets it—the art, the people, the culture, the software—with the digital arts community. What was really compelling about his work was that it got us up from our desks and engaged with the world around us. He had us dusting off old scanners, blow-drying fax paper, and cleaning out the gutters…errr wait, that was the wife. Anyway, it was sneaky, getting us out of our chairs to go collect a few leaves, but the end result was glorious—we discovered that there is a whole world out there just dying to be incorporated into our designs by our own hand. It sounds novel now, but after living day-in-and-day-out in the digital darkroom, your eyes will go from squinting like a prisoner in Plato's cave to wide-eyed revelation when exposed to the light of this sort of knowledge.

When Derek asked me to write the foreword to his next book, I was flattered and compelled. Flattered because the guy has been such an inspirational educator to me and to many of the folks with whom I've worked. Compelled because if ever a forthright handful of words need be said about one educator among the sea of digital arts instructors out there, it's Derek Lea.

He's inspiring to me because he works in much the same way I do: Crank up the tunes, let the eyes roll back and allow the mind's eye—floating in that personal, ethereal realm between magic and matter; between id and ego; between life and death—to take control, and create. Create! *Create!* He's an inspiration to the people I work with because his techniques are not only fresh, but they don't get the reader all tangled up in the overly technical tomfoolery that some use to baffle the reader with their "wisdom" rather than propel them into manifesting beauty through simplicity.

Beyond the artwork, beyond the talent, beyond the book you have in your hands, rests the reason why I've gathered these few words of praise—the man. One of the main things I've always admired about Derek—beyond all that aforementioned genius—is the fact that he's the embodiment of WYSIWYG. Simply put, Derek is a what-you-see-is-what-you-get type of guy. He doesn't put on airs pretending to be something he's not; he doesn't say that he's going to do something and not do it; and his grace rests in his candor. Just ask him about how he obtained his first copy of Photoshop and he'll bluntly relay that it was acquired through a five-finger discount—plucked from a new scanner box and plopped into an old jacket pocket—while working at a soul-sucking job as a clothing company's designer. (Hey, they needed the *scanner*, not the throwaway copy of Photoshop 2.5 that came with it, right?)

Now, thankfully, Derek has reached what many consider the summit of any digital art instructor's career: Imparting knowledge to the masses in the most rewarding and prolific way as a tenure-track digital arts professor at Centennial College in Toronto, Ontario, Canada.

The next time you're in your office, when you glance over at that empty space between the inspirational shelf and the educational shelf, if you find yourself murmuring curses about there being nothing that's inspirationally educational or educationally inspirational—and you didn't leave with this book, you and I both know, until the talent flows and the excuses ebb: You'll have no one to blame for that empty space on your self but yourself.

All the best to you and yours

–Issac Stolzenbach

Acknowledgments

This was a very difficult book to write. I underestimated the scope of the project. I underestimated the learning curve to master each program, and I underestimated the time it would take to pull it all together. I also underestimated how it would impact the lives of those around me. First and foremost, I must thank my wife, Janet. She always supports me in these projects, no matter how hard it is on her; she always recognizes the importance, tells me to go for it, and makes sure that I get it done. We have two young children: Charlotte and Isabella. Caring for young children is no easy task at the best of times, and when Dad is writing a book on top of everything else, it demands even more from Mom. So, once again: Thank you, Janet. Janet and I are also very fortunate to have supportive siblings and families. A huge thanks goes out to my sister Lisa and Janet's sister Lesley as well as brother-in-law Tom, who were always there to volunteer to help out. The kids love you all anyway, but your support during this time was huge. Oh, and thanks for all the chicken wings and quiche.

Thanks to Valerie Geary, my commissioning editor at Focal Press. She was cool as ice every time I called her with a meltdown, saying that there was no way that I could turn in the book on time (this happened a lot). However, in some ways it seems appropriate because this whole thing began as her idea. Also thanks to Carlin Reagan at Focal Press, who, alongside Valerie, bore the brunt of said meltdowns and helped out along the way. You guys are great. Seriously, I can't imagine working with anyone else.

Mike Shaw is apparently a sucker for punishment. This senior quality engineer from Adobe should have learned his lesson during his involvement with the first two editions of *Creative Photoshop*, but thankfully he did not. Mike is the guy who goes through all the details in the manuscript in microscopic detail and makes sure it all works out perfectly. This is no easy task, yet he somehow does it really fast. Thanks, Mike.

Patrick Goski is a dreadlocked Canadian 3D overlord. He was the go-to guy for all things ZBrush and Cinema 4D. If it weren't for him, I seriously don't know what I would have done with about 100 pages of this book. His input was essential, and I am thankful for his brilliance, easygoing nature, and meticulous attention to detail. Thanks, Patrick.

Issac Stolzenbach was the persuasive managing editor who convinced me to do a regular column in *Photoshop User* magazine. I really thought I was finished with magazines after I stopped contributing to *Computer Arts*, but Issac made it fun again. Issac has a writing style and wit about him that made him my first choice to write the Foreword for this book. Thankfully, he agreed. If more editors were as great to work with as Issac,

I would probably still be doing a lot more magazine work, but he is a rarity. Any title will be lucky to have him on board.

Thanks to all the companies (and people working at those companies) that supplied software and support for the contents of this book. I think the importance of what you do is evident in this book, but certainly not limited to it. Thanks for making some of the best creative tools on the planet.

And finally, thanks to you, the readers. If you guys weren't there in the forums, on the Facebook page, reading my other books and magazine articles, or simply providing feedback on my artwork, none of this would happen. I get a lot of e-mail from you, and if you don't get a reply, please don't be insulted or think it isn't appreciated; that is not the case. I am just one guy who tries to do too many things all the time. At the end of the day, there are not enough hours to respond to every message. I do my best, but time always seems to escape me at some point.

Introduction

Putting things together

My discovery of Photoshop came after I worked as a graphic designer and art director for a few years. Back then, in the pre-desktop publishing days, we learned to put things together from different sources. Photostats, illustrations, and typesetting all got pasted onto boards to create press-ready artwork. I think that the idea of putting stuff together is something that has always stuck with me, regardless of what it is exactly that I'm using or where it came from.

People are often surprised to hear me, as a digital artist, say that the computer is place to create finished ideas, not to develop one or brainstorm. But for me that is true. The computer introduces constraints in terms of interaction and reduces the sense of freedom that is essential to effectively develop ideas, because you must also focus on the process of interacting with the machine to a degree that hinders. I have been a witness to, and actively involved in, the advent of the desktop computer as an essential tool for artists. One thing that I've noticed over the years is that the computer itself becomes something other than a tool; for many it becomes a comfort zone. More specifically, the actual software that artists master can often become a comfort zone. And when engrossed in a comfort zone, innovation and fresh ideas eventually dissipate. The process of creation within a comfort zone becomes routine, and the resulting work is uninspired. The fun gets sucked out of it, and it shows.

When I first started to use Photoshop, I was more than intrigued. I was hooked. I had found my medium as an artist. But after a while, I realized that being comfortable with the program was limiting in terms of staying fresh and developing new ideas. I began to explore other programs. I had been working with Illustrator prior to Photoshop and started bringing the two programs together to produce finished compositions. At the same time, I was very interested in Painter and a variety of 3D applications as they began to appear. I started playing around in different programs and was very excited to break out of my comfort zone. My work was becoming more experimental and inspired, and I was having much more fun with it. Then I noticed a common denominator. It was Photoshop.

Even though I was spending considerable time in other programs, I was always bouncing in and out of Photoshop. For 3D applications, I would make backgrounds in Photoshop ahead of time to align elements or to ensure perfect angles. Midway through the 3D process, I would find myself back in Photoshop, creating textures and displacement maps. Then, at the end of the 3D process, I would find myself opening the finished renderings in Photoshop, adjusting them, and using them to create something new once again. This process was not limited to 3D applications; it also proved true when I combined Photoshop with other programs such as Illustrator or Painter. Photoshop becomes the cornerstone application when working this way; it is essential at many points in the process. However, take note that this process of leaving Photoshop snaps you out of the Photoshop-only induced comfort zone, injecting some excitement into the tried-and-true process of putting things together.

Why write an entire book about this?

In the first edition of my previous book, *Creative Photoshop*, the last section contained a few chapters on the subject of using Photoshop with other programs. The general feeling was that although this discussion was interesting, it was out of place among the rest of the content and did not have enough pages allocated to it to address it properly. So, when I wrote the second edition of *Creative Photoshop*, I took that material out and replaced it with other content. It was Valerie Geary at Focal Press who suggested that the content that I removed was the beginning of another, completely different book. She was right. This book was quite a challenge to write, but now you have a few hundred pages on the topic at your disposal. Doing it in a smaller way would not do the subject justice. Trust me on this. I think the next edition will be even bigger.

Why Illustrator, Cinema 4D, Painter, Poser, and ZBrush?

If you are not determined or do not have much of an attention span, you might as well put this book down now. The content of each chapter is comprehensive and involved. That is because doing it any other way would sell you short. Every application used here is powerful and deserves a fair amount of depth when it comes to exploration and explanation. Each program is unique and, in my opinion, the best of its kind.

Illustrator is Photoshop's soul mate. They have played well together for many, many years, and they are constantly getting better at it. Most designers and illustrators use both applications daily. I decided that it was my duty to devote a substantial amount of space to doing extremely diverse and cool things by combining them. Hopefully I have introduced one or two ideas that you have never thought of before.

There is nothing else out there like Painter, so it was an obvious choice for the book. It is the only application in its class, as far as I'm concerned. In early versions of the program, I used it more or less on its own. However, these days it is built to work with Photoshop. Bouncing files back and forth is effortless, and there is a wonderful Photoshop familiarity about Painter's user interface.

ZBrush is another truly astounding piece of software. When I first caught wind of it, I figured that what I'd heard had to be lies. I was wrong. ZBrush delivers. This intuitive 3D sculpting program is one of a kind. If you have never explored it before, you are in for a treat. It takes the arduous process of working with 3D out of the equation via intuitive user interaction. Working with it really is like drawing or painting in 3D space.

Deciding on Cinema 4D was more of a challenge. This is not due to any shortcomings in the program, because I have found none. It is due to the fact that there are a lot of 3D programs out there, and I had to consider them all before settling on Cinema 4D. It is not the cheapest program out there, nor is it the most expensive. However, what I have found is that it is the easiest to learn in its class. And when I talk about its class, I am talking about powerful features, flexibility, modular architecture, and fantastic user interaction. I have worked with a number of 3D applications over the years, but I am sold on the fact that if you are a serious artist looking to get into the world of 3D and do something substantial, Cinema 4D is what you need. Also, its power runs deep, and you will likely never find a limitation to what you can create as you begin to master its various tools, features, and functions.

Poser was an obvious choice for me. When I think of 3D figures, I think of Poser. I have been using it since version 1.0 and am simply amazed at what it can create in terms of figures these days. And, like all the aforementioned programs, it is like a fine wine that simply becomes better with each incarnation.

Beginner, intermediate, or advanced?

I have always had a problem with the way that one's level of skill or capability as a digital artist has been limited to one of only three words. Obviously there are more than three variations in experience or mastery from user to user. However, these words are so ingrained in the collective subconscious that I find I must, at some point, address this topic by using them so people know what the hell I'm talking about.

Chances are, if you picked up this book one of the first things you wondered was whether or not you were capable of working through the material or whether you would be bored with it due to simplicity. I will do my best to set the record straight here. As a Photoshop user, I would say that at the very least you should consider yourself an intermediate user to effectively use this book. There is simply no room for me to tell you what a layer is or where to find the Brush tool or simple things like that. If you know your way around the program, you'll do just fine. That being said, advanced users will not find it so rudimentary that they will be bored. There is a hell of a lot going on in here.

Now, when it comes to the other programs, I have tried to work from the standpoint that the reader is a beginner. There is a good chance that you are using these other programs for the first time, so I instruct you in that way. I'll tell you a bit more about where things are or include more navigational screen grabs to help you around the interface. You can work your way through this book just fine, without ever having opened a different application than Photoshop. However, when it comes to Illustrator, I am assuming some knowledge pre-exists due to the fact that you are an intermediate Photoshop user. There are similarities between certain tools and the general interface of both programs, so you won't get as much handholding when it comes to Illustrator.

Every program used in this book comes with a Help menu function of some sort built into it. If you get stuck, don't hesitate to use it. After you've figured out what the holdback is and remedied it, continue to follow along where you left off.

Which version of which program do you need?

I wrote this book with core features, principles, and workflow methods in mind, and that pertains to everything, including Photoshop. I have never been an advocate of using the latest bells and whistles just because they're new. At the end of it all, you want to learn how to get the most out of each program, to help you realize your vision as an artist. Although I was using the most recent versions of each program at the time of writing, what I do from chapter to chapter is not necessarily version specific. If you are using downright archaic versions of programs, you might run into problems. But if you are remotely current on the version you're using, you should be able to make your way through with ease.

Do you have to buy all the programs to get through this book?

Absolutely not. As a matter of fact, I was very careful to select programs that have a demo version available for download. Every program used in the book has a trial version that can be downloaded from each company's Website. You will need to purchase nothing. Website links are provided in the opening spread for each chapter. Also, if you want to use just Photoshop, that is a possibility, too. If you are using Photoshop and nothing else, each chapter has a series of tips that will guide you through the process, and there are downloadable project files that will provide the assets created in other programs, so you can focus on the Photoshop-only portions. In most cases, this will get you to the finished stage. The only real exception is the Painter chapter. That particular chapter finishes off in Painter, so you won't wrap up in Photoshop like the other chapters. To remedy this for those of you using Photoshop only, I have included a layered file of the image I created for your perusal.

How to use this book

Each chapter in this book is a stand-alone project. One chapter does not lead into the next. You can literally open the book and start with any chapter that interests you. I have decided to follow the format

I used previously in *Creative Photoshop*. Each chapter begins with an inspirational image, and then a highly detailed, step-by-step walkthrough carries you through the process of how it was created. All the files you'll need to create each image are included in the downloadable project files for that chapter at www.beyondphotoshopthebook.com. At the end of each chapter, you'll not only create something compelling—you'll walk away with the knowhow required to apply these methods to work of your own. That is the real goal here: to inspire you as well as inform you, while at the same time creating something that is visually compelling.

Using a pressure-sensitive tablet

If you purchase one piece of equipment as a digital artist, make sure it is a pressure-sensitive tablet and stylus. Seriously, drawing and painting with a mouse are like entering a perpetual fight against your computer. For your own sake, buy a tablet. It doesn't have to be large or fancy, it just needs to be something more intuitive than a mouse. To prove my point, I used a Wacom Bamboo tablet for this entire book. It is small, limited, and inexpensive, but it does the job.

Further, I did not explore any pressure-sensitivity settings in Photoshop or other programs other than defaults. The point I'm trying to make is that success is about interacting with your machine in a natural way, and in my experience, getting a tablet is the best way to achieve this goal. If you want something larger or you want to explore pressure sensitivity, tilt, rotation, and so on, go ahead and do so. I just want you to know that using a tablet can be as simple as plugging it in and installing a driver, then forgetting about it—basking in the intuitive feel of it all as you begin to use it right away. Some chapters in this book will be possible to get through without a tablet: mainly the Illustrator, Poser, and Cinema 4D chapters. However, when it comes to using Painter and ZBrush, not using a tablet will almost certainly result in total frustration.

Expert tips

In addition to step-by-step instruction and inspirational imagery, you'll find hundreds of expert tips scattered throughout this book. Some of the tips pertain to the instructions on a particular page, but many are additional hints and pieces of advice, which will prove useful for almost anything you set out to do. Feel free to flip around the book and examine different tips, just as you would randomly flip from chapter to chapter. Tips are divided into five categories, represented by these icons:

Shortcuts
These time-saving tips will shave hours off your time spent working. Whether a keyboard command or a quicker way of doing something, these tips will allow you to spend more time creating rather than spending all your time executing certain tasks the long way.

Info
These tips contain useful tidbits and extra information that might not be addressed in the step-by-step instructions in each chapter. Or additional, more detailed information is provided to accompany a specific stage in the process.

Download files
These tips point you toward the specific files required to follow along. All project files are available for download in the project files section of the *Beyond Photoshop* Website.

Caution
Be extremely careful when you see this tip. You are being warned of potential pitfalls and must carefully pay attention to prevent things from going horribly wrong.

Creative tips
Creative tips provide valuable hints and advice regarding the artistic process of creating with Photoshop. These touch on everything from unconventional tool usage within Photoshop itself to hints on how to extract resource materials from the physical world surrounding you.

Become part of the *Beyond Photoshop* community

Your exploration into combining Photoshop with other programs does not end with this book. Visit the *Beyond Photoshop* Website and explore the user forum. Share knowledge with and ask questions of other readers. Be sure to post your finished images in the user forum for everyone else to see. Submit the works you've created by following the chapters here, or post your own work, showcasing your new skills. Be sure to check it out.

Join the *Beyond Photoshop* community at www.beyondphotoshopthebook.com.

Chapter 1

Sharp Edges and Painterly Blends

Combining Illustrator with Photoshop

Photoshop contains some excellent vector tools and features. But when it comes to creating artwork, experienced digital artists, illustrators, and designers rarely limit themselves to a single software application. It is no secret that when it comes to drawing with vectors, there is no better choice than Adobe Illustrator. Illustrator has been the industry-standard vector art tool for as long as I can remember. I personally have been using it as an integral part of my digital toolset since 1991.

The features and functions within Illustrator are unparalleled indeed, but what do you do when you want all the superb vector creation possibilities offered within Illustrator, yet you also want the superb paint tool features in Photoshop? The answer is simple: You combine the two applications. And believe it or not, when it comes to creating a stunning Art Noveau masterpiece like the one you see here, you simply need to copy and paste. To put it simply: Photoshop and Illustrator play very well together.

In this chapter, we'll explore the advantages of bringing existing vector art from Illustrator into Photoshop and using it as vector building blocks to create the piece you see here. More specifically, we'll be pasting vector art into Photoshop, creating shape layers and paths as the Illustrator data makes its way into Photoshop. We'll use paths to create selection borders, and we'll duplicate and edit shape layers to suit a variety of purposes. Once the vectors are safely in place, we can employ Photoshop's marvelous paint and composition tools, resulting in a nostalgic piece of art that is a combination of both sharp vectors and soft painted elements.

Versions	**Requirements and Recommendations**
Photoshop CS4 Illustrator CS4	In addition to Photoshop, you'll need a copy of Illustrator. If you don't have a copy of Illustrator, you can download a trial version from www.adobe.com.

What you'll learn in this chapter

Creative Techniques and Working Methods

Constructing rather than outlining

The artwork in this illustration relies heavily on prominent outlines. Generally, when I witness inexperienced users of Illustrator attempting to create artwork in a similar style, they rely on stroke attributes to create the outline in the image. An unfortunate result of this method is that there is little or no expressive quality in the line-work. What makes line-work expressive in the context of an illustration is the variation in thickness and the way the ends of each line taper, are sharp, or are rounded. Granted, there are options within the Stroke palette that allow you to change the endpoints of the line; but again, like the uniform thickness of the stroke, those just aren't expressive enough. The best way to achieve the desired expressive quality is to pay attention to the sketch.

When we draw, something intuitive happens, and it becomes effortless or even a subconscious act to create expressive line-work. Within software it is a different story. We need to focus on preserving the innate, expressive quality of our drawing as we create the finished product. This goal cannot be achieved by using stroke attributes but by creating each element manually with the Pen tool. However, there is more to it than simple mastery over the Pen tool. There is a logical method of construction, which involves creating an exterior shape first. The next step is to subtract an interior. This will give you your expressive outline. After that, details are created as closed shapes, and the result is unified. The Pathfinder palette plays a central role in this systematic drawing process.

Deconstructing and inverting

When you paste your illustrated outlines into Photoshop, they will serve another purpose. By working with duplicates of the shapes, you will learn how to remove the outer regions, thus inverting the appearance of the fill. This might sound confusing, but it is a simple process that we'll go through repeatedly. It allows you to use your illustrations not only as outlines but also for creating instant solid color fills on separate layers.

Tools, Features, and Functions

Template layers

These Illustrator layers will allow you to fade the opacity of your sketch so that you can trace over it without visual distraction. Also, and perhaps more important, the imagery on the Template layer will remain visible in both Preview and Outline modes.

Outline Stroke

This nifty feature allows you to convert Illustrator's stroke attribute to an actual, editable vector object. This is helpful when you're pasting something into Photoshop. Not only do you preserve the stroke, but by converting it to an object, you can delete the exterior path on your resulting shape layer to invert the appearance as well.

An intricate illustration like this one requires quite a bit of prior planning. There is no better start than putting pencil to paper and sketching out those ideas. Here the main content is more or less worked out. Her face is looking good, but everything else requires some more refining.

Because the face itself was working already, I simply refined the other elements in this drawing. Don't fret because there is no face shown here; we'll make a composite template soon by combing the two drawings in Photoshop.

It is always a good idea to keep the components separate, even at the drawing stage. This allows you to digitally refine each component separately, affording you some flexibility when it comes time to assemble the finished composition.

PART ONE: Preparing sketches

1 Open the *sketch-1.jpg* file in Photoshop. Then open the *sketch-2.jpg* file. Use the Move tool to drag the image from the *sketch-2.jpg* file into the *sketch1.jpg* file as a new layer. Reduce the opacity of the layer so that you see the underlying layer. Use the underlying layer as a guide to position the top layer as accurately as possible. The important thing to concentrate on at this point is lining up her facial features within the outline of her face.

 Project files

All the files needed to follow along with this chapter and create the featured image are available for download on the accompanying Website, in the project files section. Visit www.beyondphotoshopthebook.com.

2 When you're satisfied with the position of the top layer, click the Add Layer Mask button at the bottom of the Layers palette to mask the layer. Ensure that the new mask is targeted in the Layers palette and select the Brush tool. In the Brushes palette, select a soft, round preset and disable any shape dynamics that are active. Your foreground color should be set to black at this point; if it isn't, press the X key to set it. Paint over her face area within the mask to reveal the underlying face. When you're satisfied with the result, return the opacity of the layer to 100%.

 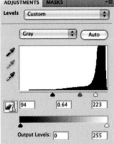

3 Click the Create New Fill or Adjustment Layer button at the bottom of the Layers palette and select the Levels option from the menu to create a new Levels adjustment layer. In the Adjustments palette, drag the left and right input level sliders inward. Drag the left slider over a little further, and then drag the middle slider to the right a little. Basically, our goal is to create a sense of clarity in the image. Don't worry if there are still some unwanted artifacts; we'll simply use this as a template in Illustrator. Save the file as *face template.psd*.

Repeat the process

Perform similar adjustments to the two remaining sketches, creating a series of clear templates for Illustrator.

1 Now open the *sketch-3.jpg* file. Press Control-L (PC)/Command-L (Mac) to perform a Levels adjustment. When the Levels dialog box appears, drag the left and right input level sliders inward to increase the contrast. Adjust the midtones slider as necessary to minimize the midtones in the drawing.

2 Save the file as *words template.psd*. Then open the *sketch-4.psd* file. You can tell just by looking at the image that you'll need to increase the contrast overall to create a clear template to trace over in Illustrator. Press Control-L (PC)/Command-L (Mac) to open the Levels adjustment dialog box.

 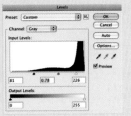

3 Perform a similar adjustment to the input level sliders as you've done previously. First, drag the left and right sliders inward, then adjust the midtones. When you're satisfied, save this file as *flower template.psd*.

PART TWO: Creating a pattern

 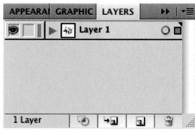

4 Launch Illustrator and create a new file. The size of the artboard is unimportant since we're simply going to paste the completed art into Photoshop. You can leave the artboard size set to the default setting. Don't worry about the document's color space, either. Choose File > Place from the menu and navigate to the *flower template.psd* file. Click the Place button. When the placed artwork appears, Shift-click and drag a corner point outward to increase the size so that you have a larger space to work within.

 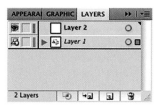

Illustrator files and workaround

If you want to follow along with this chapter yet you find the idea of creating art in Illustrator daunting, worry not. All the Illustrator files that are created throughout this chapter are included in the downloadable project files. So, if you don't feel like meticulously creating the vector components, they are there for your perusal should you decide to open them in Illustrator. And for those of you who don't want to so much as open Illustrator, we've included a file called *working.psd* that contains all the art pasted from Illustrator throughout this chapter. Following along using that file is simply a matter of enabling the visibility of the included shape layers and generating selections from included paths as necessary.

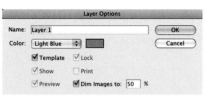

5 In the Layers palette, double-click the layer to open the Layer Options. In the Layer Options, enable the Template function. This will hide all other options except the Dim option. By default, the Dim setting will be set to 50%. Go ahead and leave it set as it is. If you ever want to change the dimness of the image, you can simply double-click the layer and reset the value. Select the Pen tool and then click the Fill swatch in the Toolbar. When the Color palette appears, set the fill to Black. Then click the Stroke swatch in the Tool Options bar and set it to None in the Color palette or by clicking the None option beneath it in the Toolbar. You cannot draw on a template layer, so click the Create New Layer button at the bottom of the Layers palette to create a layer that you can work on. Ensure that the new layer is targeted in the Layers palette.

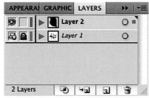

6 Use the Pen tool to begin tracing the outer left edge of the shape. Start at the bottom and work your way upward, clicking and dragging as you go, to create a path made of Bezier curves that follows the edge of the sketch. At any point you can alter a point or the handles of a curve by using the Direct Selection tool. After editing a point, continuing from the last point is as simple as clicking and dragging on the point and then creating the next point, and so on. You might find that because the object has a solid black fill attribute applied to it, it is hard to view the underlying sketch as you work. To remedy this problem, switch to Outline viewing mode by typing Control-Y (or Command-Y). You can switch back to Preview viewing mode at any time by typing the same command.

Tracing the sketch

Using the underlying template as your guide, begin to trace the contour, creating your first closed shape.

1 When you get to the top, continue along toward the right. When you get to the top-right point of the first flower, move down the right side of this flower, tracing it. Do not worry about the other flower just yet; simply keep creating your path down the right side of the first flower.

2 When you get to the part where the line on the sketch intersects with the other flower, continue to draw your path by moving to the left and then tracing the inner edge. Continue to trace the inner edge as it moves up and down and meanders along. Do not cross over any thick, black lines. Just trace this inner line all the way back to your original starting point.

3 When you get back to your original point, click it to close the shape. Now that the shape is closed, press Control-Y (or Command-Y) to preview it. While you are previewing it, perform any necessary tweaks to the shape with the Direct Selection tool, creating smooth curves.

7 Press Control-Y (or Command-Y) again to switch to outline view. You will have noticed by now that in some areas the design looks outlined, as it was intended. However, regions at the top are solid black. To remedy this situation, the next step is to use some shapes to, one by one, subtract from these regions. Use the same methods you employed previously to draw a closed shape around the inner region of the flower's petals at the top. When you're finished, select the new shape with the Selection tool, and then select the previous shape as well by Shift-clicking on it. While both shapes are selected, click the Minus Front button in the Shape Modes section of the Pathfinder palette. This will subtract the new shape from the previous shape. Press Control-Y (or Command-Y) to preview the result.

 ### Why doesn't it work?

If your Minus Front operations are producing unwanted or unpredictable results, you could be doing a few things incorrectly. First, ensure that you use the Selection tool rather than the Direct Selection tool. You need to select objects, not line segments or points. Also, ensure that the shape you're using as a tool resides above the shape you're subtracting from. You can check this in the hierarchy of the Layers palette. Finally, subtract only one shape at a time. If you select three shapes and perform the Minus Front operation, it will not work properly.

8 Press Control-Y (or Command-Y) to switch back to outline view. Draw another one of the shapes that you need to subtract from the solid black area. When you have closed the shape, select it and select the main shape with the selection tool. When both shapes are selected, perform the Minus Front operation in the pathfinder once again. Repeat this procedure as many times as required to stay true to the original drawing. Feel free to use the Direct Selection tool to modify points or Bezier handles at any point to refine the shape.

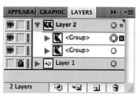

9 The only things missing from this side of the flower now are the small, black details. Carefully draw a series of closed objects to represent the missing details indicated by the underlying sketch. When you're finished, press Control-A (or Command-A) to select all the objects, and then press Control-G (or Command-G) to group them. Use the Selection tool to click the group and drag it to the right while holding down the Alt (PC)/Option (Mac) key to duplicate it.

10 While the duplicate group is selected, choose Object > Transform > Reflect from the menu. When the Reflect options appear, choose the Horizontal axis and click OK. After reflecting, Shift-drag to the right or left to adjust the horizontal position of the duplicate so that both groups are overlapping slightly in the middle. Now use the Pen tool to draw a closed shape that traces the outer edge of the central flower. Trace the entire flower and close the shape by clicking the original starting point when you've made your way back to it. It is important to bear in mind that we are using the sketch as a guide and, as is evident in the duplication procedure we just performed, alterations and/or improvements can be performed at your discretion. Never be afraid to clean up your art as you go.

 Alphonse Mucha

The work of the Czechoslovakian painter and illustrator Alphonse Mucha was my inspiration for this chapter's opening illustration. His work frequently featured women in flowing robes with lavish and flowing hair surrounded by flowers. I borrowed the style of my illustration's hair, as well as the hand-rendered typography and flowers, from his work. Mucha was one of a kind, and if you like the gentle, flowing quality of my illustration, you should investigate the work of the real master at www.muchafoundation.org.

11 Press Control-A (or Command-A) to select all the objects on the artboard, and then click the Unite button in the Shape Modes section of the Pathfinder palette. After the shapes are united, you'll notice that as a result a new group appears in the Layers palette. While the resulting shape is still selected, choose Object > Compound Path > Make from the menu. You'll see the group change to a compound shape in the Layers palette, but there will be no visible change on the artboard. Converting the group to a compound path is essential for future Pathfinder operations to work properly.

12 After you convert the group to a compound path, press Control-Y (or Command-Y) to switch to Outline mode if you're currently working in Preview mode. You'll need to switch to Outline mode to see the underlying sketch. Use the Pen tool to create a shape that that traces the inside of the flower petals outline as indicated by the sketch. Again, take your time and work your way around the entire interior of the petals only until you return to the starting point. Don't worry about the stem yet; we'll do that next. Return to the starting point to close the shape. Press Control-A (or Command-A) to select all, then click the Minus Front button in the Pathfinder palette. Switch back to Preview mode to view the result.

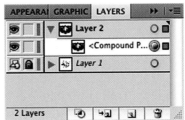

13 Again, you'll notice the result appear as a group in the Layers palette. While the new group is selected, choose Object > Compound Path > Make from the menu. After converting the group to a compound path, return to Outline mode so that you can clearly see the underlying sketch on the template layer. Use the Pen tool to create a closed shape that traces the interior of the stem. Toggle back and forth between Preview and Outline modes as necessary to both see what you're doing and to view the results accurately. When you have closed the shape, press Control-A (or Command-A) to select all, and then click the Minus Front button in the Pathfinder palette. Again, convert the resulting group to a compound path.

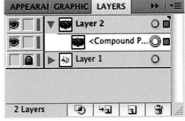

14 Use the Pen tool to create a series of closed shapes indicated by the petal details on the underlying sketch. When you're finished, select all and click the Unite button in the Pathfinder to unite all the shapes. While the new group of shapes is selected, convert it to a compound path, as you've done previously. When you're finished, disable the visibility of the template layer by clicking its Visibility icon in the left column of the Layers palette.

 Illustrator workaround 1

If you want to inspect or use the finished pattern file that was used here rather than create your own, it is included within the downloadable project files for this chapter. The name of the file is *pattern.ai*.

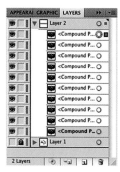

15 Zoom out considerably and use the Pan tool to position your artwork in the upper-left corner of the window. Use the Selection tool to select the compound path if it isn't already. Click it and then drag to the right while holding down the Alt (or Option) and Shift keys. This will create a duplicate that is vertically aligned with the original shape. Leave the duplicate shape selected and then press Control-D (or Command-D) to implement the Transform Again operation. This will create another instance of your shape, moving it the exact same distance as you did previously. Keep typing the same keyboard command until you've created a row of 10 shapes.

Finishing the pattern
Duplicate, offset, and duplicate until you complete the pattern in Illustrator.

1 After creating a horizontal row, press Control-A (or Command-A) to select them all. Then click any shape with the Selection tool and drag downward while holding down the Alt (or Option) key to create a duplicate row.

2 Hold down the Shift key as you drag the row to the right or left to offset it. Then press Control-A (or Command-A) to select all. After selecting everything, click any shape with the Selection tool and drag it downward while holding down the Alt (or Option) and Shift keys.

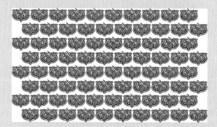

3 While the two duplicated rows are selected, press Control-D (or Command-D) twice. This will implement the Transform Again operation twice, resulting in eight rows. Press Control-A (or Command-A) to select all, and then press Control-C (or Command-C) to copy.

Illustrator preferences

To have the full gamut of options available to you when you paste your Illustrator art into Photoshop, it is necessary that your Illustrator preferences are set up properly before you copy. In the file handling and clipboard preferences, ensure that the PDF and AICB options are enabled. If these options are not enabled, your art will be automatically rasterized when you paste it into Photoshop.

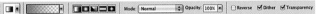

16 Launch Photoshop and create a new RGB file that is approximately 18 inches wide and 12 inches high. Set the background contents to white. Select the Gradient tool. In the Tool Options bar, choose the Linear gradient method and the Foreground to Transparent gradient preset. Click the foreground color swatch in the Toolbar to open the picker. Select a purple color from the picker and create a gradient on the background layer by clicking the left side of the canvas and dragging to the right.

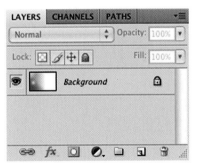

17 In the Tool Options bar, switch the gradient method to Radial. Leave the Gradient preset set to Foreground to Transparent. Now click the foreground color swatch in the Toolbar and select a yellow color from the picker. Create a large radial gradient in the upper left of the canvas area. Next, choose a darker purple foreground color and create a new gradient in the lower left. Finally, choose a very light yellow foreground color and create a smaller gradient in the area between the other two.

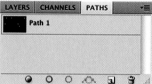

18 Press Control-V (or Command-V) to paste your copied art from Illustrator into the Photoshop file. When the Paste As options appear, choose the Path option. The artwork will be immense compared to your canvas. To remedy this problem, begin by pressing the F key as many times as necessary until the designated view switches to full Screen Mode With Menu Bar. Next, zoom out considerably until you can see the edges of the pasted artwork. Press Control-T (or Command-T) to enable the Free Transform operation. When the bounding box appears, click a corner point and drag inward while holding down the Alt (or Option) and Shift keys until the pattern is drastically reduced. Press the Enter key to apply the transformation.

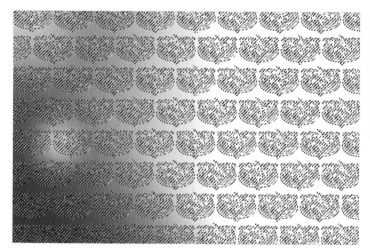

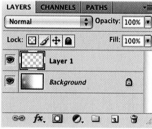

19 Ensure that you name this path in the path's palette or it will be in danger of being overwritten. Do not leave it named *work path*. If you simply double-click the path's name and then leave it set to *Path 1*, that is fine. Do this each time you add a path. Control-click (or Command-click) the path thumbnail to load it as a selection. Because it is quite intricate, it will likely take a moment for the selection to load. When the selection marquee appears, return to the Layers palette. Click the Create A New Layer button at the bottom of the Layers palette. Target the new layer.

20 Select the Gradient tool. It should still be set to the Foreground to Transparent preset. Choose the Linear method and then click the foreground color swatch in the Toolbar. When the picker appears, choose a dirty pink color and click OK. Click and drag from the left edge of the canvas to the right, filling the active selection with a gradient on the new layer. Switch to the Radial method in the Tool Options bar and then create a couple of new gradients within the selection, from the top- and bottom-left corners, moving toward the center of the canvas. Use a mauve foreground color at the bottom and a yellow color at the top. Press Control-D (or Command-D) to deactivate the selection.

PART THREE: Creating the text

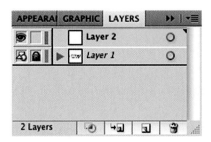

21 Return to Illustrator and create a new file. As before, the artboard size does not matter. Simply hide the artboard from view after you create the document. Choose File > Place from the menu and select the *words template.psd* file you created earlier. Click the Place button and then double-click the layer in the Layers palette. Choose the Template option from the Layer options and click OK. Click the Create New Layer Button at the bottom of the Layers palette and ensure that the new layer is targeted.

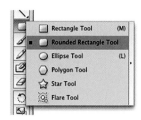

22 Click and hold the Rectangle tool in the Toolbar and then select the Rounded Rectangle tool when it appears. If your fill color is not set to Black, go ahead and change it in the Color palette. Also ensure that that the stroke attribute is set to None. Click and drag to create a new rounded rectangle about the same size as the one shown in the underlying template layer. This will define the perimeter of the text box. Press Control-Y (or Command-Y) to switch to Outline view if you are currently working in Preview mode so that you can see the underlying sketch.

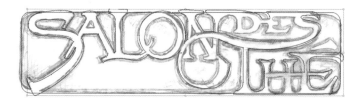

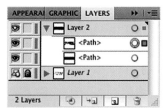

23 Use the Pen tool to carefully trace the outer line of the lettering. Concentrate only on the exterior of the letters at this point and ensure that this outer form creates a single, closed shape. This part is time consuming and requires quite a bit of patience, so relax and take your time here. It will be necessary to extend beyond the edge of the rectangle in some regions just to continue the shape. Don't worry about how the lines that extend beyond the edge of the rectangle look; they will be removed at the next stage in the process.

 Editing rounded corners

When you create a rounded rectangle, you might think that the corners are either too round or perhaps not round enough. If this is the case, delete the rectangle, then either click once or Alt-click (or Option-click) on the artboard. The rounded rectangle options will appear. Leave the width and height settings as they were so that the new rectangle will be the exact same size as the previous one. However, increase or decrease the corner radius amount as you see fit. Click OK and a new, revised, rounded rectangle will appear.

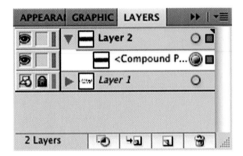

24 Press Control-A (or Command-A) to select the new shape as well as the underlying rounded rectangle. When both are selected, click the Minus Front operation in the Pathfinder palette to punch a hole in the rectangle using the new shape. View the results in Preview mode. While the resulting group is selected, choose Object > Compound Path > Make from the menu. Now use the Pen tool to carefully trace all the missing components as indicated by the sketch—things like the inside of the letter *o*, the inside of the letter *a*, and so on. Again, take your time as you draw all these little bits and pieces. It is important that they match the quality of your existing compound path. When you're finished, select all and then click the Unite button in the Pathfinder palette. After that, convert the resulting group to a compound path.

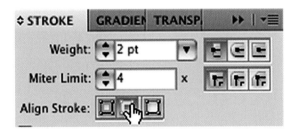

25 Switch to Outline mode and use the Pen tool to create a closed shape for the accent over the *e* in *the*. Select all and click the Minus Front button in the Pathfinder palette. Convert the result to a compound path. While the compound path is selected, click the small icon in the Toolbar that toggles the fill and stroke attributes to invert them. In the Stroke palette, choose the Align Stroke To Inside option and increase the weight to 2 points.

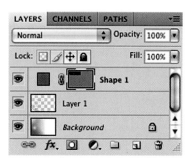

26 Choose Object > Path > Outline Stroke from the menu. This will convert the stroke attribute to an object. Select all and copy. Return to your working file in Photoshop and paste. When the Paste options appear, select the Shape Layer option and click OK. When the shape layer appears on the canvas, press Control-T (or Command-T) to access Free Transform. Shift-drag a corner point outward to increase the size of the shape and position it at the upper left of the canvas. Press the Enter key to apply the transformation. Your shape layer will use the current foreground color as its fill color. To change the color, double-click the Shape Layer thumbnail in the Layers palette. When the picker appears, choose a brighter purple color and click OK.

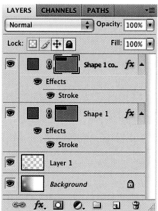

 Illustrator workaround 2

Again, if you are not inclined to draw the text components yourself or if you simply want to inspect the actual file used here, it is included within the downloadable project files for this chapter. The file is called *words.ai*.

27 Ensure that your shape layer is targeted in the Layers palette, and then choose the Stroke option from the Layer Styles menu at the bottom of the Layers palette. In the Layer style options, enable the Preview option, if it isn't already enabled, and adjust the size of the stroke so that it is about as wide as the purple stroke of the shape layer itself. Set the Position option to Outside. Click the Color swatch and choose a light peach color from the picker. Duplicate the layer by dragging it onto the Create A New Layer button at the bottom of the Layers palette.

28 Click the Stroke effect applied to your duplicate layer and drag it to the trash at the bottom of the Layers palette to remove it. Double-click the Duplicate Shape layer's thumbnail to access the picker and change its color to a lighter purple. Choose the Direct Selection tool from the toolbar. Hold down the Alt (or Option) key and click the outer path on the left side of the shape layer. This will select the outer path only, leaving the inner path untouched. Press the Delete key. As the outer path is removed, the fill is inverted, filling the inner path.

Inverting the shape layer

Removing the outer paths will cause a drastic change in the layer's shape area operations.

1 Alt-click (or Option-click) on the outer path of the shape to the upper right of the *s* with the Direct Selection tool. Again, when the outer path is selected, delete it. It is very important to hold down the Alt (or Option) key as you click an outer path.

2 If you do not hold down the Alt (or Option) key when you click, the Direct Selection tool will select a single point or line segment. Pressing the Delete key will only delete that single point or line segment until you press it a second time. Alt-click (or Option-click) on the outer path inside the *a* and then delete it.

3 Repeat this process with each shape, with the exception of the accent over the *e*. For the accent over the *e*, Alt-click (or Option-click) on the inner path this time and then press the Delete key. The result of all this selecting and deleting will look like what is shown here.

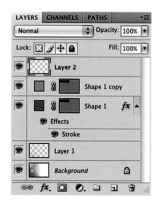

29 Control-click (or Command-click) on the duplicate shape layer's vector mask thumbnail in the Layers palette to load it as a selection. Create a new layer and ensure that it is targeted. Select the Gradient tool and set the preset to Foreground to Transparent if it isn't already. Also, ensure that the Radial method is specified in the Tool Options bar. Select a very light mauve foreground color from the picker. Click and drag from left to right within the selection on the new layer. This will create a gentle blend in this area. Deactivate the current selection.

PART FOUR: The woman's face and hair

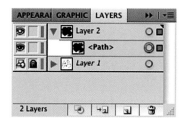

30 Return to Illustrator and create a new file. Once again, the artboard size doesn't matter. Simply hide the artboard from view. Set the Fill attribute to Black and the Stroke attribute to None. Choose File > Place from the menu and place the *face template.psd* file. As before, double-click the layer in the Layers palette and then enable the Template Layer option. Create a new layer and ensure that it remains targeted. Working in Outline mode, use the Pen tool to carefully create a large, closed shape that traces the outer contour of the woman's face and hair. Don't worry about the teacup or flowers at this point. You can simply create a simple line segment in the region that overlaps the teacup. Feel free to deviate from the sketch slightly as you see fit.

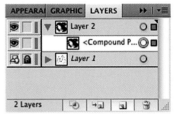

31 Now proceed to draw another shape that traces the interior of her face. This will entail tracing around the eyebrow at the left as well. Press Control-A (or Command-A) to select all and then click the Minus Front button in the Pathfinder palette to subtract the face shape from the outer shape you created previously. While the resulting group is selected, choose Object > Compound Path > Make from the menu. Next, repeat the process by tracing her neck area; take some liberty while tracing the right side of this shape. When the shape is closed, select all, perform the Minus Front operation, and then convert the resulting group to a compound path. Switch to Preview mode to view the results thus far.

 Illustrator workaround 3

Due to the intricacy of drawing required for this illustrated component, it is likely that most of you will want to at least peruse the actual file used here. If you want to use that file instead of creating your own, that is fine, too. This file is called *main.ai* and is included within the downloadable project files for this chapter. The woman's face is on its own layer in the Illustrator file. Also included in this file, on separate layers, is the finished artwork for the teacup and flower that you'll create later in the chapter. Feel free to inspect these as well, or simply use them in place of creating your own components later on.

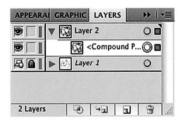

32 Now begin the task of tracing the interior of her hair area to create a single, very complicated, closed shape. Just follow the contour all the way around. In some instances you'll be moving inward to trace a detail from the sketch, then you'll double-back along the other side of the detail to get back to the interior edge and then continue on from there. This process will take a while, so allocate a fair amount of time for it. When you're finished, select all, perform the Minus Front operation, and then convert the resulting group to a compound path.

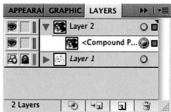

33 The next step is to trace all the solid black details. Using the template as your guide, create closed shapes to represent all the details in the woman's face and hair. When you get to areas where there are holes or spaces between strands of her hair, simply trace the outer perimeter for the time being. We'll punch holes in these regions in the next step. For now, take your time and create all the black regions. When you're happy with the result, select all and click the Unite button in the Pathfinder palette. After uniting, convert the group into a compound path.

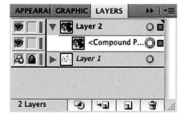

34 Now you'll need to switch back to Outline mode, because we're going to create the holes or negative spaces in the large black regions of her hair. If you work in Preview mode, you won't be able to use the underlying template as your guide. Begin by creating a single, white inner shape that traces the inner line of one of these negative spaces. Ensure that the shape is closed and then select all. After selecting all, click the Minus Front button in the Pathfinder. After doing that, convert the resulting group to a compound path. Then repeat this entire process for each hole or negative space. First create the closed shape, select all, perform the Minus Front operation, and then convert the resulting group to a compound path. Do not deviate from this workflow or things could go horribly wrong. You must work with one piece at a time. This process can be time consuming, but it is essential in ensuring that the resulting compound shape looks like the one shown here and will work properly when you bring it into Photoshop.

PART FIVE: Color, shading, and detail

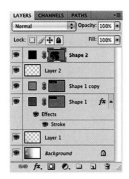

35 Select your compound shape and copy it. Save this Illustrator file and keep it open, since we will be returning to it. Return to your working file in Photoshop. Set the foreground color to black by pressing the D key on your keyboard, and then paste. When the Paste options appear, choose the Shape Layer option to paste the copied art in as a shape layer. Leave the fill color of the shape layer set to Black and use the Move tool to drag it to the left, positioning it beneath the text.

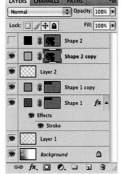

36 In the Layers palette, target your new shape layer. Hold down the Alt (or Option) key, and then drag downward in the Layers palette until you see a horizontal, thick, black line appear directly beneath the shape layer. Release the mouse button and you'll see that this is an excellent way to not only duplicate a layer but to also place your duplicate where you want it within the Layers palette. Disable the visibility of your original layer and then double-click your duplicate layer thumbnail in the Layers palette, to open the picker. Choose yellow to change the duplicate layer's fill color to yellow.

 Exporting paths

At this point, you can clearly see that there are a number of ways to incorporate Illustrator art into your Photoshop files. However, this relationship is a two-way street, and paths can also be exported from Photoshop to use within Illustrator. To export a path, choose File > Export > Paths to Illustrator. This choice allows you to create a new Illustrator file containing one of your Photoshop paths. In the Export Paths box, you can name your file and choose which path to export from the Write menu. The new file containing your path can then be opened and edited within Illustrator.

37 Choose the Direct Selection tool from the Toolbar and use it to click the outside path component of your shape layer while holding down the Alt (or Option) key. This will select the entire outer path component without selecting any of the other path components. Press the Delete key and the selected path component will disappear. This alters the behavior of other path components, inverting the effect on the shape layer. The result is a filled hair shape, but it is not perfect. Some components will invert that you don't want to invert. Alt-click (or Option-click) on any unwanted inverted components, such as her face, neck, ear, and the areas between strands of her hair. Press the Delete key to remove them. Remove any remaining details that should appear on the black layer, especially facial details.

 Saving paths as shapes

You can store any path or shape layer's vector mask as a custom shape, to be used again at any point later on. To save a path as a custom shape, first target the path in the Paths palette. Then choose Edit > Define Custom Shape from the menu. Name your shape and click OK. This will add your shape to the custom shape pop-up palette in the Tool Options bar, which is available only when you're using the Custom Shape tool. Simply choose your new custom shape from the available options in the pop-up menu. Then click and drag to create a new instance of your shape. Holding down the Shift key as you drag will ensure that your shape is proportionately accurate.

38 Disable the visibility of your new yellow hair shape layer. Alt-drag (or Option-drag) your hidden black outline shape layer again to create another duplicate shape layer that resides between the original black outline layer and the yellow hair layer in the Layers palette. Enable the visibility of your newly duplicated layer. Again, use the Direct Selection tool to Alt-click (or Option-click) the outer path. Delete the selected outer path to invert the shape layer. Then systematically delete all shape layer components that are not areas of her skin. Again, use the method of Alt-clicking (or Option-clicking) and deleting. Take care when you get to the ear. Ensure that you delete the outer path and the details but not the inner path. Double-click the Shape Layer thumbnail in the Layers palette and change the color of the shape layer to a flesh tone.

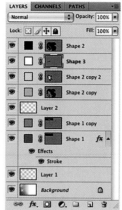

39 Enable the visibility of your black outline and yellow hair shape layers in the Layers palette. Select the Pen tool. Ensure that it is set to create a new shape layer in the Tool Options bar, and set your foreground color to White. Use the Pen tool to carefully draw a closed path that outlines her eye, creating a new shape layer. Then choose the Add to Shape Area option in the Tool Options bar and create a closed path component around her other eye, adding it to the existing shape layer.

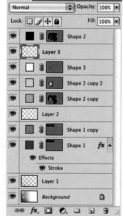

40 Now add a bit of soft, painterly shading to your artwork, in keeping with the signature appearance of authentic Art Noveau. First, Control-click (or Command-click) on your flesh-colored shape layer to load a selection based on the contents of that particular layer. Create a new layer that resides directly above your white eyes shape layer in the Layers palette. Select the Brush tool and choose a large, soft, round brush tip preset. Set the opacity of your brush around 20% in the Tool Options bar. Select a darker flesh color from the picker and begin to paint some shaded areas in the selection on the new layer.

Moving layer effects

When you apply a layer effect to a layer, it is not permanently attached to that layer. You can move it to another layer by simply clicking the layer style and dragging it onto another layer in the Layers palette. Or you can copy your layer style to another layer by clicking it and then Alt-dragging (or Option-dragging) it onto another layer.

41 Continue to paint shaded areas on the woman's face. Choose lighter or darker flesh colors from the picker and increase or decrease brush opacity as required until you've painted a sufficient amount of soft shading onto her skin. Next, use the same techniques, with much smaller brush tips and different colors, to paint shading into the whites her eyes, her iris areas, and her lips. When you're finished, deactivate the selection and select the Pen tool. Ensure that the Pen tool is set to create paths, not shape layers, and that the Add To Path Area option is selected in the Tool Options bar.

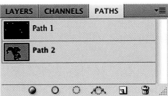

42 Now take a good look at the woman's hair and try to visualize where darker areas would naturally occur within the yellow areas. Carefully draw numerous closed path components wherever you think her hair should have some darker shading. Keep your shapes simple and use the contours indicated by the black outline layer as your guide. When you've finished creating the path components, generate a selection from the entire path by Control-clicking (or Command-clicking) it in the Paths palette.

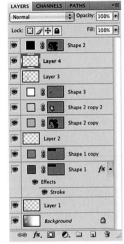

43 Return to the Layers palette. While the current selection is active, create a new layer and ensure that it is targeted. Select the Gradient tool from the Toolbar. Choose a brown foreground color from the picker and then click and drag within the active selection to add numerous gradients. Create a variety of radial, foreground-to-transparent gradients within the selection. Deactivate the selection and then select the Pen tool. Now use the Pen tool to create a series of path components to represent small highlight areas within her hair. Again, use the black outline art as your visual guide.

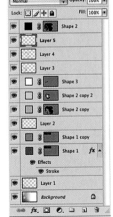

Other paste options

In addition to pasting your Illustrator art into Photoshop as paths and shape layers, there are a couple of other options. You can paste copied artwork from Illustrator into Photoshop as pixels or Smart Objects. Pasting as pixels will add your artwork to the canvas with a bounding box surrounding it. Similar to Free Transform, you can adjust size, angle, or position and then press the Enter key to apply the transformation. Once the transformation is applied, the artwork is rasterized. Smart objects are pasted in with the same bounding box surrounding them, yet they are not rasterized and remain editable. You can edit the source content of your smart object by double-clicking it in the Layers palette.

44 Load the new path as a selection and create a new layer. Choose a very light yellow foreground color from the picker. Be certain to select a yellow that is much lighter than the color of her hair. Fill the active selection with the new light yellow foreground color on the new layer by typing Alt-Delete (or Option-Delete) on the keyboard. Deactivate the selection.

45 Using the methods we used on the previous page, let's add some unnatural mauve details into our subject's hair. First, use the Pen tool to draw closed path components within her hair that will accommodate gradients of a different color. Load the entire finished path as a selection, create a new layer, and select the Gradient tool. Choose a mauve foreground color from the picker and create a series of radial, foreground-to-transparent gradients within the selection until it resembles what is shown here. Deactivate the selection when complete.

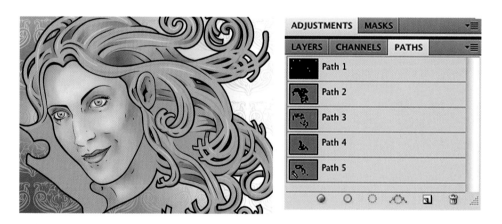

46 Now use the Pen tool to draw a number of closed path components in areas where you want to create some mauve highlights in her hair. Use the same logic and techniques that you used to create the yellow highlight path components. Also, create a closed path component that surrounds the area in her hair to the left of her cheek and neck. Generate a selection from the entire path and fill the contents of the selection with the current mauve foreground color on the same layer as your mauve gradients. Deactivate the selection.

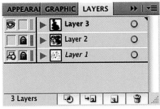

47 Return to your open Illustrator file and disable the visibility of the compound path layer by clicking the Visibility icon in the column to the left of it in the Layers palette. Then lock the layer by clicking in the column to the right of that. Create a new layer, ensure that it is targeted, and select the Pen tool. Use the Pen tool to carefully create a closed shape around the outer perimeter of the teacup and rising smoke. Just focus on tracing the exterior at this point, and feel free to improve on what is indicated by the sketch. Close the shape when you're finished.

Repeating the process

Use what is now becoming a familiar procedure to finish creating the teacup.

1 Now use the Pen tool to trace the inner region of the teacup and the smoke. Create a closed shape and then select all. When everything is selected, click the Minus Front button in the Pathfinder palette. After that, choose Object > Compound Path > Make from the menu.

2 Next, use the Pen tool to create a series of closed shapes that trace over all the solid black details in the underlying sketch. Overlap the existing shape in regions where the details should connect with it. Select all and then click the Unite button in the Pathfinder. Convert the resulting group into a compound path.

3 Switch to Outline mode if you're currently working in Preview mode, so that you can see the underlying sketch. Draw a shape that traces an inner hole or negative space within a solid black shape. Select all, perform the Minus Front operation, and then convert the resulting group to a compound path. Repeat this process as many times as necessary to punch the required holes into the solid black shapes. Switch to Preview mode to view the result.

48 Copy the compound path and save the Illustrator file. Leave it open because we'll be returning to it shortly. Return to your working file in Photoshop and press the D key to set the foreground color to black. When the Paste options appear, choose Shape Layer to paste the copied art into your file as a new shape layer. Use the Move tool to move the teacup outline to the lower left of the canvas.

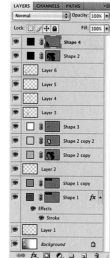

 Dragging from Illustrator

If you want to add Illustrator art to your Photoshop file as a smart object, there is a quicker method than copying and pasting. Use the Standard Screen Mode option in Illustrator and position your window so that you can see your open Photoshop destination file in the background. Then simply drag your Illustrator art with the Selection tool into your Photoshop file in the background. The dragged artwork will be added to your Photoshop file as a smart object.

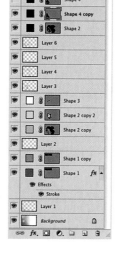

49 Create a duplicate of the shape layer underneath the original. Disable the visibility of your original layer and target the duplicate in the Layers palette. As you did with her hair and face previously, use the Direct Selection tool to Alt-click (or Option-click) a point or line segment of the outer path component in this shape layer. Press the Delete key to remove the outer path component and invert the shape layer areas. Use this same method to remove unwanted, inverted path components from the layer—places such as the inner paths that are used to define holes or negative spaces.

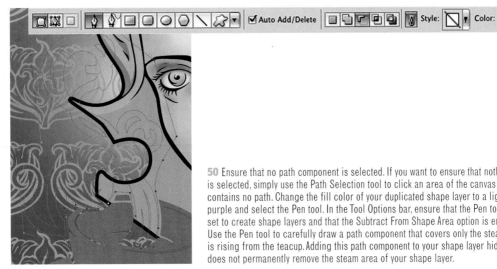

50 Ensure that no path component is selected. If you want to ensure that nothing is selected, simply use the Path Selection tool to click an area of the canvas that contains no path. Change the fill color of your duplicated shape layer to a light purple and select the Pen tool. In the Tool Options bar, ensure that the Pen tool is set to create shape layers and that the Subtract From Shape Area option is enabled. Use the Pen tool to carefully draw a path component that covers only the steam that is rising from the teacup. Adding this path component to your shape layer hides but does not permanently remove the steam area of your shape layer.

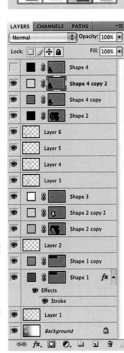

51 Duplicate the purple teacup shape layer. Target your new duplicate layer and change the fill color to a light green. Choose the Path Selection tool and use it to select the path component on your duplicate shape layer that hides the steam shape. With the path component selected, click the Intersect Shape Areas button in the Tool Options bar. Doing this will only reveal areas on the shape layer where shape components overlap.

(i) Combining

You can use components together to produce a variety of shape area effects in a single shape layer. However, you can create a final, single shape from your shape layer components by selecting them with the Path Selection tool and then clicking the Combine button in the Tool Options bar. Once you combine the different components, you will lose the ability to move or edit the components individually, because the result of combining is one single shape.

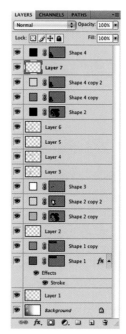

52 Create a new layer in the Layers palette and then Control-click (or Command-click) the purple teacup shape layer to generate a selection from the visible contents of the layer. Target your new layer and enable the visibility of the black outline shape layer directly above it in the Layers palette. Now select the Brush tool. Use a similar large, soft, round, brush preset and opacity setting to those used previously to paint the shading on the woman's skin. Use darker purple foreground colors to paint shading onto the teacup within the selection border. Adjust opacity and brush size as necessary. Deselect when finished.

Add shadows and highlights

Introduce a series of gradients into path-based selections to add shadows within the steam and highlights onto the cup and saucer.

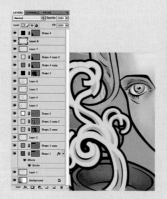

1 Select the Pen tool. Ensure that it is set to create paths and that the Add To Path Area function is enabled in the Tool Options bar. Draw a series of path components to define areas within the steam where shading should occur.

2 Load the entire path as a selection and create a new layer. Use the Gradient tool to create a series of darker green, radial, foreground-to-transparent gradients within the active selection on the new layer, to indicate shaded areas.

3 Now use the Pen tool to create closed path components on the cup and saucer and the coffee's surface. Generate a selection from the entire path and fill the selections with white or mauve, radial, foreground-to-transparent gradients on the same layer. Deselect.

PART SEVEN: Adding the flowers

53 Return to your open file in Illustrator. Disable the visibility of the teacup layer and lock it. Use the Pen tool to draw a closed shape that traces the outer edge of the flower on the teacup. After that, switch to Outline mode if necessary to view the underlying sketch. Then draw another closed shape that traces the interior of the flower. Feel free to trace the contour of some of the petal details that connect with the outline, as indicated by the sketch while you create this shape. After closing the shape, select all and perform a Minus Front operation to subtract the inner path from the outer path. Convert the resulting group to a compound path.

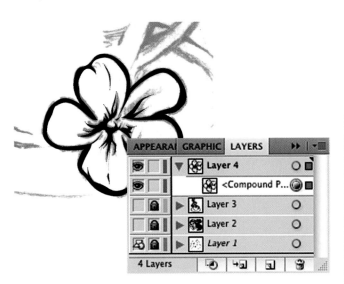

 Visibility and locks

After locking a layer or disabling the visibility, you can unlock or enable the visibility again by clicking in the same column in the Layers palette. For obvious reasons, it is good practice to keep things separate as you work. However, by keeping everything in one file, there is also the bonus of being able to reuse the same placed sketch rather than creating a new file for each component, placing the sketch each time, creating a template layer each time, and so on.

54 Use the Pen tool to create a series of closed paths that trace the details in the center of the flower as well as the details on the petals. When you are finished, select all and perform a Unite operation via the Pathfinder palette. Convert the resulting group to a compound path and copy it.

55 Return to your working file in Photoshop. Press the D key on the keyboard to set the foreground color to black. Paste the copied flower art into Photoshop as a new shape layer. Drag the layer to the top of the stack in the Layers palette. Use the Move tool to position the flower so that it overlaps the woman's hair near her temple on the canvas.

 Viewing effects

When you add an effect to your layer, it is shown beneath the layer. To hide the effect in the Layers palette, simply click the Expand/Collapse button to the right of the layer thumbnail. To view a hidden effect, click the same button to expand the layer, revealing the effects. To hide an effect on the actual canvas, click the Visibility icon (the eye) to the left of the effect. Repeat the same method to make the effect visible again.

56 Create a duplicate of this shape layer beneath the original in the Layers palette. Disable the visibility of your original flower shape layer and ensure that your duplicate is targeted. As you've done previously with the woman and the teacup, use the Direct Selection tool to click a point or line segment of the outer path while holding down the Alt (or Option) key. Press the Delete key to invert the area of your shape. Double-click the layer in the Layers palette and change the color of the shape layer to a light green, like the green steam rising from the teacup.

57 Enable the visibility of the flower black outline layer. Select the Ellipse shape tool. Ensure that it is set to create shape layers rather than paths and that the Create New Shape Layer option is enabled in the Tool Options bar. Draw an ellipse in the center of the flower to create a new shape layer just below the black outline layer. While your new shape layer is targeted, click the color swatch in the Tool Options bar and select a yellow color from the picker.

 Pasting paths

When pasting paths into Photoshop from Illustrator, it is very important to keep an eye on what is currently targeted in the Photoshop Paths palette. To paste illustrator art into Photoshop as a new path, there must be no path targeted in the Paths palette at the time of pasting. If you have a path targeted when you paste, the newly pasted vectors will be added to the currently targeted path as additional path components.

58 Load a selection from the green flower shape layer by Control-clicking (or Command-clicking) it in the Layers palette. Create a new layer and select the Brush tool. As you've done previously with the other image elements, choose a soft, round brush preset and a low opacity setting. Paint inside the selection on the new layer, using a darker green color than the flower petals to add shading. Vary brush size, color, and opacity as necessary to achieve a pleasing result. Deactivate the selection when you're finished. Click the top shape layer, the black outline layer. Then Shift-click the bottom flower layer. Press Control-G (or Command-G) to group the layers.

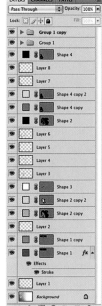

59 Duplicate your group by dragging it onto the Create A New Layer button at the bottom of the Layers palette. Choose Edit-Free Transform from the menu, and Shift-drag a bounding box corner point inward slightly to reduce the size of the flower. Click and drag within the center of the bounding box to reposition the duplicated group on the canvas. If you want to rotate your group, simply move the mouse outside the bounding box and then click and drag. When you're finished, press the Enter key to apply the transformation.

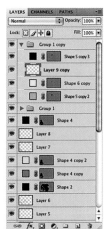

60 Once you've duplicated the flower and changed the size and position, the next step is to change the color. Inside the duplicate group, double-click the light green shape layer to open the picker. Choose a purple/blue color and click OK to change the color of the shape layer. Next, target the layer within the duplicate group that contains the painted shading. Choose Image > Adjustments > Hue/Saturation from the menu. Adjust the sliders until the shading is a darker purple/blue color.

61 Create numerous duplicates of the flower groups. Alter the color of the petals shape layer and the hue/saturation of the paint layer within various duplicate groups to add some variety in terms of flower color. Use Free Transform to resize and rotate them as necessary. Scatter the flowers around the canvas area. Move the groups up and down within the Layers palette as necessary so that some flowers overlap others on the canvas area. At this point, feel free to edit existing layers and embellish the image further using the plethora of techniques we've employed in this chapter.

Final analysis

Let's take a moment to reflect on the Illustrator and Photoshop methods that were essential to the success of creating this Art Nouveau masterpiece.

b Pasting art as shape layers gives you the option of duplicating your layers and reversing the shape area effects by methodically deleting path components. This is an excellent way to create solid color fill layers to match up with your outline art.

c Introducing painted strokes as shading into the Photoshop file allows us to soften the harsh, solid, vector appearance of working with shape layers. Underlying shape layer contents can provide the basis for selection borders, allowing you to constrain your painting to an area defined by a selection border.

d By working with different shape area options and introducing new path components to your shape layers, you are able to selectively reveal shape layer content differently from layer to layer, as we did here with the teacup and steam layers.

e By duplicating the flower group, altering the fill color of the shape layer, editing the hue of the paint layer, adjusting size, and repositioning, we are able to scatter numerous variations of the same flower throughout the scene.

a Pasting paths from Illustrator into a Photoshop document allows us to produce a sharp-edged selection border from the highly detailed Illustrator vector art. Then Photoshop paint tools can be used within the selection to introduce a pattern containing various soft, graduated colors.

Chapter 2

2D Textures and 3D Vectors

Combining Illustrator with Photoshop

Illustrator is generally the first choice of any digital artist, designer, or illustrator for creating sharp vector graphics. However, let's not forget about the myriad of vector tools and features in Photoshop. Even though they're not as comprehensive as those provided by Illustrator, they are powerful and extremely useful. The trick is to know when to use each program and for what purpose. In some cases it is logical, and convenient, to create and edit basic vector shapes in Photoshop. However, in instances where 3D vector technology, symbols, or clipping masks are required, Illustrator is the tool you're going to need to reach for.

An unfortunate byproduct of working with vectors is that an inherently digital or perfect look often prevails at the end of it all. Things can feel too perfect, too crisp, or too sharp. An excellent way to remedy this is to explore a variety of masking methods within both Illustrator and Photoshop, using image-based textures as your mask resources to distress your vectors in a convincing manner. This allows you to combine distressed textures from pixel-based imagery, with the crisp and clean artwork created with vector tools. The result is something entirely unique that resides in the mysterious realm between vectors and pixels. Getting comfortable with this newfound middle ground is essential to creating imagery that transcends the signature appearance of the tools you use.

Versions

Photoshop CS4
Illustrator CS4

Requirements and Recommendations

In addition to Photoshop, you'll need a copy of Illustrator. If you don't have a copy of Illustrator, a trial version can be downloaded from www.adobe.com.

What you'll learn in this chapter

Creative Techniques and Working Methods

Masking vectors in Photoshop

If you're holding this book in your hands, there's a good chance that you are aware of the possibilities of combining vectors and pixels in Photoshop. If you aren't aware of these possibilities, worry not; that awareness will settle in soon after you begin to read this chapter. In any case, Photoshop houses a plethora of vector creation and editing tools. And, as exemplified by the first portion of this chapter, there's a lot that you can do with vectors in Photoshop. Also, of equal importance is the fact that there are some great methods that you can employ using Photoshop to mask your vector shapes with image files, combining imagery from within alpha channels with your shape layers via layer masks.

Masking vectors in Illustrator

When people think of Illustrator, they generally don't think about masking vectors with images. The capability is there, yet we see that the process is a little different when we compare it to the same task in Photoshop. You need to designate your image as an opacity mask, which will allow you to see through the image's white regions while black regions remain hidden, exactly like the behavior of a layer mask in Photoshop. You can apply an opacity mask to a single object or an entire group. You can also edit the mask independently of your artwork in Illustrator at any time. Again, the same inherent logic prevails in Photoshop when we perform a similar task, yet the procedure is slightly different. All is explained over the following pages.

Tools, Features, and Functions

Transparency palette

This is the place in Illustrator where you can convert a placed image into an opacity mask. In addition, by clicking the mask thumbnail, you enter a mode in which you can edit the mask itself without affecting the masked artwork.

Clipping masks

Just like a vector mask in Photoshop, a clipping mask in Illustrator uses the structure of a vector shape to clip or mask artwork. You can mask a single object or a group. A clipping mask affects only the item that is directly beneath it in the Layers palette.

Symbols and 3D

You might already know that Symbol technology is a great way to manage numerous instances of the same thing in Illustrator. However, you might not be aware of the fact that Symbols can be mapped onto 3D effects, creating a surface texture or material on the resulting object.

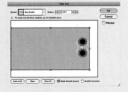

PART ONE: Building the background

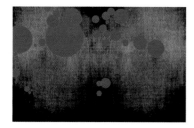

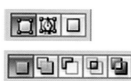

1 Open the *background.psd* file. Duplicate the background layer by dragging it onto the Create A New Layer button at the bottom of the Layers palette. Change the blending mode of the duplicate layer to Soft Light and reduce the opacity to 47%. Click the foreground color swatch in the Toolbar and select a bluish-purple foreground color from the picker. Select the Ellipse shape tool and ensure that it is set to create shape layers in the Tool Options bar. Click and drag while holding down the Shift key to create a circular shape within the new shape layer. Then click the Add To Shape Area button in the Tool Options bar. With this operation enabled, continue to click and drag while holding down the Shift key to add a number of other circles to the same shape layer. Try to create something that resembles what is shown here.

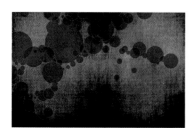

2 Change the blending mode to multiply and then reduce the opacity of the layer to 76%. Click the Create New Shape Layer button in the Tool Options bar. Select a teal-blue foreground color from the picker and then Shift-click the canvas to create a new teal circle within a new shape layer. You'll notice that the new shape layer has a multiply blending mode and an opacity setting of 76%, just like the previous shape layer. Again, click the Add To Shape Area button in the Tool Options bar. With this operation enabled, click and drag repeatedly while holding down the Shift key until the canvas looks something like the following.

 Project files

All the files needed to follow along with this chapter and create the featured image are available for download on the accompanying Website, in the project files section. Visit www.beyondphotoshopthebook.com.

 Shape size and position

If you want to move an individual shape within a shape layer, simply use the Path selection tool to click it and then drag it to the desired position. While an individual shape is selected, you can resize it via Edit > Free Transform at any point.

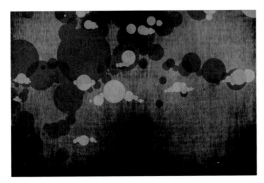

3 Duplicate the layer by dragging it onto the Create A New Layer button at the bottom of the Layers palette. Change the blending mode of the duplicate layer to color. Again, click the Create New Shape Layer button in the Tool Options bar. This time select a slightly lighter blue foreground color from the picker and then Shift-click the canvas to create a new teal circle within a new shape layer. After that, click the Add To Shape Area button in the Tool Options bar. With this operation enabled, click and drag repeatedly while holding down the Shift key until you've created some cloud shapes like those shown here. Change the blending mode of this shape layer to normal.

More circular shapes

Repeat this process a few more times to build up circular shapes on a series of layers.

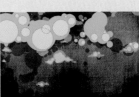

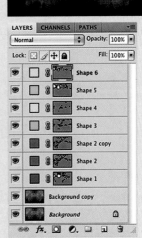

1 Repeat this entire process to create a new shape layer with a Normal blending mode and an opacity setting of 76%. Ensure that it contains a number of overlapping light blue circles. Position the shapes over the shapes on the underlying layer, making them a little bit smaller to look like highlight areas on your clouds.

2 Now use the same procedure to create another shape layer that is a slightly darker blue color. Create larger shapes this time and place them closer to the top of the canvas, as shown here. Set the blending mode of this shape layer to Normal and the opacity to 100%.

3 Again, create another shape layer. This time use a light blue color like the one you used for the cloud highlights. Use the same approach to hint at highlights over the shapes on the previous layer. Like the previous layer, this one's blending mode should be set to Normal and the opacity should be set to 100%.

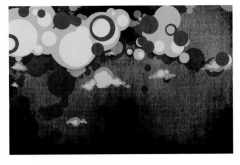

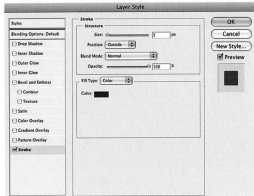

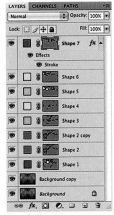

4 Repeat the same process one more time to create a shape layer that contains a number of light red circles, some of which overlap. However, to make this shape layer different from the rest, click the Subtract From Shape Area button in the Tool Options bar and then create some smaller circle shapes that overlap a few larger ones on this layer, to punch holes in them. After doing that, ensure that the layer is still targeted and then select the Stroke option from the Add a Layer Style menu at the bottom of the Layers palette. In the Layer Style dialog box, use the size slider to specify a nice, thick stroke, then click the color swatch to access the picker. Select a dark red color and click OK. Then, after exiting the picker, click OK to apply the stroke to your layer.

5 If your top shape layer is not currently targeted in the Layers palette, go ahead and click it to target it. Next, Shift-click the bottom shape layer to target all the shape layers. When all the shape layers are targeted, press Control-G (or Command-G) to group them. After the layers are grouped, target either the background layer or the background copy layer. Press Control-A (or Command-A) to select all and then press Control-C (or Command-C) to copy the selected contents. In the Channels palette, click the Create New Channel button. With the new channel targeted, press Control-V (or Command-V) to paste the copied art into the new channel.

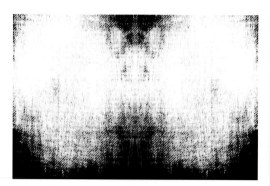

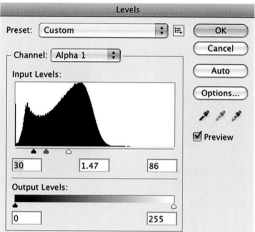

6 Ensure that the new channel is targeted and then press Control-L (or Command-L) to access Levels. In the Levels dialog box, adjust the input levels sliders drastically until the image within the channel is almost completely void of midtones, leaving behind a simple and drastic black-and-white image in the channel. Click OK and then Control-click (or Command-click) on the channel's thumbnail to load a selection from it.

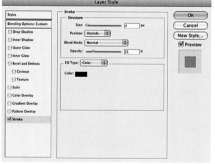

7 While the selection is active, return to the Layers palette and target the group you created previously. With the group targeted and the selection active, click the Add Layer Mask button at the bottom of the Layers palette to mask the group. Selected areas will remain visible while nonselected areas are masked. Now create one final shape layer that contains a series of overlapping white circles. Reduce the opacity of the layer to 57% and then add a Stroke Effect from the Add A Layer Style menu. Enter a Size value that is similar to what you used for the last stroke effect. Then click the color swatch to access the picker. Select a black color from the picker and click OK. Now reduce the opacity of the stroke to 21% and click OK to apply the layer style.

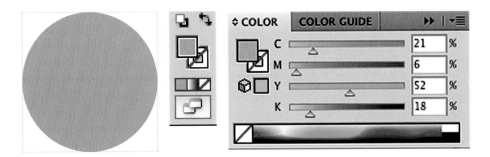

8 Launch Illustrator and create a new document by pressing Control-N (or Command-N). The size of the artboard and the document color profile do not matter for what we're going to do here. Simply go ahead and click OK when the New Document dialog box appears. Next, to avoid visual distraction as you work, choose View > Hide Artboards from the menu, to hide the artboard. Select the Ellipse tool and Shift-drag to create a large circle. While the circle remains selected, click the Fill swatch in the Toolbar to select the Fill attribute as well as open the Color palette if it is not currently visible. Choose a light green color from the CMYK spectrum at the bottom of the palette and then tweak it with the sliders until it resembles the color shown here.

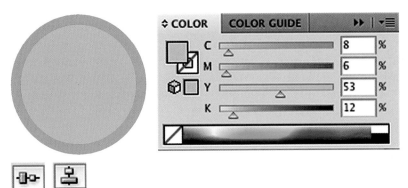

9 Shift-drag again to create another, smaller circle that overlaps the first. With the second circle selected, edit the color in the Color palette so that the green becomes lighter and less blue, more of a khaki yellow color. Use the Select tool to Shift-click the other circle to select them both, then choose the Horizontal Align Center and Vertical Align Center options in the Align palette to align the two circles.

 Color palette sliders

Depending on how you have Illustrator set up, you might see something other than CMYK sliders in the Color palette. If your color sliders are not appearing in your Color palette as they are shown here, simply go to the Color palette menu and choose the CMYK option.

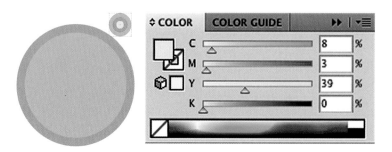

10 At this point, both circles should still be selected. Shift-click the green circle with the Selection tool to deselect it, leaving the yellow circle selected. Alt-drag (or Option-drag) the circle upward and to the right. Shift-drag one of the corners of the bounding box inward, considerably reducing the size. Draw another, slightly smaller circle that overlaps it and, while it is selected, click the original green circle with the Eyedropper tool to change the fill color of this circle to green as well. Create one more slightly smaller circle that overlaps, and create a light yellow fill color for it in the Color palette. Select all three small circles and again, then click the Horizontal Align Center and Vertical Align Center options in the Align palette.

A group of groups

Begin to create and edit a shape that consists of groups of grouped circles.

1 While all three aligned circles are selected, press Control-G (or Command-G) to group them. Hold down the Alt (or Option) key and drag the group to the left and slightly downward, as shown here.

2 Now hold down the Alt (or Option) key as you drag this group upward and to the left, duplicating it. Use the Selection tool to Shift-drag a corner point of the bounding box inward to reduce the size. Position the duplicated group as shown here.

3 Perform this same operation again so that there is another, reduced group oriented on this implied diagonal rule. Expand the newest group in the Layers palette, and then click the circular icon on the light yellow circle's sublayer to target it within the group. Press the Delete key to remove it.

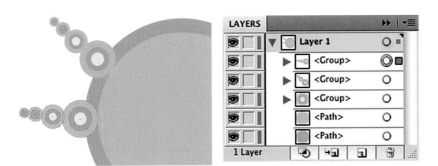

11 Create a duplicate of this edited group. Place it in the upper left like the others and reduce it in size. Select all these diagonally aligned groups and then group them into a single group. Ensure that the new group is selected and then select the Rotate tool from the Toolbar. Click once in the center of the large circle to specify this as the origin point around which the rotation will occur. An icon will remain in this area after you click. Then click the selected group and drag downward while holding down the Alt (Option) key. This will create a duplicate of the group while performing the rotate operation.

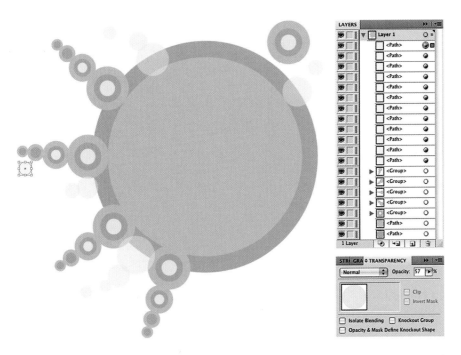

12 Repeat this process a few more times, rotating and duplicating the group around the larger circle as shown here. Create a new circle shape at the upper left of the original group that you rotated. While the circle is selected, use the Eyedropper tool to click any one of the light yellow circles within one of your groups to apply the light yellow fill color to your currently selected circle. In the Transparency palette, reduce the opacity of the object to 57%. Use the Selection tool to Alt-drag (or Option-drag) the circle, copying it to a new position. Then Shift-drag a corner point of the bounding box inward to resize it proportionately. After that, Alt-drag (or Option-drag) this circle to a new position and resize it as well. Repeat this process over and over again until there is a cluster of circles resembling what is shown here.

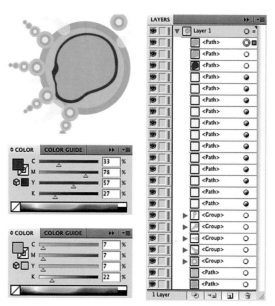

13 Use the Pen tool to create a closed shape that will indicate a thick outer edge around the skull we'll be creating next. While the object is still selected, assign a red fill attribute via the Color palette. Then use the Pen tool to draw a smaller shape inside the red shape. This will be outer edge of the skull, so take your time here and focus on creating a convincing shape. While the shape is selected, assign a light gray fill attribute in the Color palette. Duplicate the new shape by dragging it onto the Create New Layer button at the bottom of the Layers palette.

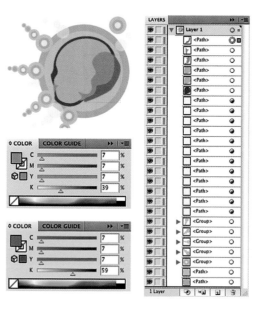

Don't feel like drawing?

I understand that the Pen tool is not for everybody and that perhaps you want to follow along but you don't want to spend your time drawing paths in Illustrator. If that is the case, the file containing the skull artwork is available in the project files you download for this chapter. The file is called *skull.ai* and includes everything we have worked on in Part 2. So if you don't want to draw all the paths but you'd like to explore the contents of the file in Illustrator, go ahead and open the *skull.ai* file and then skip ahead to Part 4.

14 Use the Pen tool to draw a couple of closed shapes to indicate shaded areas at the left and right of the skull. Your shapes will have the same gray fill color attribute as the previous shape you created. To change that, select them both and then increase the black slider to 39% in the Color palette. Then draw another shape that is smaller than the one at the right yet overlaps it. After drawing this shape, increase the black slider to 59%.

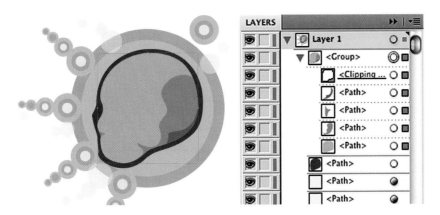

15 In the Layers palette, drag the lowest gray skull sublayer to the top of the stack within the current layer. Do not panic as it obscures the details that you just created; this is temporary. Click the Circular icon at the right of the sublayer to select it. Then Shift-click the circular icons to the right of each sublayer that contains a grey skull component. When they are all selected, choose Object > Clipping mask > Make from the menu. This will group the sublayers and use the top sublayer as a clipping mask. When it clips the layers beneath, it will become invisible, revealing the gray details that you previously obscured.

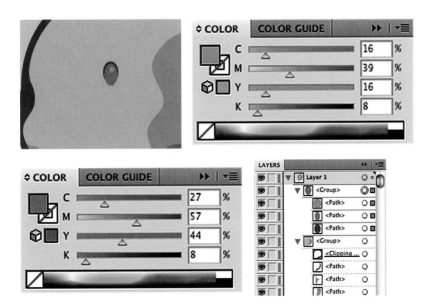

16 Use the Ellipse tool to create a small vertical ellipse. Try to envision where the eye at the right of the skull will be and position your ellipse at the top of it. While the ellipse is selected, use the Eyedropper tool to click the red shape to apply the red fill color to your currently selected ellipse. Create a smaller, somewhat elongated ellipse that overlaps and extends below the bottom of the previous red ellipse. Alter the color sliders in the Color palette until it resembles a dirtier pink color. Now create a small circle that sits inside the top portion of the ellipse, and alter the sliders in the Color palette to change the fill color to a lighter pink. Select both ellipses and the circle, then group them.

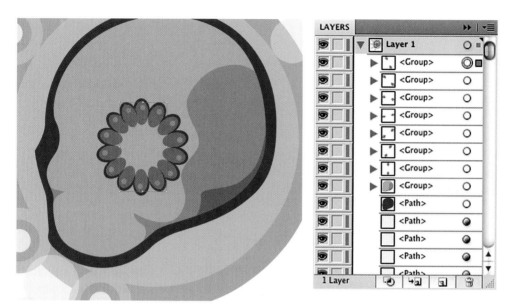

17 Use the Selection tool to drag the group downward on the artboard while holding down the Alt (or Option) and Shift keys. This will create a perfectly aligned duplicate of the group. Now click and drag outside the group's bounding box while holding down the Shift key to rotate it 180 degrees. Select both groups and then group them together. Select the Rotate tool and while the group is currently selected, begin by clicking in the registration point that is visible in the center of the group. Then click and drag while holding down the Alt (or Option) key to create a duplicate group while rotating. Repeat this process over and over again until you have created a circle of grouped shapes similar to what is shown here.

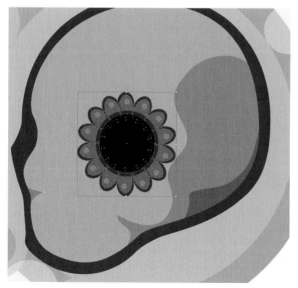

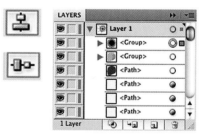

18 Create a large circle in the center of your cluster of groups. Use the Eyedropper tool to click a red object to set the fill color of your new circle to the same. Then create a somewhat small circle with a black fill color attribute. Use the Selection tool to select both circles; then, in the Align palette, click the options that will align both horizontal and vertical centers. After aligning the two circles, you might need to reposition them within your cluster. Go ahead and do so if necessary, but ensure that they are both selected before you move them. Select both circles and all of the ellipse/circle groups that surround them and then group everything into one.

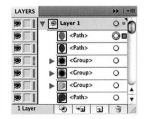

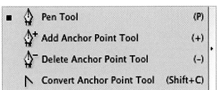

19 Use the Selection tool to drag the group to the left while holding down the Shift key to create a duplicate. Position each group as though they were eyes on the skull. Now create a vertical ellipse shape higher up, above the eye at the right. While the ellipse is selected, select the Convert Anchor Point tool. It is nested with the Pen tool in the Toolbar. Use the Convert Anchor Point tool to click the bottom anchor point, converting it from a curved point to a corner point. Next, use the selection tool to Alt-drag (or Option-drag) the shape upward, duplicating it. Then drag the top-center bounding box point downward to reduce the horizontal size of the new shape so that it fits within the original. While it is selected, use the Eyedropper to click a dirty pink shape to alter the fill color.

Create an array of petals
Add details and then use rotated duplicates to form the basis of a flower.

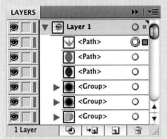

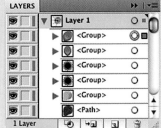

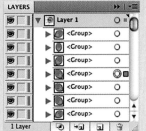

1 Use the Pen tool to draw a small detail like the one shown here. While the detail is selected, click a light pink shape with the Eyedropper tool to assign the same fill color attribute to it.

2 Select the three shapes that make up this single petal and group them. Alt-drag (or Option-drag) with the Selection tool to create a duplicate, then click and drag just outside a corner point of the bounding box to rotate the duplicate group slightly.

3 Repeat this process a number of times to create duplicates and rotate them. Position them as though they were petals on a flower. Drag groups up and down within the Layers palette to control the way they overlap each other.

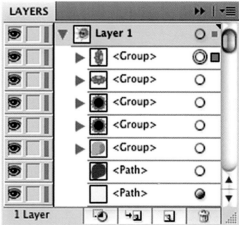

20 Draw an ellipse over the top center area of your new flower. While it is selected, use the Eyedropper to click a red area to set the fill color attribute to red. Then draw a smaller ellipse and set the fill attribute to the yellow-green color via the Color palette. Draw a smaller one inside this one and change the fill color attribute to a lighter color. Then do it one more time again, using an even lighter fill color. When you're finished, select all these ellipses as well as all the petal groups and then group everything into a single group by pressing Control-G (or Command-G). Next, Alt-drag (or Option-drag) the group to the right. Rotate it while holding down the Shift key and then position this duplicate group over the back of the skull.

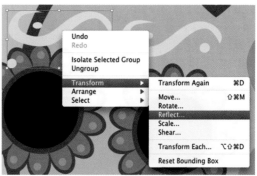

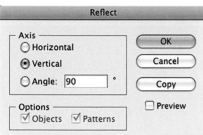

21 Use the Pen tool to create a closed shape that resembles a swirling brow. In the Color palette, assign a light yellow-green fill, similar to that used previously in the center of the flowers. Then use the Ellipse tool to create a few elliptical shapes in its proximity. Select the swirl shape and the ellipses and group them. Use the Selection tool to Alt-drag (or Option-drag) the shape to the left so that it sits above the other eye. Right-click (or Control-click) the duplicated group. When the pop-up menu appears, choose Transform > Reflect. Then, when the Reflect dialog box appears, choose the vertical axis and click OK. Next, use the bounding box handles to distort the shape. Following that, click and drag just outside a corner point to rotate it so that it looks like it belongs there.

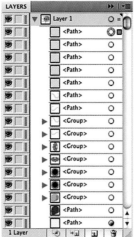

22 Double-click the group above the eye at the right to enter Isolation mode. While in Isolation mode, select just the swirl object and copy it by pressing Control-C (or Command-C). After copying, double-click anywhere else on the artboard to exit Isolation mode. After exiting, press Control-V (or Command-V) to paste the copied swirl. Resize it via the bounding box, and then click and drag outside a bounding box corner point to rotate it. Alt-drag (or Option-drag) this swirl to the left to duplicate it. Resize and rotate it using the same method you used previously, making it appear as though it belongs on the face. Use the Ellipse tool to draw a circle under these objects as well as some other circles and ellipses under the eyes.

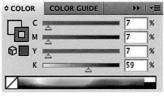

23 Create a series of ellipses in the area where the teeth should be. Ensure that they extend below the large gray skull shape. Select them all and then assign a light gray fill color attribute in the Color palette. To assign a stroke, click the Stroke icon in either the Toolbar or the Color palette to bring it to the foreground. Then specify a dark gray color in the Color palette. If necessary, feel free to edit the thickness of the stroke in the Strokes palette. While all ellipses are selected, click the Unite option in the Pathfinder palette to unite them into a single object.

Isolation mode

You can isolate a path, group, or object by double-clicking it, choosing Enter Isolation Mode from the Layers palette menu, clicking the Isolate Selected Object button in the Control palette, or right-clicking (or Control-clicking) on it and selecting the Isolate Selected option when it appears. While in Isolation mode, your isolated object, group, or path appears normal, whereas the rest of the artwork is dimmed or faded in compression. Isolation mode allows you to work exclusively with the isolated object, path, or group, leaving the rest of your artwork unaffected. You can exit Isolation mode by double-clicking the artboard, pressing the Esc key, clicking anywhere in the Isolation bar, clicking the Exit Isolation Mode button in the Control palette, or right-clicking (or Control-clicking) the object and choosing the Exit Isolation option when it appears.

24 While the unified teeth are selected, choose the Make Compound Shape option from the Pathfinder palette menu. After that, click the Expand button in the Pathfinder palette as it becomes available. Next, create a shape that covers the bottom half of the teeth. The top half of this shape should mimic the curve indicated by the underlying skull shape. If you want to see the skull shape clearly, view the artwork in Outline mode by pressing Control-Y (or Command-Y). You can return to Preview mode at any point by typing the same thing. Ensure that the shape is closed and remains selected after you create it. Shift-click the unified teeth shape with the Selection tool to select them as well. While both the teeth and the new shape are selected, choose the Minus Front option from the Pathfinder palette to trim the teeth.

Creating highlights

Once again, we'll use elliptical shapes alongside the Pathfinder to create a cluster of custom shapes.

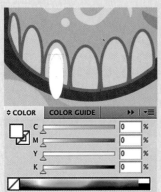  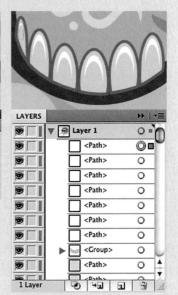

1 Create an elliptical shape that overlaps one of the teeth. In the Color palette, assign a white fill and remove the stroke. Use the Selection tool to Alt-drag (or Option-drag) the ellipse downward, creating a duplicate that overlaps the bottom.

2 While the duplicate ellipse is selected, use the Selection tool to Shift-click the original so that they are both selected. While they are both selected, click the Minus Front option in the Pathfinder palette.

3 Use the Selection tool to drag while holding down the Alt (or Option) key to create duplicates on each tool. Edit the shape and rotation of each duplicate shape via the bounding box handles or by clicking and dragging just outside a corner point.

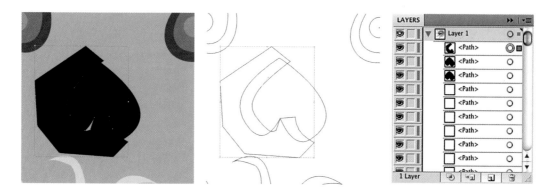

25 Use the Pen tool to draw an upside down heart-shaped nose. Specify a black fill attribute in the Color palette. After you finish creating the shape, duplicate it by dragging it onto the Create New Layer button at the bottom of the Layers palette. Now try to envision this shape as a hole in the skull and envision the thickness of the skull that would be expressed at the edges of the hole. Create a rough shape to indicate that thickness. It should look something like the one shown here, in both Preview and Outline modes. Ensure that you create only one shape, and also ensure that it is closed.

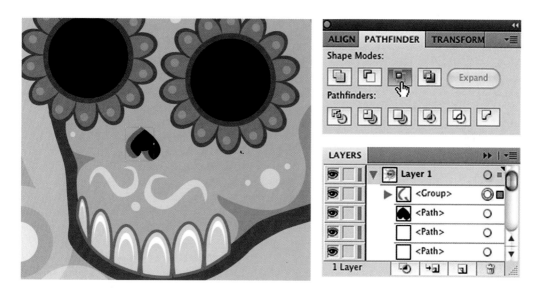

26 With this shape selected, use the Selection tool to Shift-click the upside-down heart shape directly beneath it to select them both. While both are selected, click the Intersect option in the Pathfinder. Then, while the resulting shape remains selected, create a dark gray fill color attribute in the Color palette. Select all by typing Control-A (or Command-A), and then group everything into a single group by typing Control-G (or Command-G).

Beyond Photoshop

PART THREE: Adding an opacity mask

27 Choose File > Place from the menu. Navigate to the *mask.jpg* file and click Place. Ensure that the image completely obscures the underlying art. You can move it around with the Selection tool if necessary. After placing the image into the file and positioning it properly, press Control-A (or Command-A) to select both the group and the new image. In the Transparency palette menu, choose the Make Opacity Mask option and you'll immediately see the results of the new image as an opacity mask in both the Transparency palette and on the artboard.

 Releasing a mask

Once an opacity mask is applied, you can release it, undoing the effects and taking it back to the state it was in before it was used to mask your artwork. To release a mask, simply select the artwork to which the mask is applied and then choose the Release Opacity Mask option from the Transparency palette menu.

 Illustrator workaround 1

If you are following along with the chapter but are not using Illustrator, you will need to place a couple of files that are pasted into Photoshop from Illustrator on the next page. In step 29, rather than paste, you will need choose File > Place from the menu and then navigate to the *skull.ai* file. Also, instead of pasting the altered artwork as per step 3 of the following boxout, you will need to place it as well using the same method. The name of the file is *background.ai*.

28 To edit the mask, simply click the Mask thumbnail in the Transparency palette. Uncheck the Clip option because it will hide anything that lies outside the edge parameters of the mask. Feel free to move it around, resize, rotate, or distort it if you like. Try moving it around a bit to see how the black scratches from the image affect what is hidden and what is visible. When you're satisfied, click the artwork thumbnail, not the mask, in the Transparency palette and then press Control-C (or Command-C) to copy the artwork as well as the mask applied to it.

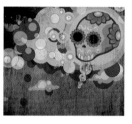

PART FOUR: Incorporating and editing Smart Objects

29 Return to your working file, which should still be open in Photoshop. If you have closed it for any reason, now is the time to open it again. Press Control-V (or Command-V) to paste the copied Illustrator art into your working Photoshop file. When the Paste dialog box appears, choose the Smart Object option and click OK. When the Smart Object appears, click inside the bounding box and drag it to the upper-right corner. Shift-drag a corner point outward to increase the size slightly while preserving proportion. When you're happy with the placement, press the Enter key. The newly pasted Smart Object should appear at the top of the stack in the Layers palette. If for any reason it appears lower down, simply drag it to the top. Immediately you'll notice how the opacity mask affects the visibility of the artwork.

Harvesting elements

Pick bits and pieces out of existing Smart Objects to create additional elements in the composition.

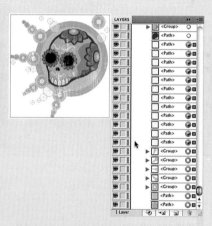

1 Duplicate the skull Smart Object by dragging it onto the Create A New Layer button at the bottom of the Layers palette. Change the blending mode to Color Burn and reduce the opacity to 39%. This will help deepen and saturate the color of the Smart Object within the Photoshop composition.

2 Double-click either Smart Object to open it in Illustrator. In the Layers palette, click the circular target next to one of the circular background elements to select it. Then click all the targets that correspond with all the other background elements until all the circles and groups that make up the background are selected.

3 Copy the selected objects and groups and close the Illustrator file. Whatever you do, do *not* save changes or you will alter the skull object. Return to Photoshop and paste the copied circles and groups into your file as a Smart Object.

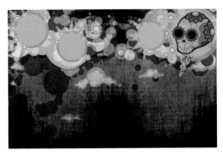

30 Shift-drag a corner point inward to reduce the size, then position the Smart Object to the left of your skull Smart Object. Use the Move tool to Alt-drag (or Option-drag) the new Smart Object to the left, duplicating it. Press Control-T (or Command-T) to access Free Transform. When the bounding box appears, click and drag outside it to rotate the Object. When you're finished, press the Enter key and make another duplicate even farther to the left. Rotate and resize this duplicate via Free Transform as well. Target all three of these background Smart Objects in the Layers palette and press Control-G (or Command-G) to group them. Duplicate the group by dragging it onto the Create A New Layer button at the bottom of the Layers palette. Change the blending mode of the duplicate group to Color Burn and reduce the opacity to 39%.

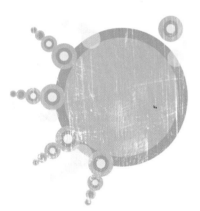

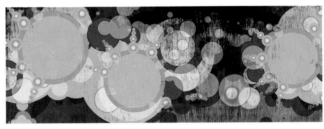

31 Expand either of these two new groups that contain your background Smart Objects and double-click a single Smart Object to open it in Illustrator. In Illustrator, choose File > Place from the menu. Navigate once again to the mask.jpg file and click Place. Resize the placed artwork so that it completely covers the vector art in the file. Position it so that a lot of the darker black areas in the bottom of the placed image cover the artwork. Select all and then choose the Make Opacity Mask option from the Transparency palette menu. Select the masked object and then disable the Clipping option in the Transparency palette. Save and close the file. When you return to Photoshop, your Smart Objects will automatically update to reflect the change.

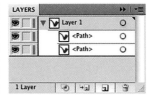

PART FIVE: Creating the walking creature

32 Return to Illustrator and create a new file. The size of the printable artboard does not matter since we're going to simply paste the finished result in Photoshop anyway. Choose View > Hide Artboards from the menu if you want to hide the edges of the artboard from view. This is just a preference of mine. If I'm not printing the art from Illustrator, generally I find the artboard edge more of a distraction than a benefit. Take a good look at the walking creature in the featured illustration at the beginning of this chapter; that's what we're going to create now. Use the Pen tool to create a closed object in the shape of one of the creature's legs. While the shape is selected, designate a Red fill color attribute in the Color palette that is similar to the one you used previously to outline the skull. Drag this sublayer onto the Create a New Layer button at the bottom of the Layers palette to duplicate it.

Adding texture to the leg
Basic shapes, pathfinder operations, replication, and clipping masks are the key ingredients in the texture applied to the creature's leg.

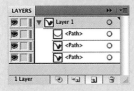  

1 Draw a small circle that overlaps a portion of the leg. This time, specify a lighter pink fill color. Use the Selection tool to Alt-drag (or Option-drag) the circle upward so that a duplicate overlaps it slightly. Then select both circles and click the Minus Front button in the Pathfinder palette.

2 Use the Selection tool to Alt-drag (or Option-drag) the new shape to the right or left. Create another duplicate on either side if necessary so that the row extends beyond either side. Continue to use this duplication method until these shapes cover much of the leg, as shown here.

3 Select all these small shapes and group them. However, ensure that you do not include either leg shape in the group. Drag the duplicate leg shape above the group in the Layers palette, temporarily obscuring it. Select this duplicated shape and the new group that resides beneath it in the Layers palette and then choose Object > Clipping Mask > Make from the menu.

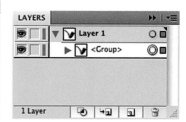

33 Now use the Pen tool to carefully create a shape that looks like the sole of the creature's foot. Take your time and use the Direct Selection tool to edit the curved line segments and points individually, if that is required to get the sole matching up nicely to the leg. Ensure that it is still selected as you create a darker red fill color attribute in the Color palette. Then create a smaller shape within the new sole shape. Use the same fill color, but in the Transparency palette change the blending mode of the shape to Multiply and reduce the opacity to 59%. Select all by pressing Control-A (or Command-A) and then group it all by pressing Control-G (or Command-G).

Again, if you don't want to draw ...

If you are still are not interested in working with the Pen tool or creating this creature, it is supplied within the downloadable project files. The file is called *creature.ai*. You can open it, investigate the contents of the file, and get ready to copy and paste it into Photoshop in Part 6.

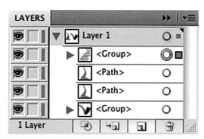

Moving within the Layers palette

Be careful when you are dragging things up or down within Illustrator's Layers palette. If you aren't careful, you can accidentally drop your object's sublayer into an existing group. When you see a dark line appear between two items in the Layers palette, it indicates that will be the new position of what you're dragging, once you release the mouse button. Stay on the lookout for this dark line. If you see bookended triangles on either side of a group, do not let go of the mouse button or you'll drop your sublayer into it.

34 Use the Pen tool to create another closed shape to represent the other leg. Use the Eyedropper to click a light pink shape from the other leg to specify that light pink and the new shape's fill color attribute. Do not be too meticulous regarding the position of this leg on the artboard; we'll move it into position later after it is finished. When you have completed the shape, duplicate it in the Layers palette. Next, to represent the texture, create a group of shapes via the Pathfinder like ones you created previously for the other leg. However, this time specify a darker red fill color for these.

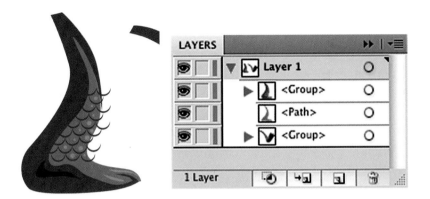

35 Use the Pen tool to create some shaded detail for this leg. Don't worry about how it overlaps the outer edge of the leg; concentrate on what is happening within. Shortly we'll clip the edges that lie outside. Specify a dark red fill color for this shading and then add some objects into the toes area to act as highlights, implying dimension. Create a new, vibrant light pink fill color for these in the Color palette. Then create a series of circles, using the same vibrant pink fill color, within the textured shapes that already exist on the leg. Finally, create a shape with a dark red fill color to add some shading to the heel. Select all these items that make up this leg via the targets that correspond to them in the Layers palette, except leave out the original leg shape you created. When all are selected, excluding the one original leg shape, group all of it by pressing Control-G (or Command-G).

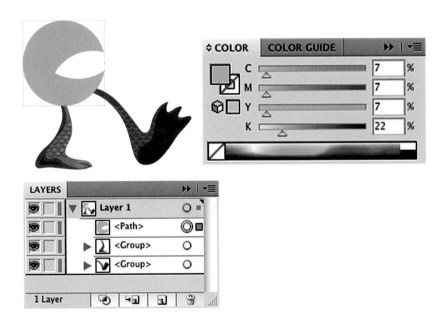

36 Next, drag the original left shape above your new group in the Layers palette and select them both. While both of them are selected, choose Object > Clipping Mask > Make from the menu. Create a large circle for the creature's body and specify a light gray fill color attribute in the Color palette. Next, draw a football shape with the Pen tool and rotate it slightly. Position it so that most of it sits within the circle but some of it overlaps the right edge. Select both this shape and the new circle. While they are both selected, click the Minus Front button in the Pathfinder palette.

37 Create a new ellipse shape that lines up nicely with the left edge and the top of the large gray shape. Then create a smaller ellipse and offset it upward a little and to the right. Select both of these shapes and perform a Minus Front operation. Change the fill color attribute of the resulting shape to dark gray in the Color palette. Next, duplicate the large, light gray shape and drag it to the top of the Layers palette. Create a rounded shape that overlaps the cutout football shape area. Select both of these shapes and click the Intersect button in the Pathfinder. Create a slightly different gray fill color for this shape.

Making some holes

We'll use what are becoming all-too-familiar methods to create holes for this creature's appendages and eyes.

1 Create a black ellipse shape in the eye region at the left and rotate it slightly. Duplicate the shape in the Layers palette. Use the Selection tool to Alt-drag (or Option-drag) the duplicate shape to the left, creating another duplicate, slightly offset.

2 Select the new duplicate and the one directly underneath it. Then click the Minus Front option in the Pathfinder to create a new shape from them. Specify a gray fill color for this new shape in the Color palette.

3 Select the new shape as well as the underlying black ellipse and group them. Then Alt-drag (or Option-drag) copies of this group around, resizing, rotating, and repositioning them as shown here.

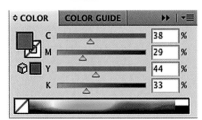

38 In the Layers palette, drag the leg at the left of the artboard upward until it sits atop everything else. Reposition it, as well as the hole nearest to it that you just created, on the gray body of the creature in a manner that looks like they belong together. The leg should appear as though it is coming out of the hole. Next, create a shape that fills the mouth area. You don't need to worry about how the edge that overlaps the gray regions looks, because the next step after creating it is to drag it beneath the other gray shapes in the Layers palette. Create a more greenish-gray fill color for this shape in the Color palette.

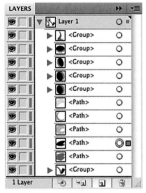

39 Next, use the Pen tool to carefully draw a black shape that is smaller than this new greenish-gray area. Leave space surrounding it to create the illusion that there is a thickness to the body of the creature and that this new black shape is an open hole. Again, you can be a little sloppy in areas that overlap the light gray shapes, because the next step is to drag it down in the Layers palette beneath these shapes so that it resides directly above the shape you just created.

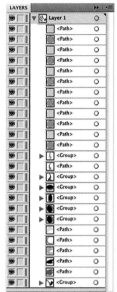

40 Now use the Pen tool to draw an arm shape that looks as though it is extending out of the hole on the creature's side. Specify a light pink fill color attribute in the Color palette. Duplicate your arm shape in the Layers palette. Next, draw a shape that indicates shaded areas at the edges of the arm, much as you've done previously for the creature's legs. Specify a dark red fill color attribute for your new shape in the Color palette. After that, drag the duplicate of the original arm shape above the new shape in the Layers palette. Then select the duplicate and the dark red shape beneath it and choose Object > Clipping Mask > Make from the menu. After clipping the shaded areas, create a number of circles on the surface of the arm, in varying shades of pink, to add some surface details.

 Deeper into Isolation mode

When you enter Isolation mode by double-clicking the group, you'll have access to all things grouped in that particular level. However, nested within that group is the clipped shadow, which you'll need to double-click to enter as well. Basically, at times you'll need to continually go deeper and deeper into Isolation mode, one step at a time. The levels are displayed as you go in the Isolation bar. You can click these to navigate through the varying levels of isolation as you work.

41 Select all these components that make up the arm and group them. Duplicate the group by dragging it onto the Create New Layer icon in the Layers palette. Use the Selection tool to move the duplicate to the other side of the creature and then rotate it into a new position. Drag the duplicated group beneath the body of the creature in the Layers palette. Double-click the duplicate group on the artboard to enter Isolation mode. While in Isolation mode, change the fill color attributes of individual objects so that the arm has an inverse or negative feeling in terms of value, compared to the other arm. When you're finished, exit Isolation mode by double-clicking a different area of the artboard.

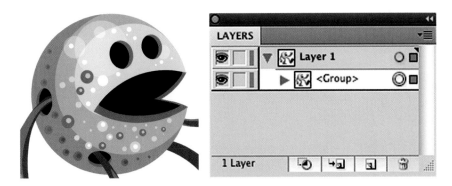

42 Now that you've completed all the difficult construction, have some fun introducing a number of circles onto the creature. Experiment with different sizes of fill colors in the Color palette. Also, play around with different blending modes and opacity settings in the Transparency palette. Have some fun placing circles lower down within the Layers palette so that pre-existing shapes can overlap them. When you're finished, select all by pressing Control-A (or Command-A) and then group it all by pressing Control-G (or Command-G).

43 Choose File > Place from the menu. Again, navigate to the *mask.jpg* file that is included within the downloadable project files. Select both the placed image and the existing group. While both are selected, choose the Make Opacity Mask option from the Transparency palette menu. Next, click the Mask thumbnail in the Layers palette to make it available for editing purposes. Resize and reposition the mask as necessary until you're satisfied with the result. You might find it necessary to disable the clip operation in the Transparency palette as well, depending on how you position the placed image. When you're finished, click the artwork thumbnail in the Transparency palette. Then select all and copy.

Is this confusing?

Although this creature looks simple, it is the direct result of a comprehensive set of procedures and operations. If, for any reason, you find this daunting and would like to consult a reference file, simply open the *creature.ai* file from this chapter's downloadable project files. You can poke through the Layers palette and analyze the opacity mask, groups, paths, and clipping masks. You can also select objects and have a look at the colors that are applied to them in the Colors palette if you like. Anything that you might be struggling with is clearly and accurately represented in this file.

Beyond Photoshop

PART SIX: Bring the creature into Photoshop

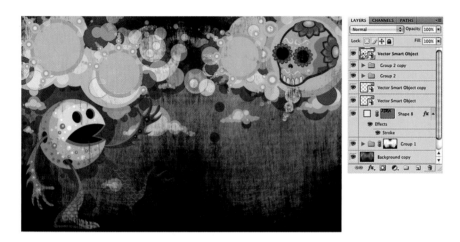

44 Return to your working file in Photoshop and paste the copied Illustrator art into it as a Smart Object. Resize the art proportionately and drag it to the lower-left corner of the canvas. Press the Enter key to apply the transformation when you're happy with the creature's relationship to the rest of the composition. If for any reason you paste into an existing group, especially one with an altered blending mode, and your object looks strange, don't worry about it. After you apply the transformation you can move the Smart Object to the top of the Layers palette so that it is unaffected by a group's blending mode as long as it is not obscured by another layer or object.

 Illustrator workaround 2

If you're following along in Photoshop and choosing not to work in Illustrator, you can directly incorporate the creature into Photoshop. Rather than copying in Illustrator and pasting in Photoshop, simply choose File > Place from the menu. Then navigate to the *creature.ai* file and place it into the composition. This sequence performs the same operation as pasting, and you can follow along exactly from the pasting point onward.

45 Drag your Smart Object onto the Create New Layer button at the bottom of the Layers palette to duplicate it. Change the blending mode of the duplicate to Color Burn and reduce the opacity to 39%. Essentially, you're trying deepen the color and enhance the saturation of this Smart Object in exactly same way that you did for all other Smart Objects that were previously pasted in. If you haven't saved the file for a while, now would be a good time to do so.

PART SEVEN: The first vector 3D creature

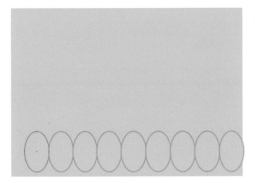
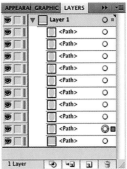

46 Return to Illustrator and create a new file. Again, the artboard size is irrelevant, but go ahead and hide it from view. After the new file is created, use the Rectangle tool to draw a large, horizontal rectangle on the artboard. Specify a lime green color fill attribute in the Color palette. Next, use the Ellipse tool to create a vertical ellipse at the bottom, within the rectangle. Use the same lime green fill color, but add a light blue stroke around the ellipse. Alt-drag (or Option-drag) with the Selection tool to the side continually to create an entire row of duplicates. Leave a bit of space at the very end. Hold down the Shift key as you drag, to ensure that duplicate shapes are aligned as you copy them.

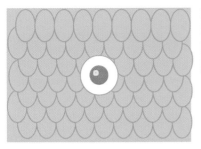

47 Select all the ellipses and Alt-drag (or Option-drag) the row upward and then offset it a little. Repeat this process again and again until the rectangle areas is filled with a pattern that resembles scales. Create a circle and then change the fill color of the circle to white. Next, create another, smaller circle, and change the fill color to a light, desaturated purple. Leave the existing stroke applied to both of these circles and select them both. In the Align palette, align the horizontal and vertical centers. While both circles remain selected and aligned, drag them to the center within the rectangle and new pattern. Finally, create a small yellow circle within the existing purple circle, to serve as a highlight. Set the stroke to None in the Color palette.

Loading symbols

Over the following pages we'll create a number of symbols to map onto 3D rotations in Illustrator. However, if you'd like to explore 3D and don't want to bother creating all the symbols, I have saved all of them into a single file that is included in this chapter's project downloads. To load the file, go to the Symbols palette menu and choose Open Symbol Library > Other Library … and then navigate to the *symbols.ai* file. Once you've loaded the symbols, you can simply map them as required over the following pages.

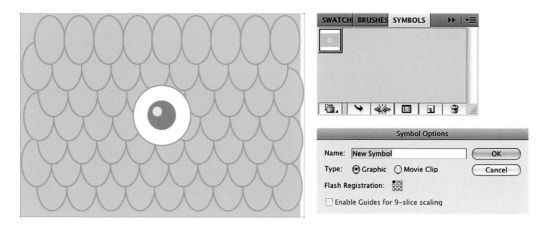

48 Open the Symbols palette. To clear it, choose Select All Unused from the Symbols palette menu and then click the Trash icon at the bottom of the palette. Agree that Yes, you do want to remove these symbols when prompted. Press Control-A (or Command-A) to select all your artwork, and then simply drag it into the now empty Symbols palette. As soon as you drag it in, the Symbols options will appear. Choose the graphic option and name it Symbol 1 before pressing the OK button. You will notice that after you do this, your artwork on the artboard will be contained within a single bounding box because it has been converted to a symbol instance. Delete the artwork from the artboard after adding it to the Symbols palette.

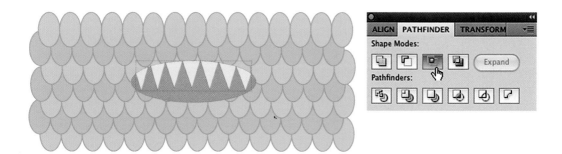

49 Next, create a row of lime green ellipses, as you did previously. After that, select them all and Alt-drag (or Option-drag) the row upward and then offset it a little, just like before. Repeat this process until you've created about seven rows. Now, select all the ellipses in every other row and alter the fill color in the Color palette so that it is a little darker. When you're done that, create a long, horizontal, orange ellipse in the center and duplicate it in the Layers palette. Ensure that there is no stroke applied to this shape. Use the Pen tool to create a polygonal shape that resembles a number of teeth and extends beyond the top edge of the orange ellipse. Select the new shape and the duplicate ellipse, then click the Intersect button in the Pathfinder. Change the fill color of the resulting shape to yellow in the Color palette.

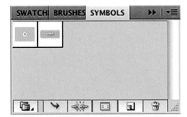

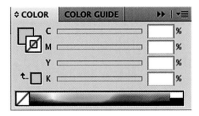

50 Select all by pressing Control-A (or Command-A) and then drag your artwork into the Symbols palette. Again, ensure that it is a graphic, not a movie, symbol, and then name it Symbol 2. Once you've added it to the Symbols palette, delete the instance of it from the artboard. Create a circle using the lime green fill color you used previously. However, it is extremely important that there is absolutely no stroke applied to this shape. Set the stroke to None in the Color palette.

Create a 3D effect

Now we'll revolve the circle into a 3D shape while using one of our new symbols as a surface texture.

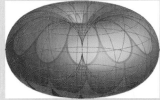

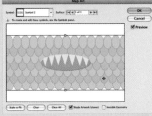
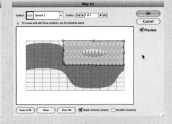

1 Choose Effect > 3D > Revolve from the menu. Enable the Preview function but leave all the other settings set to the default state. The effect of using the defaults is exactly what we're after here. If you've altered the defaults, just match them up with those shown here.

2 Click the Map Art button. When the Map Art dialog box appears, select Symbol 2 from your list of symbols. Ensure that the Preview option is enabled. The first thing you'll notice is that although it is mapped to the shape, it is not really what we're after in terms of mapping.

3 Adjust this bounding box as you would any other, then click and drag within it to reposition the art. Clicking and dragging outside the box achieves rotation. Play with the positioning and size until you're satisfied. Ensure that the Shade Artwork option is enabled and click OK. Click OK in the 3D revolve options as well.

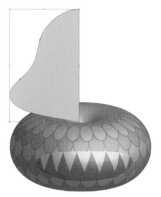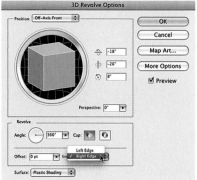

51 Next, draw a shape that resembles half the outer edge of a bell. Don't worry about closing this shape; leave the middle open. I know that is odd, considering that everything we've done in this chapter so far has been closed. However, when we use 3D Revolve, it is the outer edge that is really important. In this case, since the axis will be at the right, the left edge is what you want to concentrate on. While the open path is selected, choose Effect > 3D > Revolve from the menu. Enable the Preview option and then change the offset to occur from the Right Edge.

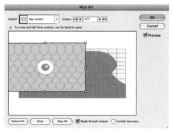

More Illustrator workarounds

If you aren't following along in Illustrator or for any reason are not comfortable working with Illustrator's 3D tools, the files for these 3D creatures are also included within the downloadable project files for this chapter. Each file contains one finished creature, complete with a mask. The files are named in the order in which they're incorporated into the Photoshop file: *3Dcreature1.ai,* *3Dcreature2.ai,* and *3Dcreature3.ai*. Rather than pasting them in when prompted, you can simply bring them into Photoshop as Smart Objects via File > Place. Also, feel free to investigate these files in detail, even if you're following along, to see how what you're doing compares to the way that these files are built.

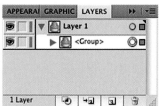

52 Click the Map Art button and then choose Symbol 1 from the list. Again, click the Preview option. Ensure that you enable the Shade Artwork option and then reposition, resize, and rotate the artwork until it appears on the shape in a similar manner to what is shown here. Click OK, and then click OK in the 3D Revolve options as well. Feel free to change the position of either object in relation to the other by moving it slightly with the Selection tool. When you're happy with how things are looking, press Control-A (or Command-A) to select all and then press Control-G (or Command-G) to group everything.

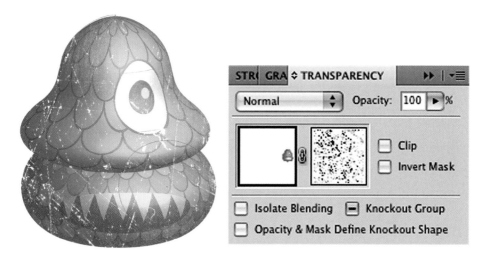

53 Select File > Place from the menu. Navigate to the *mask2.jpg* file included within the downloadable project files and click Place. After placing the image, select all by pressing Control-A (or Command-A) and then choose the Make Opacity Mask option from the Transparency palette menu. Once the mask is applied, click the Mask thumbnail in the Transparency palette. Adjust the positioning by clicking and dragging on it and alter the size via the handles on the bounding box. When you're satisfied with what you've done, click the Artwork thumbnail in the Transparency palette and then, once again, press Control-A (or Command-A) to select all. After selecting all, press Control-C (or Command-C) to copy.

54 Return to your working file in Photoshop and press Control-V (or Command-V) to paste. Paste this copied art in as a Smart Object at the top of the stack in the Layers palette, just as you've been doing all along. Increase the size of the art proportionately and place it in the upper left of the canvas so that it covers the green and yellow circles in that region. Duplicate the Smart Object and then change the blending mode of the duplicate to Color Burn. Reduce the opacity to 48%.

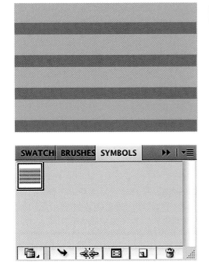

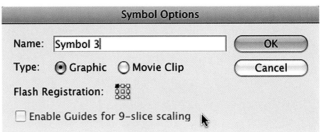

55 Create a new file in Illustrator. Use the Rectangle tool to create a large, fleshy pink rectangle. Then create a smaller, magenta-pink rectangle inside of it, near the bottom. Use the Selection tool to Alt-drag (or Option-drag) copies of the rectangle upward while holding down the Shift key until you've created something that resembles what is shown here. Clear the Symbols palette of the default swatches, as you did last time. Select all on the artboard and drag it into the Symbols palette to create a new symbol. Name it Symbol 3 and ensure that it is a graphic symbol. After adding it to the Symbols palette, select all on the artboard and delete.

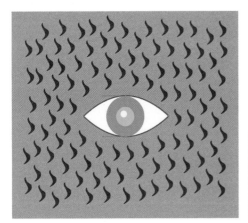

56 Create a large orange rectangle on the artboard. Then use the Pen tool to create a small, red, closed squiggle shape. Use the Selection tool to Alt-drag (or Option-drag) copies of the red squiggle all over the interior of the orange rectangle. Leave space in the center for the eye that we're going to create. In the space you've left in the center, create a wide ellipse with a white fill color attribute and a thin magenta stroke around the edge. In the center, create a smaller blue circle. Inside that, create an even smaller lime green circle. Then select the ellipse and the circles. In the Align palette, align the horizontal and vertical centers. After aligning, create a small yellow circle within the lime green circle, slightly offset, to the upper right. Finally, select the white ellipse shape and then use the Convert Point tool to click once the left point and the right point, converting them to corner points and sharpening the edges of the ellipse.

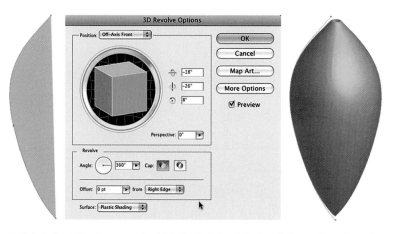

57 Select all and then drag your artwork into the Symbols palette. Specify the graphic option and name your new symbol Symbol 4. After adding it to the Symbols palette, delete the instance of that symbol from the artboard. Create a Path in the shape of an elongated *c*. Do not close the shape. Leave the right side open. Specify a fleshy pink fill color attribute in the Color palette. Choose Effect > 3D > Revolve. Again, enable the Preview option and leave all the default settings alone, except change the offset so that the Revolve effect is offset from the right edge instead of the left.

58 Click the Map Art button and select Symbol 3 from the Symbol options to be mapped. Resize, rotate, and reposition the art as required while you have the Preview option enabled. Ensure that the Shade Artwork option is enabled. When you are happy with the results, click OK, then click OK in the 3D Revolve Options dialog box as well, to return to the artboard. Use the Selection tool to Alt-drag (or Option-drag) copies of the 3D object onto the artboard until there are five objects in a row. Select a single object and then make the Appearance palette visible if it isn't currently.

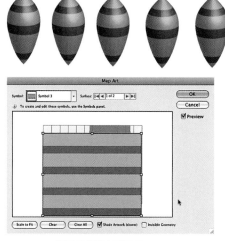

(i) More options

Within the 3D Revolve options dialog box, you'll find a button underneath the Map Art button, labeled More Options. Click this button to access (you guessed it) more options. Here, among other things, are some excellent and intuitive controls for light and shading, should you wish to go beyond what the default settings have to offer.

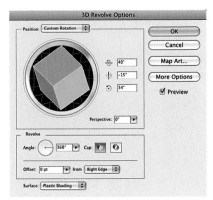

59 In the Appearance palette, click the words 3D Revolve Mapped to edit the 3D Effect. Once you click this choice, the 3D Revolve Options dialog box will open again. Again, enable the Preview option so that you can see what you're doing on the artboard. Click the different sides of the cube and drag to rotate the shape with XYZ space. With the Preview option enabled, you will immediately see the results of your rotation. When you are satisfied with the rotation, click OK, select another object, and then click 3D Revolve Mapped for that object in the Appearance palette. When the options appear, edit it, too. Repeat this process for each object until the array of objects on the artboard resembles what is shown here.

Create the top of the creature

Use what are now becoming familiar techniques to create a three-dimensional body to accompany the legs you created previously.

1 Use the Pen tool to draw the left side of a bell shape. Don't worry about closing the shape; the revolve effect will render that unnecessary. Specify an orange fill color in the Color palette.

2 While the new shape is selected, choose Effect > 3D > Rotate. Enable the Preview option and then set the offset to the right edge. You can leave all other options set at their default settings.

3 Click the Map Art button and choose Symbol 4 from the list. Position and resize the mapped symbol as required and ensure that you click the Shade artwork option. When you're happy with the result, click OK, and then click OK in the 3D Revolve options as well.

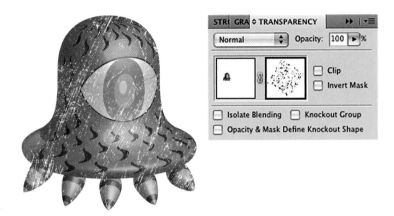

60 Select all and then group all the selected objects into a single group. Choose File > Place from the menu and navigate to the *mask2.jpg* as you did previously for the other 3D creature. Click Place and then select all again. While the underlying group and the placed image are both selected, choose the Make Opacity Mask option from the Transparency palette menu. Click the Mask thumbnail in the Transparency palette to make it editable. Resize and position it over the underlying group as necessary to achieve the masking effect you're after. Disable the clip option if necessary.

61 Click the Artwork thumbnail in the Transparency palette and then select all. Return to your Photoshop working file and paste the copied art into it as a Smart Object. Adjust the size by Shift-dragging a corner point of the bounding box as necessary. Position the creature over the yellow and green circles in the composition that are directly beside the other 3D creature. Press the Enter key to apply the transformation. Duplicate the Smart Object and change the blending mode of the duplicate to Color Burn. Then reduce the opacity of the duplicate to 10% in the Layers palette.

62 In the Layers palette, double-click the original skull Smart Object. This is the first Smart Object you pasted into Photoshop and sits beneath all the others in the Layers palette. The Smart Object will open in Illustrator. When it opens, double-click it to enter Isolation mode. While in Isolation mode, select one of the eyes as well as some of the swirl and elliptical face details. Press Control-W (or Command-W) to close the file, and do not save changes when prompted. Create a new Illustrator file. Use the rectangle tool to create a large, horizontal, light gray rectangle. Then press Control-V (or Command-V) to paste the copied objects onto the rectangle. Duplicate, rotate, resize, and reposition the objects as necessary until the arrangement resembles what is shown here.

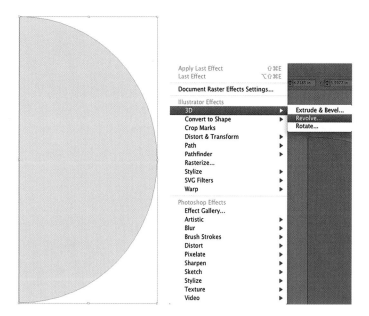

63 Clear the contents of the Symbols palette. Then select all and drag the selected artwork into the Symbols palette. Specify the Graphic option and name it when prompted. Delete the instance of the symbol from the artboard. Next, create a circle with the Ellipse tool. The color of this shape as well as the following shape is unimportant; just ensure that there is no stroke applied to either. Then use the Rectangle tool to create a shape that completely obscures the left half of the circle. Select them both and then choose the Minus Front option from the Pathfinder palette. When all that remains on the artboard is the right half of your circle, select it and then choose Effect > 3D > Revolve from the menu.

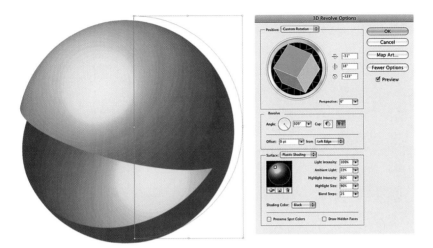

64 In the 3D Revolve options, rotate the cube or enter numeric values into the *xyz* rotation fields until your shape resembles what is shown here. Change the angle to 309 degrees and disable the end cap option. Enable the Preview option to view the results, then click the More Options button to access light and shading controls. Go ahead and alter the position of the light source as well as the numeric values of the other light options until your object resembles what is shown here.

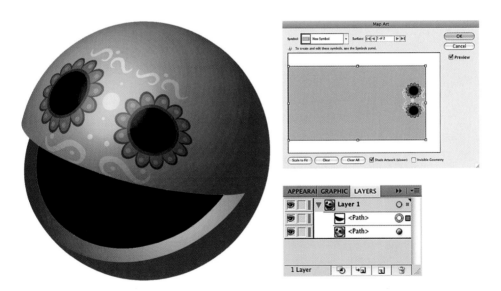

65 Click the Map Art button and then select your new symbol from the list. Use the bounding box handles to resize your symbol on the artwork and position it as necessary until your placed artwork resembles what is shown here. Be certain to enable the Preview option so that you can see what you're doing. Also, enable the Shade Artwork option. When you're satisfied with the result, click OK, and then also click OK in the 3D Revolve options. Now use the Pen tool to create a closed, black shape in the mouth region of your 3D object so that it appears as though the creature is hollow.

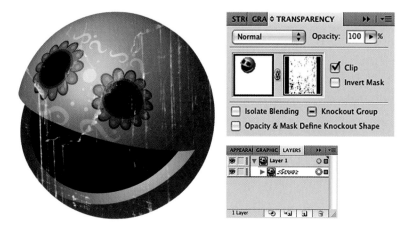

66 Press Control-A (or Command-A) to select all, then press Control-G (or Command-G) to group the selected objects. Choose File > Place from the menu and navigate to the *mask.jpg* file. Place the *mask.jpg* file and then adjust the size and position of it in the file so that the top left corner is covering the creature. When you have positioned it like this, press Control-A (or Command-A) to select all and then select the Make Opacity Mask option in the Transparency palette menu. Select the Masked object and copy it by pressing Control-C (or Command-C).

67 Return to your working file in Photoshop and paste the copied art into the file as a Smart Object. Move it over to the circle to the left of the skull, and increase or decrease the size of the pasted object as necessary by Shift-dragging on a corner point. Press the Enter key when you're satisfied with the size adjustment. Also, drag it upward to the top of the Layers palette if it is hidden underneath anything else. With the new Smart Object targeted in the Layers palette, choose the Stroke option from the Layer Style menu at the bottom of the Layers palette. Click the Color swatch to access the picker and when it opens, move the mouse over a pink region of the skull to sample that color. Then, specify a thickness that adds a generous stroke around the exterior of the object. Click OK.

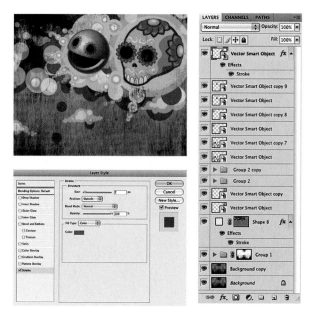

68 Duplicate the Smart Object by dragging it onto the Create New Layer button at the bottom of the Layers palette. Change the blending mode of the duplicate object to Soft Light to enhance the object's saturation and contrast in the composition. After doing this, take a good look at the composition. Remember, it is built in a way that lends itself to infinite editing. You can edit the content of the Layers palette as well as double-click on the pasted Smart Objects in the Layers palette and edit them, and their masks, in Illustrator.

Further editing

A modular composition with embedded Smart Objects lends itself to infinite, nondestructive editing. Here are a few tweaks that were performed after completion.

1 I decided that the background could use more circular shapes in a slightly lighter blue. So I created a new shape layer in the desired color, then drew a number of circular shapes on it and dragged it into the masked group containing all the other shape layers in the background. The layer was placed directly beneath the cloud layers.

2 The green creature's Smart Object was double-clicked in the Layers palette, to open it in Illustrator. Then, after selecting the object in Illustrator, we clicked the 3D effect in the Appearance palette. The mapped artwork was repositioned and scaled slightly. Then the file was saved and closed. After that, the Smart Object in Photoshop was automatically updated to reflect the changes.

3 The same method was used to edit this Smart Object in Illustrator as well. However, in addition to tweaking the mapped artwork, the position of the image within the Opacity Mask was altered. Then the file was saved and closed, instantly updating the changes within Photoshop. After this, I decided to tweak the opacity mask of each object a little using the same method.

Other examples

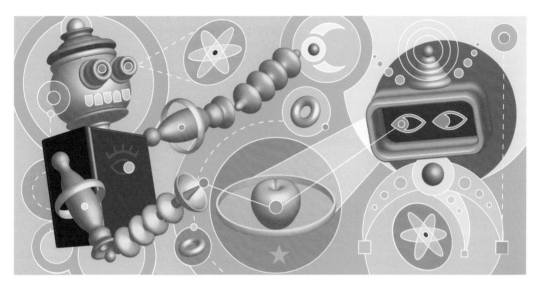

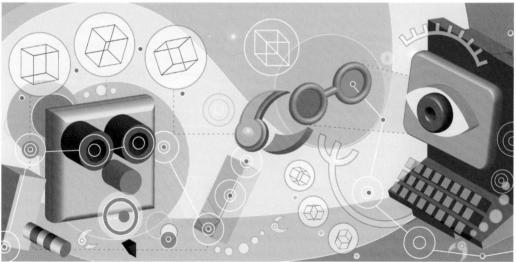

As shown here, the 3D effects in Illustrator can prove useful, even when you aren't working with texture in any capacity. In addition to the Revolve operation, you might wish to check out the Extrude method in Illustrator as well. The results of extruding are visible in the box-like and rectangular shapes above.

Here you can see the results of similar methods to those outlined in this chapter. The stripes on the plane are mapped onto a 3D shape as a symbol in Illustrator. The multilayered clouds are the results of combining circles on shape layers in Photoshop. Opacity of the layers was reduced and stroke effects were added afterward.

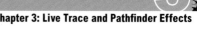

Chapter 3

Live Trace and Pathfinder Effects

Combining Illustrator with Photoshop

I remember when Illustrator introduced the Live Trace feature and the mess that ensued. No fault of Adobe's, it was a great tool and still is. However, the illustration trend that came in its wake was dreadful. It seemed like every digital art magazine had a color photograph that had been Live Traced to the extent that it resembled an old paint-by-numbers painting. A whole movement of artists seemed to be compensating for lack of drawing skills and an inability to produce decent photography by claiming that the result of the Live Trace tool was the inherent style in their work. Thankfully, this situation all fell apart and disappeared, like all empty trends, only to be replaced by another insubstantial flavor of the month.

I point this out because this trend really soured Live Trace for me. For a long time I underestimated the potential of this tool in the Illustrator/Photoshop workflow. However, one day when I was looking for a way to translate some black-and-white drawings into paths quickly and effectively, I rediscovered how useful and effective Live Trace can be. While I was in Illustrator, something possessed me to mess around with the Pathfinder palette, and I found that this was indeed a good way to play with abstract shapes and color. Although many of the same shape or path area operations can be achieved in Photoshop, I found that for some reason it felt more liberating to do this in Illustrator. Perhaps it was because I was concentrating on these particular elements only, without seeing the rest of the imagery; to tell you the truth, I don't really know why. However, it was these Pathfinder experiments, combined with Illustrator's Live Trace features, which paved the way for a strange new direction in my illustration work.

Versions	Requirements and Recommendations
Photoshop CS4 Illustrator CS4	In addition to Photoshop, you'll need a copy of Illustrator. If you don't have a copy of Illustrator, a trial version can be downloaded from www.adobe.com.

Beyond Photoshop

What you'll learn in this chapter

Creative Techniques and Working Methods

Bringing vector art down to Earth

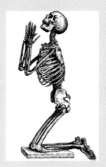

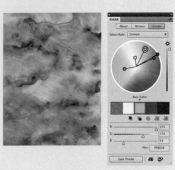

When heading into an illustration project like this one, there are a lot of things to consider ahead of time. Mainly, there is the issue of vector technology and how perfect it is. That inherent perfection can often contribute to an impersonal or inhuman feeling in your artwork. However, creating tactile or traditional components for inclusion ahead of time is an excellent way to remedy this unwanted feeling. Hence the reason for the hand-drawn skeleton, which is a recreation of an illustration in an ancient anatomical text. This hand-

drawn skeleton is the primary visual component, and although eventually converted to vectors, it retains its tactile essence. In addition, using a watercolor background really emphasizes imperfection and tactile qualities. If you allow it, watercolor paint tends to move and bleed in random ways, in stark contrast to the clear intent required to produce vector graphics. The result of all this is a strange and compelling juxtaposition between perfection and imperfection.

Color strategies

Color is one of the most important factors involved in image creation. Strategic use of color is essential when you are creating an illustration like this one. With so much detail and so many image components, a well formulated, yet restrained use of color helps reign in the chaos and allows the viewer to focus on the primary visual components. Furthermore, when we're working with two applications, preserving the color theme between them becomes very important. This is where effective use of Kuler and Adobe Swatch Exchange technology comes into play.

Tools, Features, and Functions

Live trace

This Illustrator feature is an excellent way to convert pixel-based imagery into vector art. The tracing options are flexible and powerful. And when the artwork is created with Live Trace operations in mind, precise results will always ensue.

Pathfinder

The operations contained in Illustrator's Pathfinder palette allow you to generate unique shapes from existing ones. Here these operations were used for the abstract shapes in the background; however, once you explore the possibilities it is likely you'll find use for them in a variety of vector-related tasks.

Transform Again

Illustrator's Transform Again command is a nifty feature that comes in handy in creating a number of instances of things that show progression or digression, or simply things that look cool when instances start to pile up. You can repeat the last operation you performed on your selected shape. Methodical use of this function helped create the bird groupings in this image.

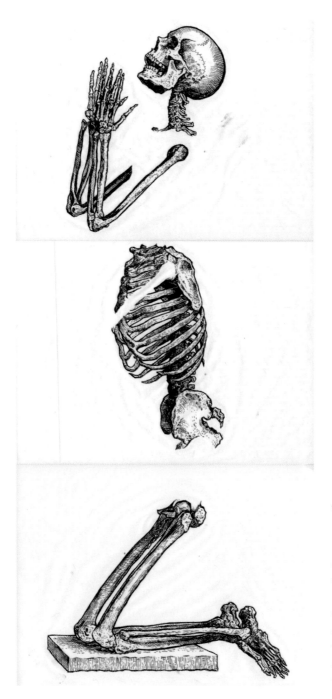

When preparing black and white for a detailed Live Trace operation, the most important thing is clarity of detail. Like most people, I use a standard-sized desktop scanner to scan drawings and other bits of tactile art as I require. However, in this instance I needed to draw the skeleton much larger, to express the detail clearly. So, in cases like this, the best thing to do is create the artwork at a large size, simply spaced over a few pages that will fit onto your scanner.

PART ONE: Devise a color strategy

1 Open the *watercolor.psd* file. You'll notice that it has a warm, earthy hue about it. Let's use this earthy hue as a jumping-off point. Before we begin creating artwork, let's formulate a limited color strategy to work within. Having a plan in terms of color will help unify our composition. And with a composition like this, where completely different elements such as watercolor paintings and sharp vector art contribute equally, unity must come from elsewhere; therefore, the logical component to provide that unity is color. I have found that the greatest tool for developing a color theme is Adobe's Internet application, called Kuler. In Photoshop, I'll usually launch Kuler by choosing Window > Extensions > Kuler from the menu. Kuler is helpful whether you want to start with a shared theme or create a theme on your own. You can either select a theme and then click the Edit Theme in Create Panel button at the bottom of the palette, or simply click the Create button at the top. Then use the Create Panel controls to edit the existing theme or modify your own.

Project files

All the files needed to follow along with this chapter and create the featured image are available for download on the accompanying Website in the project files section. Visit www.beyondphotoshopthebook.com.

2 Now, before we get too involved with Kuler, let's get the workspace ready to host our color themes as we generate them. By default, the Swatches palette in Photoshop comes equipped with a very diverse and useful set of color swatches. However, to create this image, we'll use the Swatches palette as a virtual painter's palette and store only the colors we're going to use within the image. So, in the Swatches palette menu, select the Preset Manager option. In the Preset Manager, click the first swatch and then click the last swatch while holding down the Shift key. This will select all the swatches. Press the Delete button to remove them. Click Done and you'll notice that when you return to the workspace, the Swatches panel is emptied. Next, return to the Kuler panel and click the Browse button. In the Search field, type dereklea1 to load the primary color theme that I generated earlier. As you can see, this is the primary color theme used in the main image at the beginning of the chapter. Click the Add Selected Theme to Swatches button at the bottom of the palette and you'll immediately see a change in the Swatches palette.

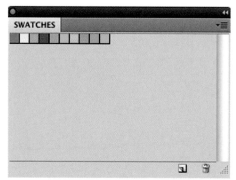

3 Next, type dereklea2 into the Kuler palette search field and you'll see the secondary color theme appear. As you did previously, add this theme to the Swatches palette. This secondary theme will be used for color accents within the main image, rather than dictating the overall feel as the first theme did; this theme provides a color strategy for embellishing the image. Next, choose Save Swatches for exchange from the Swatches palette menu. Name the file *Swatches* and specify a destination. Now, I feel it is important to point out that my strategy for using Kuler and developing themes is for reference purposes as you work. Do not feel restricted to using only these swatches in their current state. To stay on track, I like to have a visual guide as I go, that's all. It is not essential that you use only the colors in the Swatches palette. Think of them as a starting point, yet feel free to edit them or create new swatches that adhere to this theme at any point to embellish the overall color strategy.

PART TWO: Building a background

4 Leave the Photoshop workspace as it is with the current set of swatches loaded and the *watercolor.jpg* file open. Now, launch Illustrator and create a new file by pressing Control-N (or Command-N). Don't worry about multiple artboards or the document profile; we're simply going to be creating raw materials for use in Photoshop. For this reason, the artboard size doesn't matter either. Choose View > Hide Artboards from the menu, to hide the artboard. When we're using Adobe Illustrator for traditional purposes, the artboard defines the printable area. However, because we're not using Illustrator for output, the artboard is irrelevant, and hiding it simply removes a visual distraction as we work. Choose File > Place from the menu and then navigate to the *tree.jpg* file included within the downloadable project files for this chapter. Click Place to place it in the file.

Swatches

If for any reason you are not able to or are not interested in performing Kuler-related operations, do not fret. The Swatches shown here are included in the project files that you downloaded for this chapter. You can load them into the Swatches palette while clearing anything that is in the palette at the same time. Simply choose the Replace Swatches option from the palette and then navigate to the Swatches file that you downloaded. When prompted, you can save changes to your current set of swatches, if you want to preserve user-created swatches, or simply ignore the prompt to discard the current set. Then simply click the Load button.

Another way to expand

In addition to using the option under the Object menu, you can also expand your traced artwork by simply clicking the Expand button when it appears in the Control palette. Either method works.

5 While the placed image remains selected, click the Live Trace button in the Control bar at the top of the screen. You will see an achromatic, black-and-white result almost immediately. This is the default trace operation. To alter it, click the Tracing Operations button in the Control bar. When the Tracing options dialog box appears, the first thing you want to do is to click the Preview checkbox, enabling the Preview option so that you can see changes reflected in the image window as you work. After that, increase the Threshold to 140, then reduce Path Fitting to 1, set the Minimum Area to 5, and enable the Ignore White option. This will result is a more detailed tracing operation. Click the Trace button.

Illustrator workaround 1

If you aren't using Illustrator, the traced tree artwork can be found in the *watercolor.psd* file as an existing Path. Simply Target the path in the Paths palette and then, while the path is visible on the canvas, select Solid Color from the Create New Fill or Adjustment Layer menu at the bottom of the Layers palette. When the picker appears, select a dark brown color. You can do this in lieu of the procedure outlined in step 7 on the following page. After creating the solid color layer masked by the path, begin following along with step 8.

 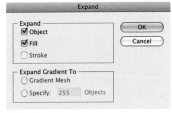

6 While the placed, traced image is still selected, choose Object > Expand from the menu. When the Expand dialog box appears, you can leave the default settings as they are. Basically, as long as the Object option is enabled, things will work fine. Click OK to convert the visual result of the Live Trace operation to a vector path that surrounds all the black regions. Press Control-C (or Command-C) to copy the expanded artwork.

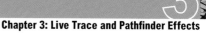

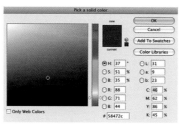

7 Return to your working Photoshop file and press Control-V (or Command-V) to paste. When the Paste dialog box appears, choose the Shape Layer option from the Paste As options. This choice will paste the copied vector art into Photoshop as a new shape layer. Double-click the Shape layer's thumbnail to access the picker and change the color of the layer from black to a dark brown instead. Click OK and then press Control-T (or Command-T) to access Free Transform. To increase the size of the shape proportionately, click and drag one of the corner points of the bounding box while holding down the Shift key, and then drag it to the lower left of the image. Press the Enter key to apply the transformation. Change the blending mode of the layer to Color Burn.

Seldon Hunt

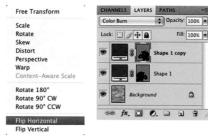

8 Drag the layer onto the Create a New Layer button at the bottom of the Layers palette to duplicate it. With the duplicate targeted, press Control-T (or Command-T) to access Free Transform and then right-click (or Control-click) within the bounding box. When the pop-up menu appears, choose the Flip Horizontal option. Then drag it to the right of the canvas while holding down the Shift key until it appears to mirror the original layer on the canvas.

Although he is mentioned in my other book, *Creative Photoshop*, it is necessary to point out the influence of this prominent Australian artist once again. If you have ever seen his work, the influence is apparent. He is the first artist to make me appreciate symmetry and inspire me to scour the Web and reference libraries for ancient drawings and etchings. Because his early work has such a signature style about it, it is hard to be influenced by him without appearing derivative. However, his newer work is moving in a distinctly different direction. Do yourself a favor and check it out at www.seldonhunt.com.

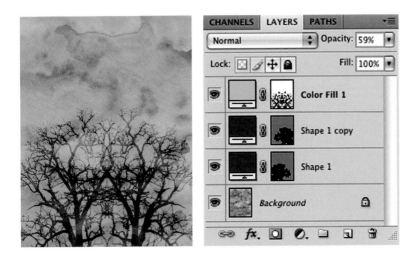

9 Hold down the Control (or Command) key and click the original layer's Vector Mask thumbnail in the Layers palette to generate a selection from its contents. Then, while the selection is active, hold down the Shift key while you Control-click (or Command-click) the duplicate layer's mask to add the masked area to the active selection. Press Control-I (or Command-I) to invert the selection and then, while the selection is active, choose the solid Color option from the Create New Adjustment or Fill Layer menu at the bottom of the Layers palette. When the picker appears, move the mouse over the top of the last swatch in the Swatches palette to select that color and click. You'll immediately see the color change on the canvas. When this happens, click OK and then reduce the opacity of the layer to 58% in the Layers palette.

10 Duplicate the solid color layer by dragging it onto the Create a New Layer button at the bottom of the Layers palette. Change the blending mode of the duplicate layer to Color. Now drag the Background layer onto the Create a New Layer button at the bottom of the Layers palette to duplicate it. Then drag the duplicate to the top of the stack in the Layers palette and change the blending mode to Linear Burn. Reduce the opacity to 27%. Now duplicate this layer as well and change the blending mode to Overlay. Control-click (or Command-click) on either solid color layer's mask to load a selection from it.

11 Select the Gradient tool and choose the Foreground to Transparent gradient preset from the preset picker in the Tool Options bar. Enable the radial method and then click the light yellow swatch in the Swatches palette. Click the Create a New Layer button at the bottom of the Layers palette to create a new layer and drag the layer to the top of the stack in the Layers palette. With the new layer targeted, click and drag from the horizontal center at the bottom of the canvas outward to create a radial gradient within the selection on the current layer.

12 Press Control-Shift-I (or Command-Shift-I) to invert the selection. Click the darkest red swatch in the Swatches palette and then choose the Linear gradient method in the Tool Options bar. Click and drag from the top of the trees downward to add a gradient into the inverted selection on the same layer. Then select the darker yellow swatch and perform the same operation, except do not drag as far down when creating this gradient. Press Control-D (or Command-D) to deactivate the selection. Choose Levels from the Create New Fill or Adjustment Layer menu at the bottom of the Layers palette to create a new Levels adjustment layer. In the Adjustment palette, adjust the input levels similarly to what is shown here, to increase the contrast and density of color of the underlying layers. Keep this file open; it will act as the main Photoshop working file from here on.

PART THREE: Adding birds and rays of light

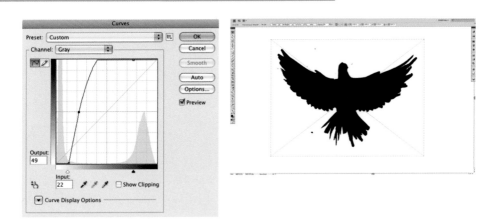

13 Open the *bird.jpg* file. Press Control-M (or Command-M) to access the Curves adjustment dialog box. In the dialog box, perform a drastic curve operation, like the one shown here, to increase the contrast in the image and remove all the midtone values between 100% black and 0% white. Apply the Curves adjustment and then save and close the *bird.jpg* file. Return to Illustrator and create a new file. Again, the artboard size or color space does not matter. Simply hide the artboard as you did before and then place the newly saved *bird.jpg* file into your document.

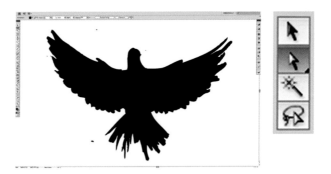

14 While the placed art is selected, click the Live Trace button in the Control palette. Next, click the Tracing Options dialog button in the Control palette as well. In the Tracing Options dialog box, decrease the threshold to 79 and enable the Ignore White operation. Press the Trace button and then choose Object > Expand from the menu. Leave the defaults as they are in the resulting dialog box and simply click OK to convert the traced artwork to vector paths. Now you'll notice that a few pieces of debris made their way into the traced artwork. Don't worry about these; we'll get rid of them now. Simply select the Direct Selection tool from the Toolbar. Click anywhere on the artboard to deselect the expanded vector art.

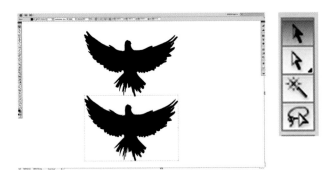

15 Use the Direct Selection tool to click anywhere on a single piece of debris. This will select a single point or line segment of the object, but that is fine. Next, simply press the Delete key twice to remove the debris. Repeat this process with every unwanted piece of debris until all that remains is your solitary bird shape. Choose the Selection tool from the Toolbar. Zoom out by pressing Control (or Command) until there is more visible space around the bird. Click the bird shape and drag down while holding down the Alt (or Option) and Shift keys to create a duplicate of the bird directly beneath the original.

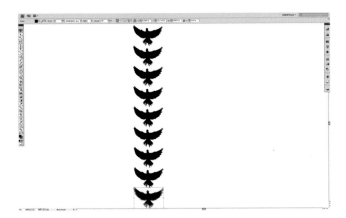

16 Ensure that your duplicate shape remains selected. Zoom out some more, then click and drag upward while holding down the Spacebar to temporarily access the Pan tool. Release the Spacebar to revert to the Selection tool, and then press Control-D (or Command-D) to perform the Transform Again command. This will repeat the duplication process exactly with your selected shape. Keep typing press Control-D (or Command-D) until there are nine birds stacked on top of each other.

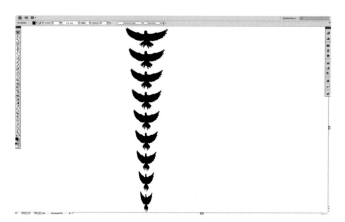

17 The bottom-most bird will be selected at the end of this series of Transform Again operations. Click the midpoint of the bounding box's vertical line at the left or right and drag it toward the center considerably while holding down the Alt (or Option) key. This step will horizontally scale the shape toward the central point. Next, select the bird above it and perform the operation to a lesser degree. Repeat this process, selecting the bird above each time, until a large, tapered shape made out of birds begins to appear. After doing this a few times, you'll find that it is necessary to drag outward while performing the scale operation.

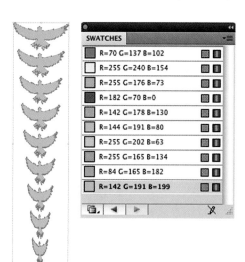

 Viewing Swatches

You'll notice that the default swatch display in Illustrator differs from the way that swatches are displayed in Photoshop. However, you can alter the way they are displayed in either program by simply choosing a different display option in the Swatches palette menu. You can view choose a list view or a different size of thumbnail if you like.

18 In Illustrator's Swatches palette, choose Open Swatch Library > Other Library from the Swatches Palette menu. Navigate to the *Swatches.ase* file you created earlier. When you click the Open button, the Swatches will load in a new palette. Press Control-A (or Command-A) to select all the bird shapes and then click the lightest blue swatch in your new Swatches palette. While all the birds are selected, press Control-C (or Command-C) to copy them.

19 Return to your Photoshop file and press Control-V (or Command-V) to paste. When the Paste dialog box appears, choose the Smart Object option. The artwork will be pasted into the file with a bounding box surrounding it. Simply press the Enter key, and don't worry about performing any transformation operations for the time being. Just leave the pasted art where it is. However, if your Smart Object is not at the top of the stack in the Layers palette, drag it there. Change the blending mode of the Smart Object to Overlay in the Layers palette.

Illustrator workaround 2

If you aren't using Illustrator, you can import the *birds* file as a Smart Object by doing the following: Choose File < Place from the menu in Photoshop. Then navigate to the *birds.ai* file included with the downloadable project files. This will give you the same result as pasting the art from Illustrator, as outlined in step 19.

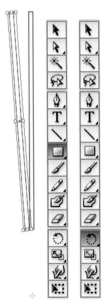

20 Return to Illustrator and create a new document. Select the Rectangle tool from the Toolbar and then draw a tall, thin rectangle. Ensure that this rectangle remains selected. Next, select the Rotate tool from the Toolbar and click once directly below the rectangle to create an origin point for the rotation. Hold down the Alt (or Option) key while you click the rectangle and drag it just slightly to the left. This will create a duplicate while rotating around the origin point. Ensure that the duplicate remains selected.

Smart Object advantages

A main advantage of working with a Smart Object is that it can be edited at any point. However, when you're pasting from Illustrator into Photoshop, there are other benefits. First, a Smart Object retains its assigned color from Illustrator. If this file were pasted as a Shape Layer, it would automatically have the foreground color applied to it. Second, a Smart Object is automatically fitted to the canvas area. This Illustrator file is immense compared to the Photoshop canvas, so pasting as a Smart Object saves us the trouble of scaling as well.

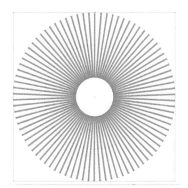

Illustrator workaround 3

Again, if you aren't using Illustrator, you can import the rectangles file as a Smart Object by choosing File > Place from the menu in Photoshop. Then navigate to the *rectangles.ai* file included with the downloadable project files. This will give you the same result as step 22, where the art is copied from Illustrator and pasted into Photoshop.

21 Press Control-D (or Command-D) over and over again to perform a number of Transform Again operations. This will create a circular shape made of rectangles. Don't worry about how the last instance of the rectangle meets up with the first one at the top. It isn't important. When you're finished, press Control-A (or Command-A) to select all and then click the pink, flesh-colored swatch to fill the objects with that color. Then press Control-C (or Command-C) to copy everything and return to your working file in Photoshop.

22 Press Control-V (or Command-V) to paste the copied vector art into Photoshop. Paste it into the file as a Smart Object and then hold down the Alt (or Option) and Shift keys as you drag a corner point of the bounding box outward to proportionately scale it out from the center. Click and drag within the bounding box to position in the horizontal center of the canvas and just a bit higher than the vertical center. When you're happy with the result, press the Enter key to apply the transformation. Change the blending mode of the Smart Object to Soft Light in the Layers palette.

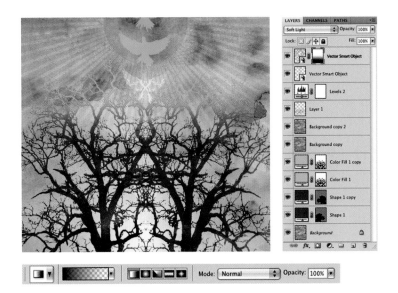

23 Click the Add Layer Mask button at the bottom of the Layers palette to add a mask to the Smart Object. Target the mask in the Layers palette and then select the Gradient tool. If the foreground color is not currently set to black, press the X key and then ensure that you have the Foreground to Transparent preset and the Linear method selected in the Tool Options bar. Click at the bottom of the canvas and drag upward about halfway, to create a soft transition between the lower rectangles and the background.

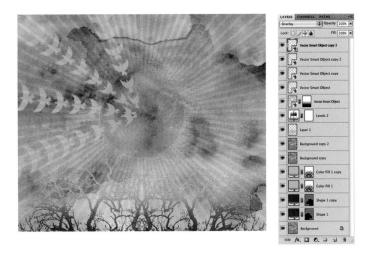

24 Drag the bird Smart Object above the rectangles Smart Object in the Layers palette. With the bird Smart Object targeted, press Control-T (or Command-T) to access Free Transform. When the bounding box appears, Shift-click a corner point and begin to drag inward to reduce the size proportionately. Then click and drag outside the box to rotate it. Try to match the angle of the rotated birds with the angle of the rectangle rays on the underlying smart object. Press Enter to apply the transformation and then Alt-drag (or Option-drag) the Smart Object with the Move tool to duplicate it. Use Free Transform to rotate and reposition the duplicate so that there is a gap between the two Smart Objects. Repeat the process a couple more times until the top corner of the canvas resembles what is shown here.

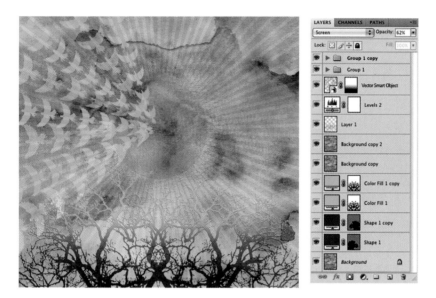

25 With the top bird Smart Object targeted in the Layers palette, hold down the Shift key and click the bottom bird Smart Object. This will target them all. When they're all targeted, press Control-G (or Command-G) to group them. Duplicate the group by dragging it onto the Create A New Layer button at the bottom of the Layers palette. Then, with the duplicate group selected, press Control-T (or Command-T) to access Free Transform. Increase the size proportionately, then rotate the group slightly so that the gaps between the rows of birds are filled. Press the Enter key to apply the transformation and then change the blending mode of the group to Screen. Reduce the opacity to 62%.

Grouping and duplicating

Fill the entire sky with birds by methodically, grouping, duplicating, and flipping.

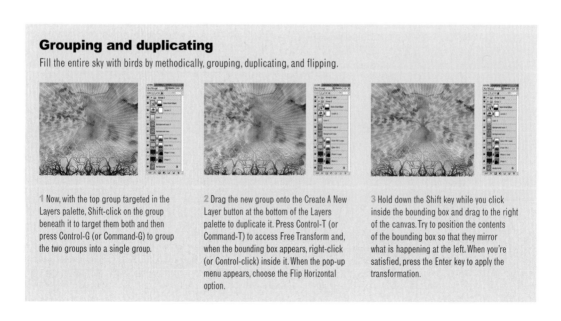

1 Now, with the top group targeted in the Layers palette, Shift-click on the group beneath it to target them both and then press Control-G (or Command-G) to group the two groups into a single group.

2 Drag the new group onto the Create A New Layer button at the bottom of the Layers palette to duplicate it. Press Control-T (or Command-T) to access Free Transform and, when the bounding box appears, right-click (or Control-click) inside it. When the pop-up menu appears, choose the Flip Horizontal option.

3 Hold down the Shift key while you click inside the bounding box and drag to the right of the canvas. Try to position the contents of the bounding box so that they mirror what is happening at the left. When you're satisfied, press the Enter key to apply the transformation.

PART FOUR: Creating shapes with the Pathfinder

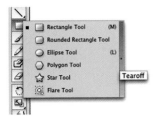

Align and Pathfinder

When you launch Illustrator in its default state, you will not see the Pathfinder palette or the Align palette. Both of these palettes are essential to following along with this chapter, so, to view them, simply choose Window > Pathfinder or Window > Align from the menu. When you do so, a floating palette will appear with tabs allowing you access to either of these palettes along with the Transform palette.

26 Okay, now would be a good time to save your Photoshop working file, because we're going to abandon it for a while and focus on Illustrator for the time being. In Illustrator, create a new document. Again, the size of the artboard and the color space are irrelevant. Simply hide the artboard via the View menu to avoid visual distractions as you work. If you click and hold the Rectangle tool, you'll notice all the other shape tools available when the tool is expanded. Basically, we're going to want to access the Ellipse tool and the Rectangle tool often. So, simply tear off this subtool palette by clicking and holding the tool until all the subtools are displayed. Then drag to the right until the tear-off bar becomes highlighted and let go. Once you've torn off the palette, you can place it anywhere.

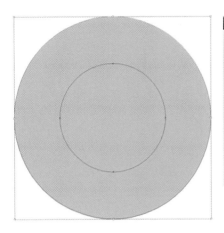

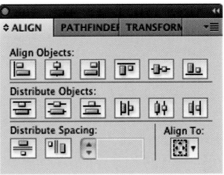

27 Select the Ellipse tool and then Shift-drag on the artboard to create a large circle. While the new circle is selected, click the dark yellow swatch to fill it with that color. Use the Selection tool to then Alt-click (or Option-click) the shape and drag to duplicate it. Shift-drag a corner point of the shape's bounding box inward to reduce the size of it proportionately. While the duplicate is selected, Shift-click the original shape to select it, too. With both shapes selected, click the Horizontal Align Center and Vertical Align Center buttons in the Align palette.

28 In the Pathfinder palette, click the Minus
Front button in the Shape Modes section. This
will nicely punch a hole in the big circle, using
the circle that was overlapping it as a tool. Now
draw a rectangle that overlaps the entire left
side of the resulting shape. Then select both the
rectangle and the underlying shape and, again,
click the Minus Front button.

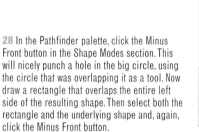

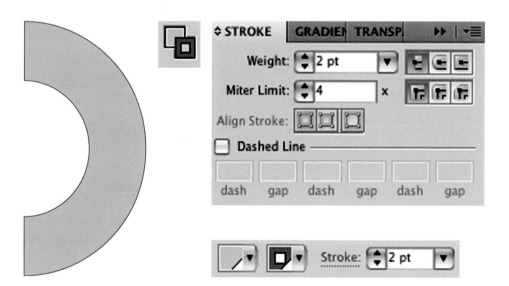

29 Click the Stroke swatch in the Toolbar, bringing it to the front so that it overlaps the fill swatch. Then, in the Swatches palette, click
the darkest red swatch, to apply a dark red stroke to the yellow shape. Now, depending on how large you've drawn your shape, you
might need to adjust the size relationship of the stroke to the object. While the object is selected, you can do this by altering the stroke
weight in either the Stroke palette or the Control palette.

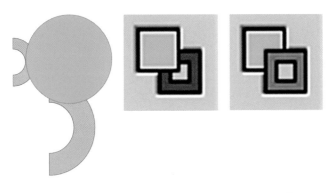

Toggling fill and stroke

A quicker way to toggle between fill and stroke than always returning to the Toolbar and clicking the one you want is to simply press the X key. Pressing X will invert them. So, if the stroke is in the background, pressing X will bring it to the foreground, sending the fill swatch to the background, or vice versa.

30 Use the Selection tool to Alt-drag (or Option-drag) this shape to a different area of the artboard; then Shift-drag a corner point inward to reduce the size of the duplicate proportionally. Now draw another large circle. Because you edited the stroke of your object last, clicking a color swatch will apply that color to your stroke, not the fill. So, to edit the fill rather than the stroke color, click the Fill swatch in the Toolbar to bring it to the foreground. Then, with the Fill swatch overlapping the stroke swatch, click a light green color swatch in the floating Swatches palette to fill the new circle shape. Then click the Stroke swatch in the Toolbar and select a darker green-colored swatch from the floating Swatches palette to alter the color of the object's stroke. Again, feel free to alter stroke width as necessary in the Stroke palette.

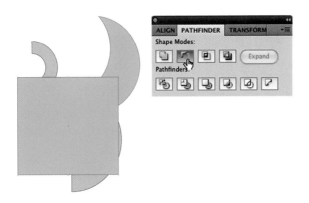

Quick jump to a Selection tool

When you're using a shape tool such as the Rectangle or the Ellipse tool, a quick way to access the last Selection tool used is to simply hold down the Control (or Command) key. Releasing the Control (or Command) key will immediately revert to the shape tool you were using. Because the Selection tool was the last tool we used here, that is what will show up when you hold down the Control (or Command) key. However, if the Direct Selection tool was the last tool used, then holding down the Control (or Command) key will temporarily access it instead.

31 Use the Selection tool to Alt-drag (or Option-drag) this shape upward a little and over to the left, creating a duplicate that overlaps it. Shift-click the original so that both green circles are selected; then click the Minus Front button in the Pathfinder palette. Now draw a rectangle that overlaps the lower-left portion of the resulting half-moon shape.

32 Use the Selection tool to Shift-click the underlying half-moon shape so that both are selected; then once again click the Minus Front button in the Pathfinder palette. Use this same Minus Front method to create a slimmer half-moon shape out of two circles, lower down on the artboard. Make it look more like a quarter moon this time around. Then draw a circle that overlaps the top of the quarter-moon shape. Note that your shapes will always possess the same stroke and fill attributes as the previous shapes you created—that is, until you alter these attributes. Use the Selection tool to Shift-click the underlying quarter-moon shape so that both are selected, then click the Unite button in the Pathfinder palette to unite them into a single shape.

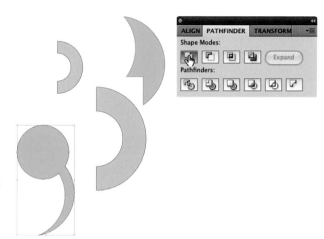

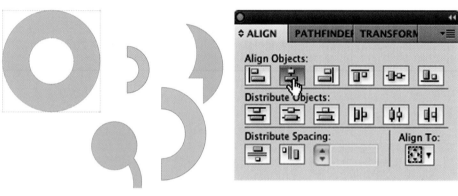

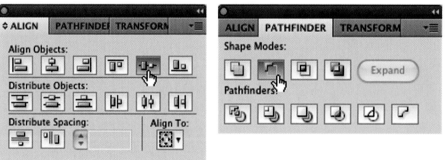

33 Now draw a large circle. Change the fill color to the lightest blue swatch in the floating Swatches palette and then change the stroke color to a slightly darker blue swatch. As always, feel free to alter the width of the stroke in the Stroke palette as you see fit. Next, create smaller circle that over laps this one in some way. Shift-click the underlying, larger circle with the Selection tool to select them both. Then direct your attention to the Align palette. In the Align palette, first click the Horizontal Align Center button and then click the Vertical Align Center button. After both circles are aligned, return to the Pathfinder palette and click the Minus Front button.

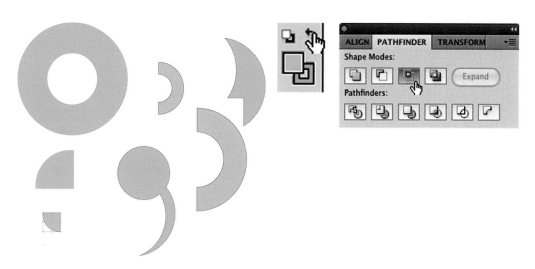

34 Draw another circle and, while that circle is selected, click the Swap Fill and Stroke icon just above the Fill and Stroke swatches in the Toolbar, to invert the colors. Next, draw a square that overlaps the top left of the circle. Use the Selection tool to Shift-click the underlying circle so that both are selected, then click the Intersect button in the Pathfinder to create a shape that is a result of only the regions that overlap. Use the Selection tool to Alt-drag (or Option-drag) this shape lower down on the artboard; then click and drag outside the bounding box once the mouse pointer changes to indicate rotation. Hold down the Shift key as you rotate to constrain the rotation to 45° increments. Shift-drag a corner point inward to proportionally reduce the size as well.

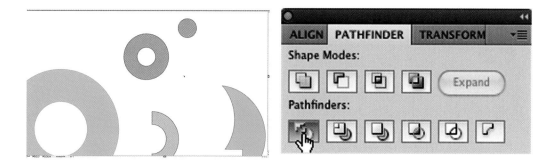

35 Now draw a circle using the pink swatch for the fill color and the red swatch for the stroke. Then draw another, smaller circle that overlaps it. Select both circles and then align them both vertically and horizontally using the same options we used previously in the Align palette. Next, click the Trim button in the Pathfinder palette. The result of the Trim operation is not immediately evident; it groups the two shapes together. To ungroup them, type Control-Shift-G (or Command-Shift-G). Then type Control-Shift-A (or Command-Shift-A) to deselect them. Next, use the Selection tool to click the smaller circle and drag it outside the other shape. Moving one of the shapes allows you to see the kind of result the trim operation will give you.

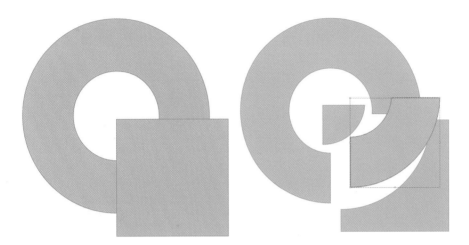

36 Now that you've witnessed the possibilities of the Trim operation, let's perform it again on an existing shape. Click once on the big blue donut shape we created previously. This will pick up the fill and stroke attributes that were used for this shape and apply those attributes to any subsequent shapes we create until you change them. Draw a square that overlaps the bottom-right corner of the big blue donut. Select both shapes and then click the Trim button. Again, ungroup and then deselect. Now use the Selection tool to select and move around the resulting individual shapes as you see fit.

Create additional shapes

Use Pathfinder operations and Align functions to add more shapes to the cluster.

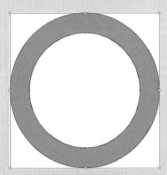

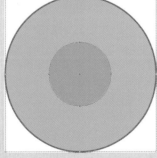

1 Create a circle using the pink swatch for the fill color and the red swatch for the stroke color. Then draw another circle overlapping it. Use the Vertical and Horizontal alignment options employed previously in the Align palette. Select them both and perform the Minus Front operation in the Pathfinder.

2 Next, create a couple of circles. Begin with a large one, then create a considerably smaller one. Specify different stroke and fill attributes for each circle and then select them both. While both are selected, align their Vertical and Horizontal centers via the Align palette.

3 Create some more shapes until you're satisfied that there is a nice cluster of objects to work with. Here's a glimpse at all the shapes that I created so far. You can use more or fewer shapes; it is up to you.

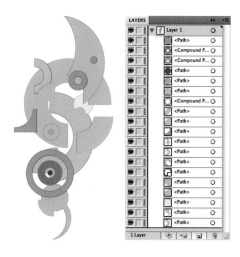

37 Use the Selection tool to move the shapes around to begin creating a somewhat designed cluster. Feel free to rotate and resize shapes as necessary until you like what you see. In addition, use the colors in the floating Swatches palette to change the stroke or fill color attributes of individual shapes as you work. Also, if you don't like the way that the shapes overlap, have a look in the Layers palette. Click the triangle that corresponds to Layer 1 to expand it. You'll see that every individual shape resides within Layer 1 on its own sublayer. You can drag sublayers up and down within the layer in the Layers palette to change the way that things overlap.

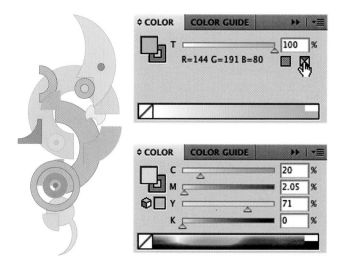

Moving forward and backward

In addition to moving shapes forward or backward in the Layers palette, options are also available in the Arrange menu. However, there are some keyboard shortcuts in Illustrator that will have you moving your shapes forward and backward even more quickly. Press Control-] (or Command-]) to move your selected shape forward, or press Control-[(or Command-[ ) to move your shape backward. If you want to move your shape all the way to the front, press Control-Shift-] (or Command-Shift-]), and inversely, to move it all the way to the back, press Control-Shift-[(or Command-Shift-[ ).

38 Now, I mentioned much earlier that the whole point of developing a group of swatches was to use them as a reference while formulating a color strategy within the illustration. However, until now we've been employing these colors quite literally. That is fine, but it is important to remember that you can alter things at any point as you go along. So, take a good look at the cluster of shapes and examine how the colors are working. To customize the color of a shape, select it and then click either the stroke or the fill swatch in the Color palette to gain access to the desired color on that shape. Then click the CMYK conversion icon to convert the color to an editable CMYK equivalent. Now go ahead and alter the color via the CMYK sliders. Use this method to tweak individual colors within the composition.

PART FIVE: Incorporating shapes into the composition

39 Press Control-A (or Command-A) to select all the shapes, then press Control-C (or Command-C) to copy them. Return to your working file in Photoshop and press Control-V (or Command-V) to paste. When the Paste dialog box appears, choose Smart Object from the Paste As options, to paste the copied art as a Smart Object. Shift-drag one of the top corners of the bounding box inward to reduce the size of the pasted art proportionately, and then drag within the box to visually center the object horizontally. Press the Enter key to apply the transformation and then reduce the opacity of the Smart Object to 65% in the Layers palette.

 Illustrator workaround 4

Again, for those of you who are following along but aren't using Illustrator, this Smart Object is available. Rather than pasting it, simply use the File > Place option in the menu to place the *shapes.ai* file included within the downloadable project files.

40 Duplicate the Smart Object, and then use Free Transform to rotate it 180° and flip it horizontally. Duplicate this Smart Object and use Free Transform to proportionately reduce the size and move it up considerably on the canvas area so that it extends beyond the top edge. Next, create another duplicate, increase the size a little, and move it down on the canvas. Create another, reduce the size, and move it down even more. Create another duplicate, move it up on the canvas area, and then rotate it 90°. Basically, t he goal here is to create a unique, abstract cluster from the vector shapes you brought in from Illustrator.

41 Continue duplicating the Smart Object and using Free Transform to resize, rotate, and reposition the duplicates on the canvas area. Carry on in this manner until you're satisfied with the coverage in the background. It should roughly resemble a cross shape and give off a sort of stained-glass feel when you're finished. It won't take long until an alarming number of duplicate Smart Objects begin to fill the Layers palette. To remedy this, target the top shape Smart Object. Then scroll down in the Layers palette until you find the bottom shape Smart Object. Click the bottom one while holding down the Shift key. This will target all the shape Smart Objects. When they are all targeted, press Control-G (or Command-G) to group them.

Blending the shapes

Stack up duplicate groups with varying blending modes to better integrate the vector shapes into the existing composition.

1 Begin by changing the blending mode of the group to Linear Burn in the Layers palette. Don't worry if it appears to dark and well, burned, at this stage. We'll fix that.

2 Duplicate the group and then change the blending mode of the duplicate group to Normal. To minimize the intensity, reduce the opacity of this duplicate group to 82%.

3 Finally, duplicate this group and change the blending mode of this new, second duplicate group to Overlay. Reduce the opacity of this group to 28%.

42 One of the advantages of working with a layered composition is the opportunity to edit any single component at any time without affecting the rest of the artwork. When I look at the green, watercolor sky in the top corners, I feel that it could be darker, more intense. To intensify this region, target the first duplicate you made of the background layer and increase the opacity to 50%. Choose the Hue/Saturation option from the Create New Fill or Adjustment Layer menu at the bottom of the Layers palette. Drag the new Hue/Saturation adjustment layer above both duplicates of the background layer in the Layers palette. In the Adjustments palette, decrease the saturation by 15 and the lightness by 4.

PART SIX: Adding the skeletons

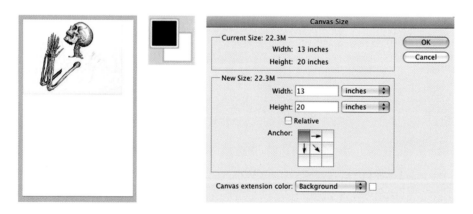

43 Open the *skeleton1.psd* file. Press the d key to ensure that the background color is set to its default, which is white. We are going to extend the canvas, and the default setting for extension color is the current background color. Although there is opportunity to change the extension color in the Canvas Size dialog box, hitting the d key ahead of time simply makes it go a little more quickly. Next, choose Image > Canvas Size from the menu. In the Canvas Size dialog box, click the top-left anchor and then change the size so that the resulting canvas will be 13 inches wide and 20 inches high. This will give us plenty of space to put the rest of the skeleton together within this file.

 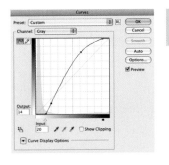 

44 Press Control-M (or Command-M) to access Curves. In the Curves dialog box, edit the curve as you see here to eliminate midtones while increasing contrast and preserving detail. Click OK to apply the Curves adjustment, and press the b key to select the Brush tool. Press the x key to make white the current foreground color, then click the Toggle the Brushes Panel icon in the Tool Options bar. When the Brushes palette appears, disable any dynamic functions except Smoothing and increase the brush diameter as you see fit. Then use this brush, with an opacity setting of 100, to paint white over areas of the background that remain gray even after performing the Curves Adjustment.

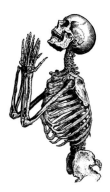 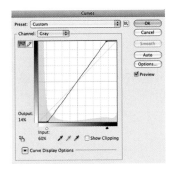 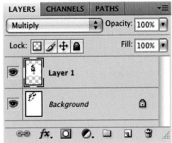

45 Choose File > Save As from the menu and save this file as *skeleton complete.psd*. After saving, open the *skeleton2.psd* file. Use the Move tool to drag the image from the *skeleton2.psd* file into your new *skeleton complete.psd* file as a new layer. Change the blending mode of the new layer to Multiply. Then, when the underlying image becomes visible, use the Move tool position the layer in its appropriate position on the canvas. Press Control-M (or Command-M) and then perform a Curves adjustment to this layer that yields a similar result to the adjustment you performed on the previous layer. Use the Brush tool to paint white over any gray areas that remain in the background on this layer.

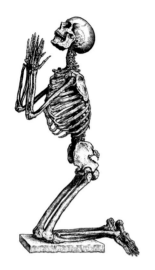

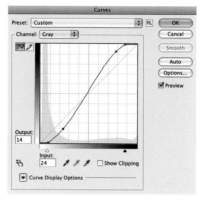

46 Now open the *skeleton.psd* file. As you did previously, drag the image into your *skeleton complete.psd* file and change the layer blending mode to Multiply. Use the Move tool to position it properly and then perform a similar Curves adjustment to the step you've performed previously on the other layers. Use the Brush tool to paint white over leftover gray regions in the background of this layer, too. Save and close the *skeleton complete.psd* file. The only file open in Photoshop right now should be the working file you've been building all along.

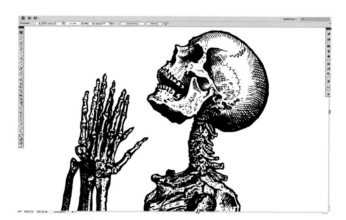

 Ancient resources

When you're working with vectors, there is a risk of things coming out too "cold and digital" at the end of it all. That's why I always try to add to the composition something prominent that feels organic.

47 Return to Illustrator and create a new document. Again, the size of the artboard doesn't matter, because we're just going to hide it anyway. Place the *skeleton complete.psd* file into the new Illustrator file and then click the Live Trace button in the Control palette. In this instance, the default setting performs an ideal tracing operation, so no further editing of the tracing options is required. Click the Expand button in the Control palette. After Expanding, press Control-Shift-G (or Command-Shift-G) to ungroup the expanded art and then press Control-Shift-A (or Command-Shift-A) to deselect.

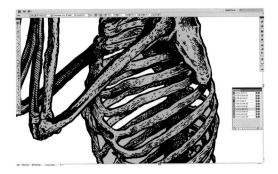

48 Use the Selection tool to click any white shape within the skeleton. Once that shape is selected, choose Select > Same > Fill Color from the menu to select all the objects in the file that have the same white fill color. With all the white shapes selected, click the dark yellow swatch in the floating Swatches palette. After changing all white objects to dark yellow, press Control-Shift-A (or Command-Shift-A) to deselect them. Use the Selection tool to click the rectangular background shape, and press the Delete key to delete it. Now, click all of the dark yellow shapes that are not actually bones. Click all shapes that were portions of the background and delete them. Do this to address the regions between the ribs, the open areas within his arms and legs, and so on.

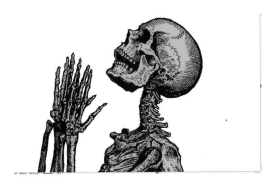

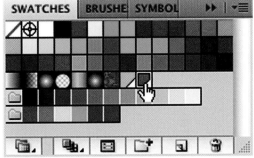

49 Next, use the Selection tool to click any black shape. Again, choose Select > Same > Fill Color from the menu to select all the objects in the file that have a black fill. When they are all selected, click the dark red swatch in the floating Swatches Library palette to change the fill of all selected regions to red instead of black. Now, looking at the image, I feel that we need more contrast between the colors. To remedy this, leave all the red shapes selected and direct your attention to the Swatches palette—not the floating Swatches Library you loaded but the actual Swatches palette. You might not have noticed, but as you click a swatch in the floating Swatches Library palette, it is also added to the Swatches palette. Your swatch will appear at the end of the default swatches, above the default color groups. Click your red swatch and then the Swatch Options button at the bottom of the palette. Alter the CMYK values of the red to match those shown here and click OK.

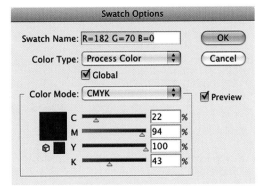

Illustrator workaround 5

If you're focusing solely on the Photoshop portions of this chapter, you can place the *skeleton.ai* file included in the downloadable project files. Use this as an alternative to pasting in step 50.

50 Press Control-A (or Command-A) to select all the shapes that make up the skeleton; then Press Control-C (or Command-C) to copy. Save your skeleton file if you like, but leave it open for the time being. Return to your working file in Photoshop and paste the copied art into the file as a Smart Object. Reduce the size of the pasted art proportionately by Shift-dragging a corner of the bounding box inward, and then press the Enter key to apply the transformation. Drag the newly pasted Smart Object to the top of the stack in the Layers palette. Use the Move tool to position the skeleton on the canvas similarly to is the one shown here.

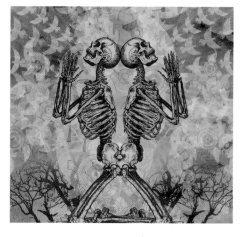

51 Drag the Smart Object onto the Create A New Layer button at the bottom of the Layers palette to duplicate it. Press Control-T (or Command-T) to access Free Transform, and then right-click (or Control-click) inside the bounding box. When the pop-up menu appears, choose the Flip Horizontal option. Then click inside the bounding box and drag to the right while holding down the Shift key. Position it so that the backs of the skeleton heads are touching; then press the Enter key to apply the transformation. Now, if you still need to move both skeletons up or down or to the left or right, simply target both Smart Objects and either drag with the Move tool or nudge the positioning with the arrow keys on the keyboard.

PART SEVEN: Other vector elements

52 Return to your open *skeleton* file in Illustrator. If you haven't saved it yet, do so now. Select all and then delete so that the file is empty. Now, you're probably wondering why we aren't simply creating a new file at this point. The reason is that if we create a new file, our two custom swatches will no longer exist in the Swatches palette of that new file. Granted, you could edit the contents of the Swatches palette, export the Swatches, and then load them in the new file. But really, why bother? This way just seems more direct for the limited tasks were asking of the swatches. Use the Ellipse tool to create a circle. Use your red swatch for the fill color and your yellow swatch for the stroke color. As always, feel free to edit the thickness of the stroke in the Stroke palette.

53 Create a number of new circles. Vary the sizes and try to position them so that, vertically, they more or less line up like the ones shown here. Also remember that you can control which circles overlap each other and in what order by altering the positions of sublayers within the Layers palette. Press Control-A (or Command-A) to select all, then the click the Horizontal Align Center button in the Pathfinder. Feel free to Shift-drag individual circles up or down after aligning. Holding down the Shift key will help prevent the circles from moving horizontally. Choose File > Save As from the menu and name the file *circles.ai*. Select all and copy.

54 Return to your Photoshop working file and paste the copied art into the file as a Smart Object. Increase the size of the Smart Object proportionately and press the Enter key. Drag the circle's Smart Object below the skeleton Smart Objects on the Layers palette. Use Free Transform to adjust the size again if necessary. Try to create a similar positioning and establish a size relationship between the circles and the skeletons that resembles what is shown here.

  Illustrator workaround 6

Okay, if you're not using Illustrator, you've no doubt figured out the routine by now. Just like last time, you can use File > Place to place the *circles.ai* file into your Photoshop working file as a Smart Object rather than pasting it from Illustrator.

55 Using the Move tool, click the Smart Object and drag it lower down on the canvas while holding down the Alt (or Option) and Shift keys to create a duplicate that is horizontally aligned. Position it on the canvas so that the pelvic regions of the skeletons are more or less in the center. Perform this operation a couple more times. However, in addition to duplicating, also use Free Transform to proportionately reduce the size of the duplicated Smart Objects. Position one duplicate Smart Object between the skeletons' backs and another behind the feet area.

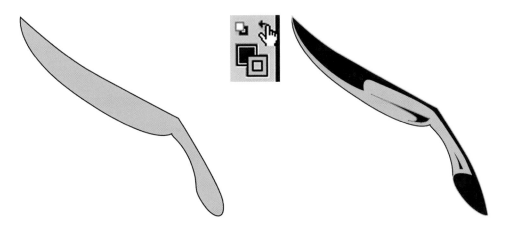

56 Return to your *circles.ai* file, which should still be open in Illustrator. Select and delete the circle shapes. Use the Pen tool to draw a closed shape like the one shown here. Use the yellow swatch for the fill color and the red swatch for the stroke color. Next, carefully draw a shape that covers select portions of the original shape, like the one shown here. When you draw the shape, it will automatically have the same stroke and fill attributes as the previous shape. That is fine for now. However, when you finish drawing the shape, click the Swap Fill and Stroke icon in the Toolbar to, well, swap the fill and stroke. Now, with the swap and fill colors in their current state, draw some details on the visible yellow regions of the first shape.

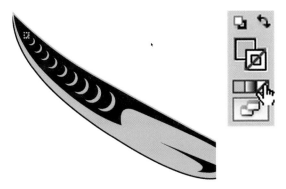

Illustrator starting point

For those of you who find creating custom shapes from scratch with the Pen tool a daunting task, I have included the shape created in step 56 in the downloadable project files. If you want to use this shape rather than creating your own, simply open the *wing start.ai* file and proceed to step 57.

57 Draw a small circle that sits on top of the red region at the upper left. Then use the Selection tool to click it and drag to the left slightly while holding down the Alt (or Option) key to create an overlapping duplicate. Hold down the Shift key and then click the original so that they are both selected. While they are both selected, click the Minus Front button in the Pathfinder palette. After performing the Minus Front operation, swap the stroke and fill colors. Next, click the Stroke icon in the Toolbar and then click the None option beneath it to remove the stroke from the shape. Alt-drag (or Option-drag) with the Selection tool to create a series of duplicates that fill the red region of the underlying wing shape. Shift-click the corner points of individual bounding boxes to reduce the size of each subsequent shape a little more than the last.

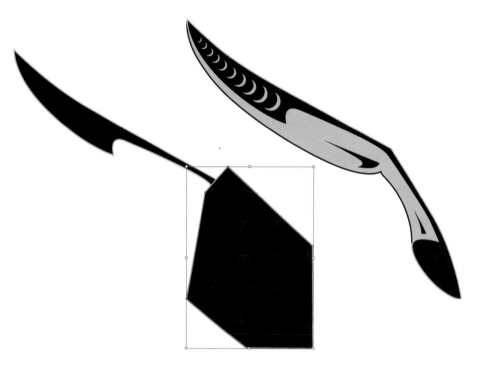

58 Use the Selection tool to click the large red shape and Press Control-C (or Command-C) to copy it. After copying, Press Control-A (or Command-A) to select all the shapes and then Press Control-G (or Command-G) to group them. After grouping, press Control-V (or Command-V) to paste the copied shape back into the file. Move it away from the group so that it does not overlap for the time being. Then draw a rough shape with the Pen tool that completely covers the right portion of the red shape.

Subtract, duplicate, and rotate
Use the Pathfinder, and overlapping, rotated instances of the same shape to create a new section of wing detail.

1 Use the Selection tool to select both of the overlapping shapes, then click the Minus Front button in the Pathfinder palette.

2 Alt-drag (or Option-drag) the shape with the Selection tool to duplicate it. Then do the same thing to create a copy of the duplicate.

3 Select each shape, then click and drag just outside of a bounding box corner point to rotate it. The result should look something like this.

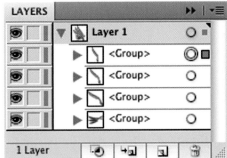

59 Select these three shapes and group them. Then use the Selection tool to drag the new group over to the other group so that it overlaps the region at the lower right. Rotate the shape and then press Control-[(or Command-[ ) to tuck this group behind the other group. Now select the other group and use the same method employed on the previous page to create a couple of duplicates of this group. Rotate each group and reposition them so that the result resembles what is shown here.

60 Select all and copy. Return to your Photoshop working file and paste the copied art into it as a Smart Object. Rotate and resize the pasted art. Position it in the region of one skeleton's forearms. Press the Enter key and then drag it beneath all of the skeleton and circle Smart Objects in the Layers palette. Duplicate the Smart Object and use Free Transform to flip it horizontally. While holding down the Shift key, use the Move tool to drag the Smart Object into position at the opposite side of the canvas.

Illustrator workaround 7

If you aren't using Illustrator, the final file you'll need to place containing the wing artwork can be found in the downloaded project files. Choose File > Place from the menu and navigate to the *wing.ai* file.

There is a lot you can do while working within in the parameters of what we created in this chapter. The preceding image is a bit simpler in terms of elements involved. Granted, there are more tree shapes in the background, but there are no abstract Pathfinder-based shapes included here. However, even without these Pathfinder-based shapes, the composition remains powerful and focused.

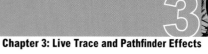

Here we see a similar approach in terms of the fact that there are two skeletons mirroring each other. Also, Pathfinder-based shapes are quite abundant in the background here, too. However, what makes this composition unique is the way that Pathfinder-based shapes are also used to create some primary components that surround the scarab-like brain creature at the top of the canvas.

Chapter 4

Hand-Painted Magic

Combining Painter with Photoshop

The first time I used Painter, it was still sold in a can. Back then it was owned by Fractal Design and there was nothing else like it. That is true today as well, but I must digress here to put things into perspective. I remember that period when even layers in Photoshop were thought of as an exciting new development. I was one of the many digital artists rejoicing in the glory of the new layer-based Photoshop workflow when I launched Painter for the first time.

What I found in Painter was confusion. There was a drawer-based interface and everything felt all over the place. After some experimentation I was able to get to work and really explore the power of what the program had to offer. That power, for those of you who don't know, is the nearly flawless simulation of real-world art materials. I was blown away by how natural it felt, even at that early stage. However, there was a handicap: The interface felt cumbersome next to what was happening in the most recent versions of Photoshop at that time. For that reason I drifted away from Painter. You see, Photoshop was really hitting its stride in terms of interface organization, and that was an easy thing to get used to. So, when I would decide to use Painter, it just felt laborious next to using Photoshop, and so I abandoned it entirely for years.

Now, let's fast-forward to what is happening currently with Painter. It is now owned by Corel and has been with that company for quite a while. Under the Corel umbrella, Painter has really blossomed. The materials and natural-feeling painterly workflow have done nothing but improve. But something else has happened during Painter's term at Corel: It has begun to play nicely with Photoshop. Right now it has an interface that will no longer confuse Photoshop users, and bouncing back and forth between applications is intuitive and comfortable. All this contributes to realizing your vision without obstacles. You no longer have to get hung up on the workflow and can instead spend your time being creative. And Painter is one hell of a creative tool.

Versions

Photoshop CS4
Painter 11

Requirements and Recommendations

In addition to Photoshop, you'll need a copy of Painter. If you don't have a copy of Painter, a trial version can be downloaded from www.corel.com. If you don't have a pressure-sensitive tablet, this chapter is the excuse you need to go out and buy one. Without a tablet, painting can feel laborious. Furthermore, to really make use of Painter's full potential, a tablet is essential. Some of the content of this chapter will be nearly impossible to follow without using a tablet.

What you'll learn in this chapter

Creative Techniques and Working Methods

Building from bits and pieces

In the first portions of this chapter, you'll learn to prepare a photographic composition to use as an underlying template in Painter. Although this form of preparation is essential and obvious to many, it is the pre-Photoshop preparation that must be considered as well. Here this was done while we were shooting the model in the studio. Knowing that something can be built up from bits and pieces in Photoshop will make the process of shooting the components much easier, and the outcome will be better. In this case, hair, fabric, and the figure were shot separately in the studio, according to plan. Then everything was compiled against a separate background shot in Photoshop. The initial pages of this chapter will shed light on the logic and benefits of this process as you work your way through.

Doing a lot with very little

Painter, like Photoshop, or perhaps even more so, has a massive arsenal of powerful tools. The temptation for many neophytes is to employ as many as possible out of sheer enthusiasm. Doing so can result in cluttered, chaotic, and disconnected results. Here we focus on a handful of powerful tools that work quite nicely together. Using a limited toolset is an excellent way to produce stunning results while avoiding the daunting task of mastering and implementing a vast number of tools.

Tools, Features, and Functions

Artists' Oils

Almost single-handedly, this Brush Category rekindled my interest in Painter. Depositing a limited amount of paint as you go might not sound like much, but the Artists' Oils are frighteningly close to the real deal.

Picking up underlying colors

It is just a little check box for each layer in Painter, but it is an unrelenting powerhouse of a feature. Picking up paint from underlying layers simply adds to authentic effect already brought home by the Artists' Oils.

Pattern Chalk

A variant of the Pattern Pens category in Painter, this amazing feature lets you use imagery to define the mark made by your brushes. Do not confuse this function with defining a brush in Photoshop; it goes deeper than that.

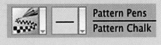

Having an idea of what you want ahead of time is always important, even if you don't feel like creating a preliminary sketch. For example, I knew that I wanted unrealistic flowing hair. So we decided to shoot the model's hair separately, as she lay on the ground. I had similar thoughts regarding the fabric. I wanted to have it flowing around her, to create an ethereal feeling. Rather than blowing a fan on the model while she was draped, we simply shot the fabric separately as well. The photography process can be much more effective if you consider capturing all the bits and pieces separately, knowing you can combine them in Photoshop afterward.

Model: Josie Lee; Hair and Makeup: Angela Veel; Photography: Vincent Lions

Beyond Photoshop

PART ONE: Building a well-composed, photographic base

1 Begin by opening the *ships.tif* file. This file will serve as the background layer in our working file, which will move back and forth between Photoshop and Painter. Next, open the *model.tif* file. Use the Move tool to click the image in the *model.tif* file and drag it into the *ships.tif* file as a new layer. Now, before we add any further images to the composition, we'll focus on the strategic placement of elements within the composition. Press Control-R (or Command-R) to show rulers.

 Project files

All the files needed to follow along with this chapter and create the featured image are available for download on the accompanying Website in the project files section. Visit www.beyondphotoshopthebook.com.

2 Click the vertical ruler at the left and begin to drag to the right while you are still holding down the mouse button. When you're about a third of the way into the image, release the mouse button. This will create a vertical guide. Repeat this process again, placing a guide further along toward the right so that the two vertical guides divide the image into thirds. There is no need for mathematical precision at this point. Simply position the guides visually. If you want to adjust the position of a guide after you've placed it, just click and drag it to where you want it to be. You can move your guides at any point.

Andrew Jones

If it wasn't for the work of Andrew Jones, there probably wouldn't be any geometric or abstract shapes swirling about in this composition. His work is unique and innovative, and because of him I decided to investigate the use of patterns in Painter—something that I never thought about before. If you scour the Web, you'll see that he integrates ZBrush into his work as well. He is a true contemporary master. Visit his site at www.androidjones.com.

3 Now direct your attention to the horizontal ruler at the top of the page. Click it and drag downward approximately a third of the way into the image. Then release the mouse button to create a horizontal guide. Repeat this process again, dragging further down until you've divided the vertical space of the image into thirds as well. At this point, you have broken the image into vertical and horizontal thirds, dividing the image into nine parts. Although you'll never see these guides in the finished image, we will use them to place elements in the image to create a balanced and interesting composition. This technique is commonly referred to as the *rule of thirds*.

4 The core principle behind the rule of thirds is that if you place the points of interest in your image where the lines intersect, the viewer can perceive or interact with them in a natural manner. However, in addition to intersection points, the lines are also useful for positioning elements within the scene. Ensure that Layer 1 is targeted and then use the Move tool to drag the contents of the layer so that the model is placed along the left vertical grid line. This will help remedy the visual awkwardness of her placement in the middle of the canvas. Now drag her down until her head is placed on the intersection point of the grid at the upper left. This is a natural point of focus for the viewer, so it is an ideal position for our primary point of interest in the image. In addition, her elbow becomes a secondary point of interest due to its placement.

5 Press Control-R (or Command-R) to hide the rulers and then press Control-; (or Command-;) to hide the guides. Worry not; your grid lines are not gone, and neither are the rulers. To enable the visibility of either at any point later on, simply use the same keyboard commands you used to hide them. Now that we've effectively placed the model in the scene, we need to remove the gray background behind her. Use the rectangular Marquee tool to draw a rough selection border that completely surrounds the rectangular background behind the model. While the selection is active, choose Select > Color Range from the menu.

Locking Guides

Once you've placed your guides where you want them, they could be accidentally moved with the Move tool. In order to prevent this, simply choose View > Lock Guides from the menu or type Control-Alt-; (or Command-Option-;) to lock them. Unlocking them is as simple as revisiting the same menu item or typing the same keyboard command.

6 When the Color Range dialog box opens, move it to the side if necessary so that it does not obscure your image. Move the mouse over the image and you will see the mouse pointer turn into an Eyedropper icon. Click an area of the gray background within the selection. Immediately you'll see that the range of color you clicked is selected, as it will be indicated by white in the Color Range Preview. All nonselected regions will appear as black. Hold down the Shift key and click other regions of the gray background to add them to the selected region of color. You can also preview the regions of color that will be selected by choosing an option from the Selection Preview menu. Select the White Matte option to show all nonselected regions as white.

Masked/selected areas

When you enter Quick Mask mode, by default selected areas are not covered by the overlay, and areas that fall outside the selection border are. If you want to invert this so that selected areas are covered by the color overlay, simply double-click the Quick Mask Mode icon at the bottom of the Toolbar. When the Quick Mask options appear, simply change the setting so that color indicates selected areas rather than masked areas.

7 You will notice in both the Color Range Preview as well as in the White Matte Preview in the image window that there are some nonbackground regions that are working their way into the selected range. To remedy this, try reducing the fuzziness in the Color Ranges dialog box by dragging the fuzziness slider to the left. This will make the Color Range tool less liberal when it comes to including similar regions of color in the selected range. In addition, you can Alt-click (or Option-click) any regions you want to subtract from the selected range in the image window. Do not expect the selected range to be a perfect selection, but when you're satisfied that it is a good starting point, click OK to exit the color range and generate a selection.

8 This selection doesn't need to be perfect, since we'll be using this photographic composition as a basis for our painting in Painter later. However, we are going to delete the selected contents from the layer. Before we do that, it is very important to ensure that no key image components are selected. The best way to preview the selection and alter it if necessary is to use Quick Mask. To enter Quick Mask mode, simply press the Q key on your keyboard. Alternatively, you can click the Quick Mask Mode icon at the bottom of the Toolbar. As soon as you enter Quick Mask mode, this icon will change to indicate it. Your selected regions will remain visible, yet all regions that fall outside your selection border will be covered with a red overlay on the canvas.

9 Select the Brush tool and choose a round, soft preset from either the preset picker in the Tool Options bar or the Brushes palette. Ensure that the opacity is set to 100% and that the current foreground color is black. If the foreground color is white, simply press the X key to remedy this. Use the Brush tool to paint over any regions that are selected that shouldn't be. In this case, we painted over her eyes because they were similar to the selected color range in the background. Inversely, you can switch the foreground color to white and add any unselected regions of the background to the selection by painting over them with white, removing the red overlay in these regions.

10 When you're satisfied with the edits you've made to the selection border within Quick Mask, simply press the Q key again to exit Quick Mask mode. When the selection loads, press the Delete key to remove the selected contents from the current layer, then press Control-D (or Command-D) to deactivate the selection. If there are artifacts left over after you delete, you can erase them with the Eraser tool or you can simply leave them alone if they're insignificant. It is important to remember that although we want to create a nice composition at this point, it does not need to be perfect by photographic standards because this composition is simply a building block for your painting.

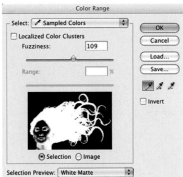

11 Open the *hair.tif* file. Again, choose Select > Color Range from the menu. When the Color Range options appear, click an area of her hair in the image window. You will see this indicated as the targeted range of color immediately in the Color Range preview. If you haven't changed anything, the Selection preview in the image window will still be set to White Matte, which is also very helpful for previewing your selected range. Next, hold down the Shift key and click other brown regions of her hair to add them to the selected range. Try increasing the Fuzziness as you do this as well. The goal is to select all the ranges of color within her hair only. When you're satisfied, click OK to load the selection.

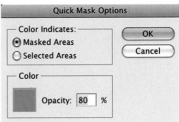

12 Press the Q key on your keyboard to enter Quick Mask mode. Here you can see that sometimes the translucent red overlay is not the most helpful device to view the areas of your image that are selected. In this case, due to the color of her hair and the color and value of her skin, it is a little hard to distinguish what's what. To remedy this, double-click the Quick Mask icon at the bottom of the Toolbar. You will exit Quick Mask mode and at the same time, the Quick Mask options will appear. Click the Color swatch and then choose something drastically different, such as a luminous blue, from the picker. Then increase the opacity of the overlay to something like 80% and click OK. After that, press the Q key again to view the difference in Quick Mask mode.

13 As you did previously, select the Brush tool and use it to edit the Quick Mask. Paint black over areas you want to mask and paint with white over areas you want to reveal. Increase and decrease the brush diameter as necessary, but leave the opacity set to 100%, since we do not want subtlety here, simply selected or not selected. Ensure that you mask her face and neck and then press the Q key to exit Quick Mask mode. Use the Move tool to click inside the selection border, and drag the selected contents into your working file as a new layer.

14 While your new layer is targeted in the Layers palette, press Control-T (or Command-T) to access Free Transform. When the bounding box appears, Shift-click and drag a corner point inward to reduce the content proportionately. Click and drag within the box to move the content on the canvas and try to place it so that it looks as though the hair is flowing from her head to the right. Press the Enter key to apply the transformation, then drag the hair layer beneath the model layer in the Layers palette to see how it works in the composition. If you need to tweak the size, feel free to use Free Transform again. Don't worry about how multiple transformations will affect the image quality. Remember, image deterioration is not really an issue here, because we're building a template for a painting.

 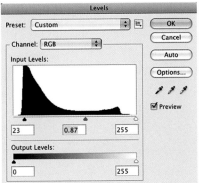

15 Our goal at this point is to draw attention to the interesting spaces within the composition, which are divided by light and dark shapes. In particular, we want the hair we added to look as though it is part of the model in terms of value, so that the model and her hair are one continuous shape. Ensure that the hair layer is targeted and then press Control-L (or Command-L) to access Levels. When the Levels options appear, drag the left Input Levels slider to the right to darken the shadow regions within the hair. Then drag the midpoint slider to the right a little as well, to darken the hair's midtones. Adjust the sliders as you see fit until the value of the hair on the current layer matches up to the value of the hair on the back of the model's head. When you're satisfied, click OK.

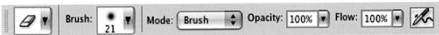

16 Target the model layer in the Layers palette and select the Eraser tool. Yes, that's right, I said the Eraser. I know that usually I'll mask things I want to remove, but again, I want to point out that we're creating a painting template across a series of layers, not a finished image at this point. And normally I would mask the layers anyway rather than erase. However, I have noticed that certain tools in Painter, which pick up underlying colors, can see past a mask and will pick up color that is hidden. That can get confusing, so we're going to erase rather than mask in this particular section. Ensure that the Eraser is set to Brush mode and then select an appropriate brush in the Tool Options bar. Erase the hair to the left of the model's face. I suggest using a small, round, soft-edged preset while you are erasing the area close to her face. Then I would increase the brush diameter for other regions that aren't as sensitive. Feel free to erase any portions of hair at the top or back of her head that you deem unsightly.

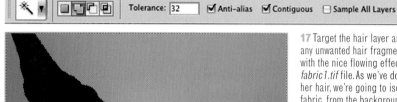

17 Target the hair layer and use the Eraser to remove any unwanted hair fragments that you feel interfere with the nice flowing effect in the image. Now open the *fabric1.tif* file. As we've done so far with the model and her hair, we're going to isolate the subject, this time the fabric, from the background. If you take a good look at the fabric, you'll see that it will be difficult to isolate using the previous Color Range method, because so much of the background shows through. Instead of using Color Range, select the Magic Wand tool. Ensure that the Contiguous option is enabled in the Tool Options bar and then click the gray background of the image. The selection will not include all regions of the background, so go ahead and Shift-click any unselected regions until the entire background is selected.

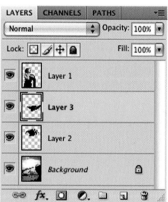

18 Press Control-Shift-I (or Command-Shift-I) to invert the selection, and then use the Move tool to drag the selected fabric into your working file as a new layer. Drag the fabric layer beneath the model layer in the Layers palette if it isn't there already, and then press Control-T (or Command-T) to access Free Transform. This time, move the mouse outside the bounding box, then click and drag to rotate the contents. In addition, feel free to position the bounding box and scale the contents as well at this point, until the new piece of fabric looks as though it is flowing out from her arm in the same direction as her hair. When you're satisfied, press Enter to apply the transformation.

19 Target the model layer and select the Lasso tool. Draw a rough selection that surrounds most of the piece of fabric that hangs down from the model's arm. Leave some space where it meets her skin; just isolate the big piece that extends to the bottom of the image. When your selection is complete, press the Delete key. Then press Control-D (or Command-D) to deactivate the selection. After the selection is deactivated, select the Eraser tool. Use the same method you used before when erasing her hair to erase the remaining bit of fabric that is hanging down just below the skin of her arm. Use extra care while erasing the region that meets her skin.

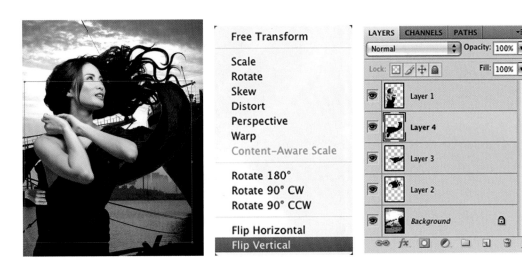

20 Open the *fabric2.tif* file. Again, use the Magic Wand tool with the Contiguous option enabled to click on a gray region of the background. Then, Shift-click in the remaining unselected gray regions until the entire background is selected. After that, invert the selection by pressing Control-Shift-I (or Command-Shift-I) and drag the selected fabric into the working file as a new layer. Press Control-T (or Command-T) to access Free Transform, and when the bounding box appears, right-click (or Control-click) inside the bounding box. When the pop-up menu appears, choose the Flip Vertical option.

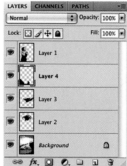

21 Click and drag outside the bounding box to rotate the contents, and then click and drag within the bounding box to move the fabric over to the lower-left corner of the canvas. The goal here is to make it look as though this piece of fabric is flowing in from the left side and curving upward slightly, as shown here. When you're satisfied with the transformation, press the Enter key to apply it.

Minimizing visual confusion

In order for the composition to be perceived naturally by the viewer, we need to alter the balance of positive and negative space by lightening some of the background elements.

1 Create a new layer and drag it down in the Layers palette until it sits directly above the Background layer. Change the blending mode of the layer to Lighten in the Layers palette.

2 Select the Gradient tool. Choose the Radial method and the Foreground to Transparent preset in the Tool Options bar. Alt-click (or Option-click) the darkest blue color present in the image's factory buildings to sample it as the current foreground color.

3 Click and drag to create a radial gradient on the new layer that overlaps the bow of the ship at the right. Then do this over the bow of the ship at the left. Then methodically sample colors from the hazy skyline and build up a series of gradients on this layer.

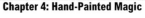

 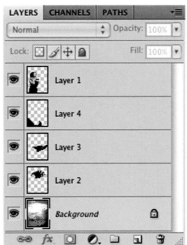

22 Feel free to take your time and experiment with the gradients you're introducing. You'll notice that I had you create them on a separate layer. That is because if things really go awry and you make a mess of it, you can simply delete the layer and start again. However, when you're satisfied with the way your gradients on the new layer affect the contrast in the background, it is safe to merge the layers. Ensure that the layer containing the gradients is targeted, and then Shift-click the Background layer in the Layers palette so that they are both targeted. When both layers are targeted, press Control-E (or Command-E) to merge them.

 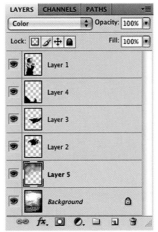 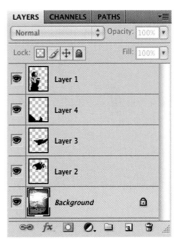

23 You'll likely notice that after you've filled the middle region of the canvas with all those gradients, there is some unity there in terms of color. This is due to the fact that all the colors used in the gradients were sampled from the horizon region, which in itself uses a limited color theme. When you analyze this result, you will then notice that the upper portion of the background does not feel unified since it adheres to a somewhat different color theme. To remedy this, create a new layer that sits directly above the background layer. Change the blending mode of the new layer to Color. Ensure that the new layer is targeted, and then create some gradients on the new layer at the top of the canvas using colors sampled from the horizon region used previously. Merge this layer with the background when you're satisfied with the results.

PART TWO: Divine proportion in Painter

24 Save your file and quit Photoshop. Launch Painter and then open your working file. Immediately you will see the guides you created in Photoshop. In Painter they will be displayed as black lines. These can still serve as compositional tools, but let's hide them for the time being because Painter has an amazing compositional tool of its own. Press Control-; (or Command-;), just as you would in Photoshop, to hide the guides from view. Choose Window > Divine Proportion from the menu, to display the Divine Proportion palette. Click the Enable Divine Proportion option at the top left of the palette to show the Divine Proportion Guide on the canvas. Initially, the guide is placed horizontally, which doesn't suit our composition thus far.

Not using Painter?

If you aren't using Painter, you can skip ahead to Part 9 of this chapter and follow along with the next round of Photoshop work. However, because the image in this chapter culminates in Painter rather than Photoshop, you won't get to the completion stage without using Painter. I do strongly recommend that you download Painter and follow along, since the user interface and method for building layered files is very similar. That being said, if you do not want to follow along with Painter, you can still have a peek at the final layered file; I've included it within the downloadable project files for this chapter. The file is called *reference.psd*. This is the finished file that is achieved at the end of the chapter.

25 In the Divine Proportion palette, select the Portrait Top Left orientation option. Now you might find it useful to increase the opacity to 100% near the bottom of the palette so that you can see the Divine Proportion Guide clearly on the canvas. When the orientation of the guide changes, you'll immediately see that using the rule of thirds to compose our image has paid off. The idea here is to use the spiral and triangles as a guide to create a composition that allows our eyes to flow around it, taking in the elements with ease in a natural manner. The Divine Proportion tool can be used as a compositional guide when you begin, or it can be used as guide for cropping after the fact. However, in this case we'll use it as a guide to refine the composition.

26 In Painter's Layers palette, click the Model layer to target it. Then hold down the Shift key and click the layers that contain her hair and the fabric fragments. This will result in every layer except the background layer being targeted. Select the Layer Adjuster tool from the Tool palette and use it to click the model and drag her to the left and slightly downward. Position the model and the other targeted layers so that her eye is aligned with the center of the spiral.

Divine Proportion

Painter's inclusion of a Divine Proportion tool is further testament to the theory that anyone who applies the principles of divine proportion can create a balanced composition. When you use the Divine Proportion tool as guide for placing the main focal points in your image, you can't go wrong. The Divine Proportion tool is based on the divine triangle, used by classical artists to compose visually pleasing paintings. This tool allows you to create a sense of proportion in your work and is the optical guide that was used for centuries by the Old Masters. Originally written about by Euclid, divine proportion naturally occurs all around us. It can be found in the proportions of the human face and more obviously in the contour of a nautilus shell. Perhaps the reason we respond to it compositionally is that it is something that is natural to us as human beings.

27 Immediately you'll see the difference this slight movement to adhere to the Divine Proportion Guide makes in our composition. When you're happy with the way the image is composed, go ahead and disable the visibility of the Divine Proportion Guide by unchecking the Enable Divine Proportion check box in the Divine Proportion palette. The guide is still there and remains in the same position relative to the image; it is simply hidden from view to avoid visual distraction while you work. Like the horizontal and vertical guides that exist in the file, you can enable the visibility of the Divine Proportion Guide at any point later by clicking on the (now familiar) check box within the Divine Proportion palette.

Beyond Photoshop

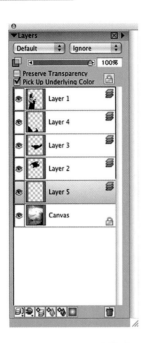

28 We're going to be building up paint on a series of new layers, so the content within the Layers palette is going to grow and grow. To see more of the content in the Layers palette, click the Layers palette bar at the top of the palette and drag it away. This will remove the Layers palette from its grouping with the Channels palette and let it float freely on its own. The main advantage of doing this is that you can then click and drag on the bottom-right corner of the palette to increase the size so that you don't have to scroll within the palette to view the content. Do this, and then click the New Layer button at the bottom of the Layers palette. Click the new layer in the Layers palette to target it. Click the Pick Up Underlying Color option and drag the layer into position so that it sits directly above the Canvas layer in the Layers palette. The Canvas layer is the same as Photoshop's Background layer; it just has a different name in Painter.

29 Double-click your new layer to access the Layer Attributes box. In this box, rename the new layer canvas paint and click OK. Don't worry about the other options in the Layer Attributes; we just want to change the name for the sake of clarity as we continue. Next, double-click the layer that contains her hair and name it hair in the Layer Attributes box. After that, double-click the layer that contains the fabric near her arm and name it fabric. Then double-click the layer that contains the fabric near the bottom and name it fabric bottom. Finally, double-click the layer that contains our model and name it figure. This might seem a little inconsistent with what I've done in other chapters, but in this chapter we're going to be painting on specific layers in the layer hierarchy, and painting on the wrong layer at any point will cause confusion and adversely affect the desired results. All the new layers should automatically have the Pick Up Underlying Color option enabled. Check each one and enable this function if necessary.

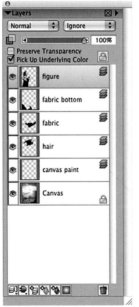

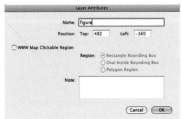

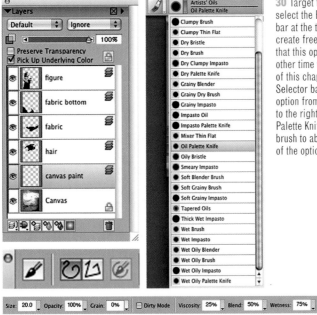

30 Target the canvas paint layer in the Layers palette and select the Brush tool from the Tool palette. In the Property bar at the top of the interface, ensure that the Brush is set to create freehand strokes. It is likely that it will be, but ensure that this option is enabled for this instance as well as every other time we use the Brush tool in Painter for the duration of this chapter. Click the Brush Category icon in the Brush Selector bar at the upper right and choose the Artists' Oils option from the Brush Category list. Then click the Variant icon to the right of it in the Brush Selector bar and choose the Oil Palette Knife option from the variant list. Set the size of the brush to about 20 pixels in the Property bar and leave the rest of the options set to their defaults for the time being.

PART FOUR: Using the Palette Knife on existing imagery

31 Begin to paint on the new layer in the clouds region at the top of the canvas. The Palette Knife will use the color and imagery from underlying layers and spread it around on the new layer, creating a paint effect. Paint a series of strokes in different regions to remove the initial photographic appearance of the image. If this is your first foray into Painter, it might feel a little weird. Spend some time experimenting with how the brush feels and reacts with the imagery in the clouds area until you get the hang of it. Try to create strokes that mimic the contour and fluffiness of the cloud. After you spend some time doing this, a painterly feeling will become more and more evident in the background. Go back and forth over the cable above the model's head, using multiple strokes until it becomes obscured by blended paint. You can smooth the effect by gently painting over regions more than once.

32 Scroll down to the bottom of the image and repeat the same process to create a similar effect at the bottom regions. At this point, focus on regions that lack fine detail, such as the large sections of the ships and the water. These regions are ideal to address while using such a large brush size. Take your time and use small strokes while painting with the Palette Knife to gently push the underlying imagery around like paint. In many instances, gently pushing in one direction and then pushing back from the other direction, over and over again, achieves the best effect. Try this method to move imagery around in the regions where the two ropes overlap the water until they disappear completely.

Common keyboard shortcuts

For those of you who are familiar with Photoshop's navigational and brush resizing shortcuts, you'll feel right at home on Painter. You can zoom in or out with the Control−+/− (or Command−+/−) keys, and holding down the Spacebar will allow you to pan around the canvas. Furthermore, the square bracket ([ ]) keys allow you to increase or decrease the size of the brush. The main difference there is that in Photoshop, resizing occurs in increments of 10; in Painter it does not.

33 When it comes to regions such as the skyline or the railings on the ships, you're going to want to reduce the size of the brush considerably in the Property bar. After reducing the size of the brush, zoom in on the skyline and then repeat the process to blend the imagery around with the Palette Knife. Be careful to ensure that you do not alter the structure of the buildings while smoothing them. You will frequently need to alter brush size and pay attention to which directions you push the paint; there should be some consistency at the end of it all. If you push paint in too many directions, the composition will appear chaotic. Here you can see that I've kept a left-to-right aesthetic when applying brush strokes so that the skyline feels unified with the water beneath it.

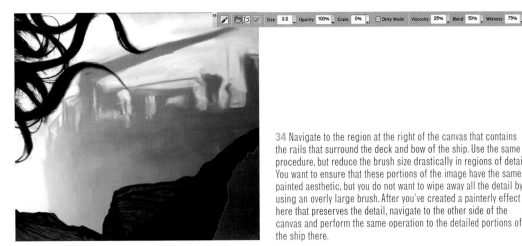

34 Navigate to the region at the right of the canvas that contains the rails that surround the deck and bow of the ship. Use the same procedure, but reduce the brush size drastically in regions of detail. You want to ensure that these portions of the image have the same painted aesthetic, but you do not want to wipe away all the detail by using an overly large brush. After you've created a painterly effect here that preserves the detail, navigate to the other side of the canvas and perform the same operation to the detailed portions of the ship there.

35 Click the New Layer button at the bottom of the Layers palette and then drag the new layer into position just above the hair layer. Double-click the new layer and then change the name to hair paint in the Layer Attributes box. Ensure that this new layer remains targeted, and then zoom in closely on the hair in the image to the right of her face. Specify a brush size that is somewhere between the size you used for the clouds and the size you used for the detailed railing areas. Brush size will vary from user to user, but try a test stroke on a region of her hair. Ideally, it will create a painterly effect while preserving the overall detail. Increase or decrease the brush size as necessary, and then set to work painting over her hair in this region, emulating the flow and direction of her hair with your brush strokes.

 Mind the edges

When you are using Artists' Oils and painting along the edges of the canvas, be careful not to pull the Palette Knife inward from the edge of the canvas. If you do this, you'll notice that it drags a very dark color in from the edge, mixing it with your paint. You can remedy this situation by pushing color back into it so that it is by no means a disaster; it can merely prove annoying after a while. It is for this reason that I am always careful, when working around the edges, to push paint outward when I reach the very edge of the canvas.

36 When you get to the region at the right, where the individual strands of her hair flow out into the sky, you can exercise some creative license. Depending on where you begin your stroke, you will be pushing light color into dark or dark color into light. With repeated strokes you can alter the structure of things. For example, the flow of some of these strands feels chunky and not fluid enough against the sky. Also, some of the strands appear too thick. Try starting your stroke in a white region and then brushing it into a dark strand, altering the flow and thickness. Repeat this on both sides of the strand as many times as necessary until you're satisfied. Use this method to reshape and alter the contour and thickness of these strands. After a bit of practice, the process will feel quite intuitive, especially if you have any previous experience with actual oil paints. Increase and decrease the brush size as necessary.

37 Create a new layer and drag it up so that it sits above the fabric layer in the Layers palette. Double-click the new layer and name it fabric paint in the Layer Attributes. Ensure that the new layer is targeted, and then zoom in on the flowing piece of fabric to the right of the model's arms. Use the same method to paint over the fabric with the same Artist Oils' Oil Palette Knife you've been using all along. Vary the brush size as necessary, and be certain to pay attention to the natural flow of the cloth as you introduce your strokes, since they should be similar in terms of direction and contour.

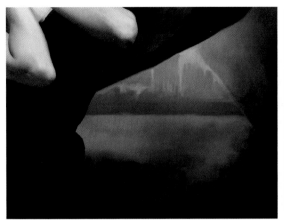

38 Create a new layer and drag it above the fabric bottom layer in the Layers palette. Double-click the new layer and name it fabric bottom paint. Ensure that this new layer is targeted and then use what is now becoming a familiar procedure to create a painted effect in this area on the new layer. Use the same brush category and variant as you've been using all along. Alter brush size as necessary, and when it comes to the edges, adjust the contour by pushing light into dark or dark into light, just as you did previously with the model's hair. Really spend some time making this fabric look softer around the edges and altering the curvature so that it feels more integrated into the background.

 Canvas Rotation

When you're painting traditionally it is only natural to change the angle of your arm as you paint, depending on the direction of the stroke. In Painter, you can rotate the canvas as well by using either the options available under the Canvas menu or by using the Rotate Page tool in the Tool palette. The Rotate Page tool is arguably the most natural way to rotate the canvas because it is a simple as clicking and dragging. When the canvas has been rotated, you can go ahead and paint at the new angle and then, when finished, you can undo the rotation by simply double-clicking it.

39 Create another new layer and drag it above the figure layer in the Layers palette so that it sits at the top of the stack. Name the new layer figure paint and then adjust your brush size so that it is quite large. With the large brush size, paint over the cloth sections of the figure at the bottom left and across her chest and midsection. Also paint over her visible stomach as well as her arms. Focus on areas that are large and do not contain fine detail while using the large brush size. Leave her neck, hair, and face alone for the time being and simply focus on the larger, less detailed regions of the figure.

40 Reduce the size of your brush and zoom in closely on the model's hands, neck, and shoulder. Take a moment to study how the image is basically made up of regions of color. As you'll see, her hands are not simply a flesh color with lighter highlights and darker shaded values of the same color. It is important to pay attention to how color indicates value when you're painting, or things will become lifeless. Carefully use the brush to blend color within each region of color, but do not alter the structure of the regions. If color blends together too much, you will lose the defined regions and your painting will look flat. Take a look at what I've done here and you'll see that although it has a painterly effect, subtle regions of different color remain separate.

41 When you are satisfied with the model's hands and arms, move on to her neck and perform the same operation of carefully smoothing regions of color and introducing Palette Knife strokes, without removing the defined edges of the separate regions. You'll find that you need to increase the brush size for the neck compared to what you were using for her hands, since there are less fine details or small regions of color. If your brush is too small, the strokes will be too prominent and look out of place in the composition. When you're finished with her neck, work on the visible areas of her ear and the region to the right of it where the fine strands of hair fall over her face. Don't touch the face yet; we'll save that for last.

42 Now direct your attention to the model's hair at the left of her face. Use a brush size that's similar to the one you used previously to paint over the hair at the right. Again, carefully introduce a series of strokes that follow the contour and flow of her hair. Take your time and be aware of where you start each stroke and how that affects where color is placed. It is certain by now that you are developing a feel for the process. However, use extra care in painting the areas where her hair meets the skin of her face. Try to paint along the division line that exists and not across it. You want to be careful not to pull light color into her hair by starting too close to her skin and then brushing it into her hair and vice versa.

And finally ... the face

Here we'll use the same process but gradually get more focused as we proceed to apply the painterly affect to her face while preserving important details.

1 Okay, begin by zooming in closely on the model's face. Increase the size of your brush compared to what you were using on her hair and begin to paint over large regions of color only. Focus on areas such as her forehead, her cheek at the left, and her chin. Avoid areas of detail while using this large brush size.

2 Reduce the brush size, making it a bit smaller than that used for her hair. Do not reduce the size dramatically; we'll get to that next. Use this medium-sized brush to paint over areas of her face such as her nose and the regions above her lips. In addition, begin to work on her eyebrows and the areas above her eyes. Stay away from her eyes and lips while using this brush size.

3 Now reduce the size of the brush considerably. Make it small enough that you can work within the regions of her eyes, teeth, and lips without destroying them. Remember to be careful not to blend regions of color together while you work on these minute areas, and be open to the idea that you'll need to make your brush even smaller. Paint over the remaining regions of the model's face.

Examine your progress

Try temporarily turning off the visibility of all the original layers in the Layers palette so that only your painted layers are visible. You can simply click the Visibility icon (the eye) to the left of each layer in the Layers palette to do this. When only your painted layers are visible, it gives you good insight into what exactly is happening every time you create a stroke that picks up underlying color.

Artists' Oils
Soft Blender Brush

43 Create a new layer in the Layers palette and name it additional paint. In the Brush Selector bar at the right, leave the Brush Category set to Artists' Oils, but change the Brush Variant to Soft Blender Brush. Zoom in closely on her face and ensure that your new layer is targeted in the Layers palette. Adjust the size of the brush in the Property bar so that it is a bit smaller than what you were using for her hair yet not as small as what you were using for the details of her face. Examine areas of transition in her face, neck, and hands. What I mean by transition is regions where one region of color meets another, such as where the shadow under her chin meets the light area of her jaw. Now identify a region. Hold down the Alt (or Option) key to temporarily switch the brush to the Dropper tool. Click a region of her lips that is similar in value to the transition, to sample that color. Then use that color to paint some strokes onto the transition area.

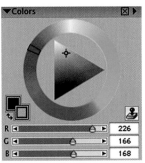

On-screen brush resizing

As you paint, it is likely that you'll want to resize your brush often and on the fly. Sometimes returning to the Property bar can interrupt the creative process and feel like a nuisance. To remedy this, painter has a nifty option that allows you to resize your brush on-screen as you work. While you're painting, simply hold down the Alt (or Option) and Control (or Command) keys and then click and drag. You'll see the brush diameter change size immediately as you drag. Simply release the keys when you're happy with the size and resume painting.

44 Use this method to look for areas of transition in the model's face, neck, and hands. Begin sampling colors from her lips and then painting those colors into areas of transition in similar values to the colors you select. Also, if you want a color that you cannot sample from the image with the Dropper, don't forget about the Color palette at the right of the screen. To choose color from the Color palette, begin by clicking the color of your choice on the hue ring. Then, after specifying a hue, you can refine your color choice by choosing the desired shade and value from the triangle inside the ring.

PART SIX: Blend paint and create colors in the Mixer palette

45 The Color palette is a great resource for getting any color you want instantly. However, in a tactile art studio, paint is mixed on a palette, and there it sits in front of you. When I am painting traditionally, I not only find this useful in terms of visual reference as I paint, but I also think that it somewhat forces me to develop a harmonious color theme as I work. You spend time thinking about the colors you use and how they work together when you see them before you on a palette. I have found that many digital artists neglect to think of color themes due to the limitless color options within a typical color picker. I really believe that color is an integral ingredient when it comes to unifying your imagery, and Painter's Mixer is a valuable asset when using this approach. If you are using the default workspace, the Mixer will not be immediately visible. You'll see the word *Mixer* appear on a palette bar beneath the Color palette. Drag the palette bar out onto the canvas area to remove the Mixer from its current grouping, making it a floating palette of its own.

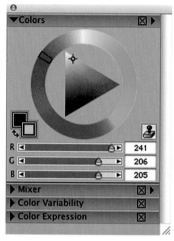

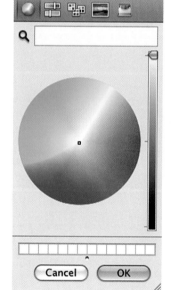

46 Click the Disclosure Triangle at the left in the Mixer palette bar to open the palette. Then click the Disclosure bar at the right and choose Clear Mixer Pad from the palette menu, to empty the Mixer. If the background is something other than white, click the Disclosure bar at the right again and then select the Change Mixer Background option from the list. Simply select white from the floating Colors picker and then click OK. This will give you an empty, white Mixer to use as your artist's palette from here on.

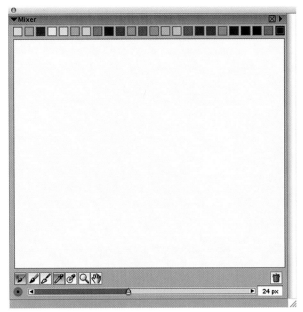

47 When the Mixer palette is floating on its own, you can resize it. Click the lower-right corner and drag outward to make it larger. Having a lot of space to mix your colors is ideal. You will also notice as you increase the size of the palette that more colors appear across the top. The colors that appear right now don't really suit our specific purpose. However, we can replace them with colors from within our own image. This will provide an appropriate resource when it comes to mixing. To do this, simply hold down the Alt (or Option) key to temporarily access the Dropper tool and click a color within your image. Then, in the Mixer palette, click one of the colored squares at the top while holding down the Control (or Command) key. This will change the color of the square to your currently selected color. Repeat this process, choosing prominent colors from within the image and replacing the boxes in the Mixer with them, until all the boxes are changed.

48 Drag the bottom corner further out to make the palette larger and you will notice even more squares appear. This time, instead of sampling existing colors from within the image, select colors from the Color palette. Then use these colors to replace the colors in the new squares that appear at the top of the Mixer palette. Choose some colors that are brighter to use as accent colors in the painting. Select some oranges, golds, yellows, bight pinks, purples, and blues. Select the Apply Color tool by clicking the second button from the left at the bottom of the Mixer palette. Then choose a dark gray color from the boxes at the top and paint some of it into the space in the Mixer palette. Select a lighter gray color and paint it next to it until the two begin to blend together. Use this method to paint some blue above these two grays and then some purple below them.

49 Now choose the Mix Color tool by selecting the third button from the left at the bottom of the Mixer palette. Use this tool to paint over areas within the Mixer palette where different colors connect. The Mix Color tool does an excellent job of blending the colors together as you paint with it. In essence, this is the same procedure as working with a traditional artist's palette. The protocol is to add paint, then mix the colors and so on. Go ahead and continue to create some more purple, blue, and gray blends using this method. First select the Apply Color tool. Then choose a color from a square at the top. Paint the color into the Mixer, adjacent to another color, and then use the Mix Color tool to blend them.

 Resizing the Mixer

You might find that this huge Mixer palette interferes with your workspace. If this is the case, simply drag the lower-right corner inward to reduce the size of the palette. When you see your colored squares and your mixed colors begin to disappear, worry not. You can access your colored squares at any point by simply making the palette larger again. This is true for your mixed colors as well. However, you can use the Pan tool at the bottom right of the row of buttons at the bottom of the palette to pan around the mixed colors. Nothing is cropped or lost when you reduce the palette; it is simply hidden from view.

50 Go ahead and have some fun creating a variety of color mixtures in the Mixer palette using this method. Note that there are tools at the bottom of the Mixer palette that will let you select individual or multiple colors from within your mix and then paint with them; so you aren't limited to simply using the squares at the top of the palette. Also, at any point you can simply select a color from the Color palette and introduce it into the mix via the Apply Color tool. This proves true for any color selected from within the image via the Dropper tool as well. The possibilities are endless.

51 Reduce the size of the Mixer if necessary and then use the Mixer's Pan tool to pan to a range of mixed gray, blue, and purple colors. Then select the Mixer's Sample Color tool, which is the one that resembles the Dropper in the Tool palette. Click a light gray-blue color to select it with the Sample Color tool. You will know when a color from the Mixer (or anywhere else, actually) has been selected, because it will appear as the main color, which is the swatch in the foreground in both the Color palette and the Tool palette. Zoom in close on a region of fabric and paint some light gray over some of the fabric highlight areas. Ensure that your additional paint layer is targeted in the Layers palette as you paint.

PART SEVEN: Adding subtle colors and accents

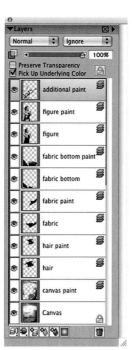

Artists' Oils
Soft Blender Brush

52 Use the Mixer's Sample Color tool to select different colors from the mixer and paint them into highlighted regions of the fabric on the new layer. Select purples, blues, and grays from the Mixer palette. Keep the Brush Category set to Artists' Oils and the Brush Variant set to Soft Blender Brush. Increase and decrease the size of the brush as you see fit until there is a nice array of strokes in the fabric that add color accents to the highlights as well as accentuate them in select regions.

53 When you're finished with the fabric, zoom in on the model's hair. When you analyze the image, you'll notice that although the composition appears balanced due to the placement of the elements, her hair looks out of place. Why is this? Well, even though it matches up nicely with the fabric in terms of value, the hue is wrong for the rest of the image. Simply put, the hair is too warm. It is shades of brown, which are distinctly different from the predominately cool color palette of the image thus far. Even though there are warm regions in the clouds in the background, these regions are predominately made up of cool blues, grays, and purples. Use the same method you used previously with the fabric to begin adding some colored strokes into her hair, helping to unify it with the rest of the composition. Again, use the current layer, brush category, and variant. Simply adjust the brush size as necessary. Start to work on her eyebrows, too.

54 Now move over to the hair at the right of her face. Continue to add strokes in this region as you did on the other side. Look at the cluster of hair and you'll notice that the highlight areas are mainly situated at the top, with the shadow regions below. This gives the hair a nice sense of depth, so be careful not to alter this relationship of values within her hair. Simply put, add lighter strokes in the light regions; add darker strokes in the dark regions. Be careful to apply strokes that integrate nicely with the contour of her hair. In this region, the shape and contour of her hair strands are very important against the background. Alter the size of the brush as necessary.

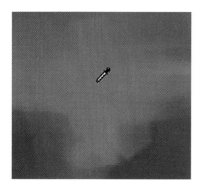 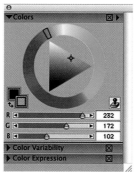

55 When you are finished adding colored strokes to the figure, her fabric, and her hair, direct your attention to the sky. Examine the colors that are already hinted at in the sky as it stands. There is a certain amount of warmth hinted at through subtle orange hues. Even the blues feel warm next to these, since they appear to have a high yellow content. We're going to accentuate these colors on the canvas with more saturated accents. Hold down the Alt (or Option) key to temporarily access the Dropper tool. Click a region of the sky or background that contains the color that is closest to orange. Then direct your attention to the Color palette to view the color you just selected. If it seems too pink or too red, begin by selecting a neighboring hue from the hue ring that is more orange. Then adjust the shade and value of the color in the triangle until your main color is a more vibrant orange.

Create a new mix of colors

Now use colors from the sky and their luminous counterparts to create a series of accent colors for use in the background.

1 With your new luminous orange as your main color, direct your attention to the Mixer palette. Select the Pan tool from the far right of the row of buttons at the bottom of the palette. Use the Pan tool to push the current mixture of colors out of view.

2 Now select the Apply Color tool from the row of tool buttons along the bottom of the palette. Use the Apply Color tool to paint some of the new orange into the Mixer palette. Then create some variations of the color in the Color palette and paint them adjacent to this color in the Mixer palette.

3 Select the Mix Color tool from the buttons at the bottom of the palette and use it to blend all the colors together until you're satisfied that you have a nice mix to use for accents in the warmer regions of the background.

56 Choose the Sample Color tool from the row of buttons along the bottom of the Mixer palette and use it to sample one of the luminous orange colors from within the palette. Zoom in closely on the skyline in the image. Adjust the size of your brush so that you can paint fine strokes between the buildings. Begin to paint some small dabs low down, between the buildings. Continue in this manner, using different colors sampled from the Mixer palette. The goal is, through these colors, to create an effect like a sunset or light shining from behind the buildings. In a region like this, try to resist the temptation of adding too much of the luminous color. We don't want this region to become too prominent as a result of high contrast. If you paint anything that feels too intense after the fact, you can simply undo what you've done by pressing Control-Z (or Command-Z) on the keyboard.

57 Now try to visualize the reflection that would occur in the water directly beneath the skyline on the canvas. Do your best to create a subtle mirrored effect of the accents you just painted above. It doesn't have to match up exactly with what you've done, but at a glance it should look as though the luminous colors are somewhat reflected. Now increase the size of your brush a little and get ready to hint at the reflections of the buildings as well. Don't worry about going to the Mixer for your colors for this. Simply hold down the Alt (or Option) key and click a color in one of the buildings on the canvas. Then release the key to return to the Brush tool and paint a slight impression of the shape in the water below. Sample various colors from different regions and use this method to paint their impressions reflected in the water. It is beneficial if your reflection has less detail or clarity than its original counterpart.

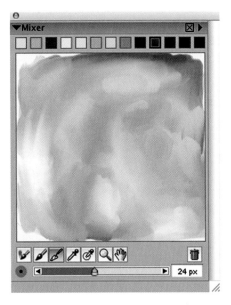

58 When you're satisfied with your reflection, pan upward in the image to the clouds at the top where they surround her hair. Hold down the Alt (or Option) key to temporarily access the Dropper tool and click the warmest region of light color you can find. Then, in the Mixer palette, use the Apply Color tool to paint that color into the mixer. Paint it into a region that contains a light color. Feel free to paint it into more than one region, because it is likely that you will have numerous light colors in the palette, and we're going to mix this color with them to create a series of colors that will blend into the image better. If the accent colors are too drastic in the clouds, it will cause confusion in the image. Feel free to sample a variety of colors from the image and paint them into the Mixer. Then use the Mix Color tool to blend it all together.

59 Now that you have a nice mixture of light, warm colors, select one of them via the Mixer palette's Sample Color tool. Then find an appropriate region in the clouds and paint a small stroke. The thickness of the stroke and the color you use will depend on the destination on the canvas. The general idea here is to sample colors from the Mixer and paint them into regions of the clouds that are light and warm, to enhance that feeling. Be certain to focus on regions where blue meets light pink or orange. In addition, you'll want to emphasize these divisions. Spend some time creating a number of strokes in these regions of the clouds, altering thickness and color. If a stroke appears too stark against a neighboring color, you can then sample that neighboring color by holding down the Alt (or Option) key and clicking it. Once you sample that color, you can use it to slowly paint it back into the stoke that appears too stark, lessening the contrast.

PART EIGHT: Blending with the Oil Palette Knife

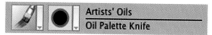

Artists' Oils
Oil Palette Knife

60 In the Brush Selector bar, choose the Oil Palette Knife option from the list of Variants. Ensure that you are using a brush size that is similar to what you used to paint the strokes into the sky. Then begin to paint over the highlight and accent strokes in the clouds to the left of the canvas. Take your time and gently paint over the strokes. In areas that are too dark, begin your stroke in a light region and rag onto the dark region. In areas that are too light, do the opposite. Remember that when using the Oil Palette Knife, it is the color that you press down on at the beginning of the stroke that is the initial color that is dragged through your stroke. However, at the same time, colors are blending into each other as well, until the stroke runs out. It is a very natural feeling.

61 When you're satisfied with the blending you've achieved at the left, direct your attention to the right side of the canvas and, again, use short strokes to blend the highlights and accent colors of the clouds into the background. Take your time and bear in mind how the direction and origin point of your strokes affects the outcome. When you get close to her hair, you'll likely need to reduce the size of the brush so that you don't blend the strands of hair into the background. Admittedly, at some point it will be impossible to blend effectively without affecting areas adjacent to your color. My suggestion is to use a large brush for the majority of the sky, getting as close to her hair and the details of the ship as possible without affecting these areas too much. Then reduce the size of the brush and move in closer to smooth any remaining regions.

62 So far we've been working with default properties and controls as we've used the Oil Palette Knife to blend paint and initially the imagery. The only thing we've really spent any time altering is the size of the brush. This is fine and it works well for our purposes thus far. Continue in this manner to smooth any necessary areas in the sky or the large ship at the right. Feel free to begin working your way into the flowing fabric in this region as well. One negative aspect of working this way is that at the end of it all, your painting might appear too smooth. Something I have always liked about working with real paint is the mark of the brush. Generally, I don't like to make everything perfectly smooth. I like to see some obvious brush marks.

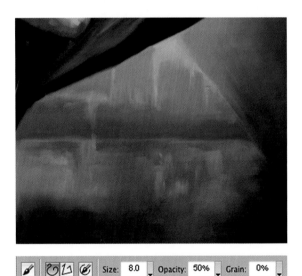

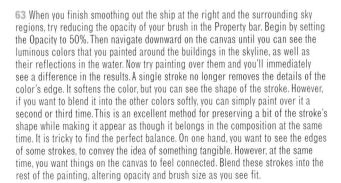

63 When you finish smoothing out the ship at the right and the surrounding sky regions, try reducing the opacity of your brush in the Property bar. Begin by setting the Opacity to 50%. Then navigate downward on the canvas until you can see the luminous colors that you painted around the buildings in the skyline, as well as their reflections in the water. Now try painting over them and you'll immediately see a difference in the results. A single stroke no longer removes the details of the color's edge. It softens the color, but you can see the shape of the stroke. However, if you want to blend it into the other colors softly, you can simply paint over it a second or third time. This is an excellent method for preserving a bit of the stroke's shape while making it appear as though it belongs in the composition at the same time. It is tricky to find the perfect balance. On one hand, you want to see the edges of some strokes, to convey the idea of something tangible. However, at the same time, you want things on the canvas to feel connected. Blend these strokes into the rest of the painting, altering opacity and brush size as you see fit.

 Opacity

A quick way to adjust the opacity of your brush in Painter is to use the number keys on your keyboard. Painter automatically multiplies your number by 10. For instance, 2 is 20, 3 is 30, 10 is 100, and so on.

64 Move over to the left and continue to use the Oil Palette Knife to soften all the accent colors painted onto the regions of fabric. Alter size and opacity as you see fit. Don't worry about the model's arms, face, shoulders, or hair at this point. Simply concentrate on the draped fabric and her stomach for the time being. After working with the Oil Palette Knife variant for a while, you're bound to get the hang of how it works. However, the Artists' Oils tool has much more flexibility built into it. Although you can see some of the Artists' Oils controls at the right side of the Property bar, you really need to see them all to understand the scope of what is possible. Choose Window > Brush Controls > Artists' Oils from the menu.

| ☐ Dirty Mode | Viscosity: 25% | Blend: 50% | Wetness: 75% |

Artists' Oils Controls

The options to customize how you paint with Artists' Oils are almost limitless when you begin to explore the palette contents.

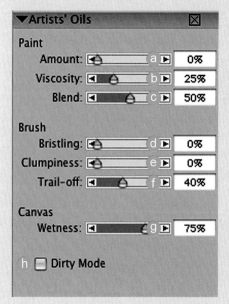

a The Amount slider controls how much paint you load onto a stroke. Just like in the real world, the more paint you use, the longer the stroke will last. This tool is set to 0 while using the Oil Palette Knife.

b The Viscosity slider controls how quickly the paint is transferred onto the canvas. The higher the value, the faster the brush will run out of paint. A higher value equals shorter strokes.

c The Blend slider adjusts how easily the paint blends with existing paint on the canvas. A high value results in an easy blend.

d The Bristling slider controls the regularity of bristles at the beginning and end of each stroke. The higher the value, the more irregular it becomes.

e The Clumpiness slider controls how clumpy the bristles appear. A high value results in more variation, increasing the clumpy effect.

f The Trail-off slider affects the length, within the stroke, of the effect of the brush running out of paint. The higher the value, the longer the Trail-off.

g The Wetness slider controls how wet the canvas is. This affects the way newly applied paint interacts with existing paint. A high value increases the amount of mixing that will occur.

h If you enable Dirty mode, any remaining paint on your brush is left on the brush. It will then interact with paint loaded for the next color.

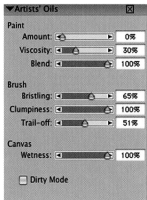

65 Zoom in on the model's hair and try adjusting some of the controls in the Artists' Oils Controls palette. Paint in her hair with different combinations here and there to test how each control adjustment affects the stroke and its interaction with the canvas. Her hair is a good region to use for experimentation because as long as you follow the contour of what exists, you won't really affect any important image details. In addition, note that you can always undo a stroke if you don't like the effect by pressing Control-Z (or Command-Z) on the keyboard.

66 After experimenting with the model's hair, you'll likely get a feel for the combinations of settings you like. Use this newfound knowledge to address her face, neck, shoulders, and arms. When you approach these regions, the fine details are absolutely essential and must remain sharp and clear. So, in addition to altering Artists' Oils controls as you work, you will need to consider size and opacity as well. For regions such as her forearms and forehead, you can use a large brush, but ensure that you steer clear of the finer regions and edge areas. Then you can work with smaller and smaller brush sizes as you work your way into detailed regions such as her facial features and fingers.

(i) Custom palettes

In Painter, you can create your own custom palette by simply dragging an icon out of a palette onto the workspace. I find this capability especially useful for keeping groupings of different brushes that I like to work with. Basically, when you customize a brush the way you like it, simply drag the icon from the Brush selector bar into the workspace. A new palette appears containing your brush. Then, when you create another brush that is different, you can drag it into the same palette. Here they will be safely stored for quick access, and you won't have to remember the way you set up the controls each time you want to replicate the effects of a brush.

161

Beyond Photoshop

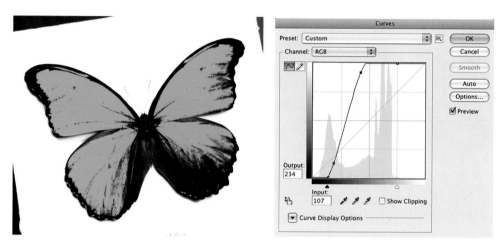

67 Save your working file in Painter and then launch Photoshop. In Photoshop, open the *butterfly.tif* file. Choose Image > Adjustments > Curves from the menu. Drastically adjust the curve as you see here to significantly increase the contrast in the image. This will essentially remove all midtones as well as remove any trace of color from the white regions. Click OK to apply the Curves adjustment when you're satisfied with the result.

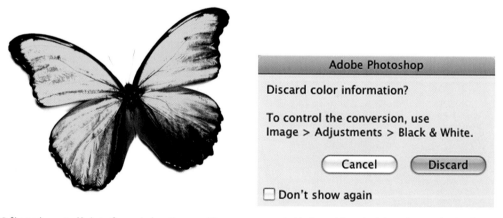

68 Choose Image > Mode > Grayscale from the menu. When you are prompted to discard the color information, go ahead and click the Discard button. After the image is converted to grayscale, select the Lasso tool from the Toolbar. Use the Lasso tool to draw a closed selection that surrounds the butterfly but does not include any of the dark areas where the paper under the butterfly ends around the canvas edges. press Control-Shift-I (or Command-Shift-I) to invert the selection. Press the I key to access the Eyedropper tool. Use the Eyedropper to click a white region of the background to sample it. The sampled color then becomes the current foreground color. Press Alt-Delete (or Option-Delete) to fill the selection with the new foreground color. Press Control-D (or Command-D) to deactivate the selection. Save and close the file.

69 In Photoshop, create a new file that is 6 inches wide and 6 inches high, at a resolution of 72 pixels per inch. Specify an RGB color mode and a white background color. Now, click the Rectangular Shape tool in the Toolbar and hold it until the shape menu appears. Choose the Ellipse tool option from the menu and press the D key to set the foreground color to black. In the Tool Options bar, click the Fill Pixels button from the group of buttons at the left. Now hold down the Shift key while you click and drag a few times to create some black circles on the canvas.

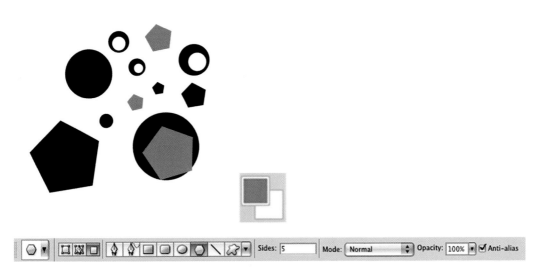

70 Now press the X key to bring the white background color to the foreground. Create a series of smaller white circles on the canvas so that they reside in the center of some of the black circles. Next, select the Polygon tool from the Tool Options bar. Leave the Sides value set to the default setting of 5. Press the X key to set the foreground color to black once again and create some polygonal shapes as shown here. Just remember that when you create a polygon it is created from the center outward. After that, click the foreground color swatch to access the picker. Select a medium gray value from the picker and create a couple of gray polygons, as shown here.

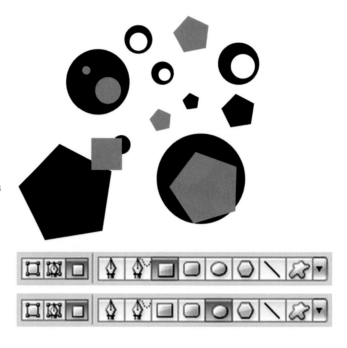

71 Select the Rectangle option from the shapes available in the Tool Options bar and then Shift-drag on the canvas to create a gray square to the upper right of the big black polygon. Next, select the Ellipse option from the available shapes in the Tool Options bar. Then Shift-drag twice to create a couple of gray circles that overlap the large black circle at the upper left. Press the X key to set the foreground color to white and then Shift-drag to create a white circle that overlaps the gray polygon at the upper right.

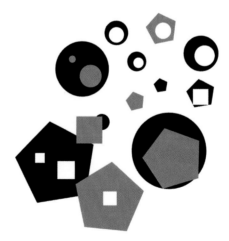

72 Now select the Polygon shape again in the Tool Options bar and press the X key to return the foreground color to gray. Create a large, gray, five-sided polygon at the lower left. After that, press the X key again to set the foreground color to white. Then select the Rectangle shape option again in the Tool Options bar. Shift-drag a few times to create some white squares inside the polygons at the lower left. Now select the Ellipse shape option and Shift-drag inside the gray polygon at the upper right to create a white circle inside it. Save the file as *pattern.tif* and then close it.

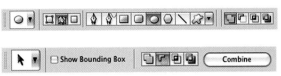

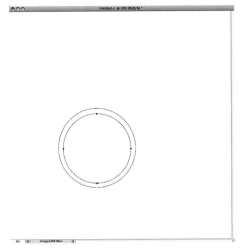

73 Create a new file that is the same as the previous file: 6 inches wide and 6 inches high, with a resolution of 72 pixels per inch, in RGB format, on a white canvas. You should still have the Ellipse shape tool selected, but now choose the Paths option in the Tool Options bar. Click and drag while holding down the Shift key, to create a circular path component at the lower portion of the canvas, just to the left of the center. While this path is selected, ensure that the Add To Path Area operation is enabled. Then draw a smaller, circular path in the same region. Select it with the Path Selection tool and move it so that it sits within the larger circle. While the new path is selected, select the Subtract From Shape Area option in the Tool Options bar.

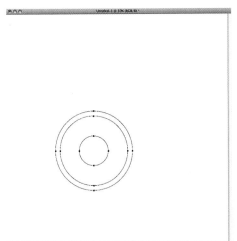

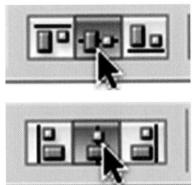

74 Shift-drag again with the Ellipse shape tool to create another circular path component. Make this one smaller than the previous two. Use the Path Selection tool to move into in the center of the previous two. While it is selected, click the Add To Path Area function in the Tool Options bar. Now hold down the Shift key and click the other two outer circles with the Path Selection tool so that all three circles are selected. When all three path components are selected, choose the Align Vertical Centers and the Align Horizontal Centers options in the Tool Options bar.

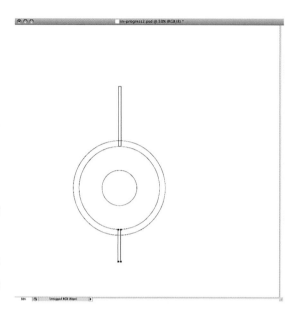

75 Now select the Rectangle shape tool. Ensure that the paths option is still selected in the Tool Options bar and that the Add To Path Area option is enabled as well. Then click and drag on the canvas to create a very thin, vertical rectangle at the top of the outer circle. Next, use the Path Selection tool to click this new shape and drag it downward while holding the Alt (or Option) key to copy it. Drag down so that this copied shape sits below the outer circle. Press Control-T (or Command-T) to access Free Transform. When the bounding box appears, Shift-drag the bottom midpoint upward, to reduce the scale of the shape vertically. Press the Enter key to apply the transformation.

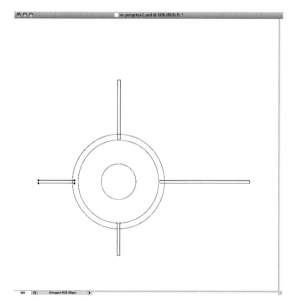

76 Use the Path Selection tool to click the top rectangle and Alt (or Option) drag it to the right to copy it. After copying it, press Control-T (or Command-T) to access Free Transform. When the bounding box appears, click and drag outside it while holding down the Shift key to rotate it incrementally. When you have rotated it 90°, press the Enter key to apply the transformation and then move it into position with the Path Selection tool so that it meets the outer circle like the other two rectangles. Click the shape and Alt-Shift (or Option-Shift) drag it to the right side of the circle to copy it and preserve the vertical alignment to the original. While the copied rectangle is selected, press Control-T (or Command-T) to access Free Transform. Drag either the left or right midpoint handle inward while holding down the Shift key to reduce the horizontal scale. Press Enter to apply the transformation and then Shift-drag the shape into position so that it meets the outer circle like the others.

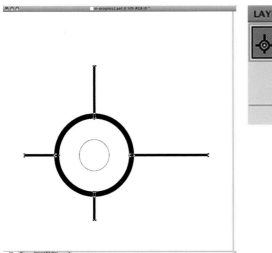

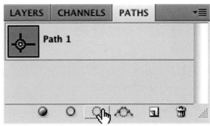

77 While this rectangular path component is still selected, Shift-click the other three with the Path Selection tool to select them as well. Then Shift-click the two outer circle path components to select them, too. At this point, all the path components except the smaller, inner circle are selected. In the Paths palette, click the Load Path As A Selection button at the bottom of the palette. This will generate a selection based on your selected path components. While the selection is active, press the D key to set the foreground color to black. Press Alt-Delete (or Option-Delete) to fill the active selection with black and then press Control-D (or Command-D) to deactivate the selection.

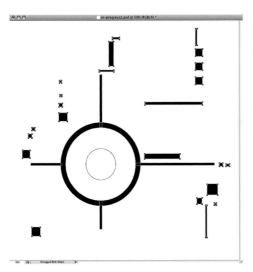

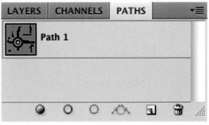

78 Use the Rectangle shape tool to Shift-drag in the upper right of the canvas to create a small square path component. Hold down the Alt (or Option) key while you click it and drag it downward. After you start dragging, hold down the Shift key to ensure perfect vertical alignment as you copy the path component. Repeat this process again until you have a stack of three squares in the upper right. After that, create a long, thin rectangular path component beneath them, and then create another square at the bottom left. Now just have a bit of fun creating more rectangular and square shapes as you fit in different areas of the canvas. Select them all with the Path Selection tool and then load them as a selection. Fill the selection with black and then deselect.

Beyond Photoshop

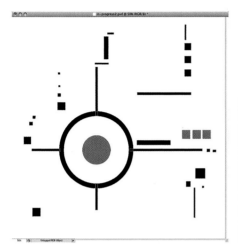

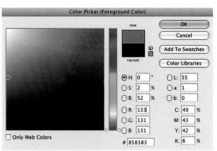

79 Click the foreground color swatch in the Toolbar to access the picker. When the picker opens, choose a lighter gray color and click OK. Use the Rectangle shape tool to create a square path component at the right and then duplicate it a couple of times. Then use the Path Selection tool to select each of these as well as the small, inner circle path component that you created previously but have not used. Load these components as a selection and fill them with the lighter gray color. Deactivate the selection.

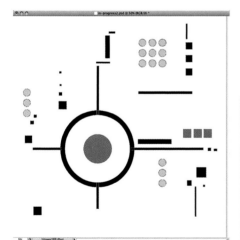

80 Now switch to the Ellipse shape tool in the Toolbar or the Tool Options bar. Shift-drag in the upper right region of the canvas to create a circular path component. Then Alt-drag (or Option-drag) it to duplicate it. While dragging, hold down the Shift key to ensure alignment. Create a row of three circular path components using this method. Then use the Path Selection tool to select all three and create a couple of duplicates of the group of three. This will result in a nice square grid of nine circular path components. Select a row of three and Alt-drag (or Option-drag) it down to duplicate it. Repeat this same procedure to create another duplicate group at the far left. Select all these new circular path components with the Path Selection tool and load them as a selection. Click the foreground color swatch in the Toolbar to access the picker and choose an even lighter gray this time. Fill the current selection with the new gray and deselect.

168

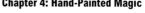

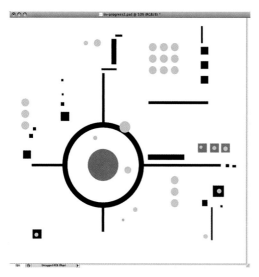

81 Creating path components and filling them is especially useful when you want to create a number of duplicate shapes with the same color fill. However, this time around, we're just going to create shapes randomly, with no predetermined alignment or organization within the composition. When you have a shape tool selected in the Toolbar, you can save the step of creating a path component by choosing the Fill Pixels option in the Tool Options bar. Go ahead and select this option. Then go ahead and Shift-drag a number of times while you still have the Ellipse shape tool selected and are using a light gray foreground color.

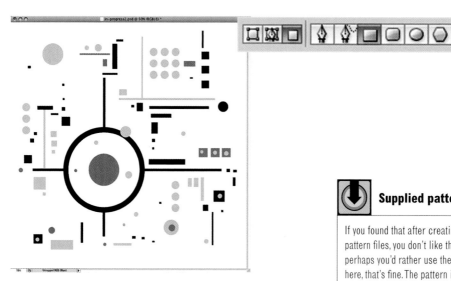

82 Have some fun creating circles here and there, using different grays as well as black foreground colors. Now switch to the Rectangle shape tool in the Tool Options bar. Ensure that the Fill Pixels option remains selected and then create numerous rectangles across the canvas in different places. Vary size and gray value considerably. Make some squares, and then also create some very thin horizontal squares as well as some very thin vertical squares. When you are satisfied with the result, save the file as *pattern1.tif*.

Supplied patterns

If you found that after creating your two pattern files, you don't like them or that perhaps you'd rather use the ones I used here, that's fine. The pattern images that I have created over the last few pages are included in the downloadable project files for this chapter. The files are called *pattern.tif* and *pattern1.tif*. Feel free to use them in place of your own further along in the chapter.

PART TEN: F-X Brushes and layer masks in Painter

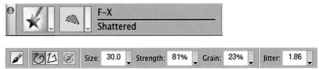

83 After saving your file, quit Photoshop. Then return to your working file in Painter. In the Layers palette, click your additional paint layer at the top of the stack to target it. Choose Layers > Duplicate Layer from the menu to duplicate it. Ensure that the duplicate layer is targeted in the Layers palette and then select the Brush tool from the Tool palette, if it isn't already selected. In the Brush Selector bar, choose the F-X option from the list of Brush Categories. Then select the Shattered option from the list of Brush Variants. You can leave the properties set to their defaults in the Property bar with the exception of the size. You'll want to reduce this considerably before you begin.

84 Begin to paint over regions such as the edges of the model's hair, her shoulders, hands, and flowing fabric. Immediately, you'll see that there are nice broken-glass effects appearing everywhere you paint on this layer. Don't worry about overdoing it at this point; we can remove the glass effect afterward via masking. After you paint over these regions, increase the brush size substantially and paint over regions in the background and over the sky as well. When you're satisfied that you've created enough of the shattered-glass effect throughout the image, choose Layers > Create Layer Mask from the menu to add a mask to the layer.

85 Click the New Mask thumbnail next to your layer in the Layers palette to target it. In the Brush Selector bar, choose the Artists' Oils option from the Brush Category List. Then select the Clumpy Brush option from the Variant List. Reduce the size of the brush as well as the opacity on the Property bar. In the Color palette, select black as the Main Color. Use the Brush to paint within the mask to hide the layer contents in select regions. Simply paint over areas of the canvas where you feel the shattered-glass effect is too strong. Working at a lower opacity allows you to vary the degree to which things are hidden by building up strokes within the mask. Work your way around the canvas, altering brush size and opacity as you paint over unwanted regions of glass detail within the mask.

PART ELEVEN: Painting with patterns

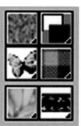

86 Open the *butterfly.tif* file that you altered previously in Photoshop. Click the Pattern Selector icon in the Tool palette. The Pattern selector is the middle left Content Selector icon. When the list of patterns appears, click in the upper right and then select the Capture Pattern option from the list. When the Capture Pattern dialog box appears, simply leave all the settings as they are, name the pattern butterfly, and click OK. You will immediately notice your new pattern appear on the Pattern Selector icon at the bottom of the Tool palette. Close the *butterfly.tif* file and return to your working file.

171

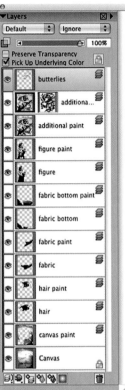

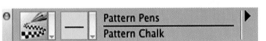

87 Create a new layer and name it butterflies. Ensure that the new layer is targeted in the Layers palette and then select the Pattern Pens option from the Brush Category list in the Brush Selector bar. Then choose the Pattern Chalk option from the Variant List. In the Property bar, adjust the size so that your brush is about as wide as one her widest hair strands. Hold down the Alt (or Option) key to temporarily access the Dropper tool. Click a region of yellow from the sky to select it as the main color. Then release the Alt (or Option) key and begin to paint some quick strokes in and around her hair. Really concentrate on how pressure affects the stroke as you paint with this category and variant. Press very lightly at the beginning and the end of each stroke so that the strokes you paint taper at the ends and are wide in the middle. Sample different warm colors from the sky and continue to paint in this manner.

88 Use this method to paint numerous tapered butterfly strokes throughout the image. Have some fun working with different sampled colors, and don't worry about overdoing it, because we'll simply mask the layer after the fact and remove anything that is too overpowering or that obscures essential detail on the underlying layers. Now drastically increase the size of the brush and add some larger butterflies into the lower regions of the canvas. Experiment with holding the brush in one place for slightly longer periods as well as twisting the stylus in your hand. You'll start to see some interesting abstractions occur as the butterflies are applied.

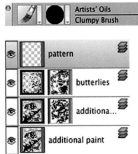

89 When you're satisfied with the amount of butterflies you've created, choose Layers > Create Layer Mask to add a mask to the layer. Target the mask in the Layers palette and then select the Artists' Oils Brush Category in the Brush Selector bar. The Variant should still be set to Clumpy Brush. If it is not, please reset it so that it is. In the Color palette, select black as the main color. While varying the size and opacity of your brush, begin to paint over butterflies within the mask that you feel are too strong or prominent. Again, a gentle effect is achieved via building up strokes with a low opacity setting. When you're happy with the way you've masked the layer, create a new layer and name it pattern.

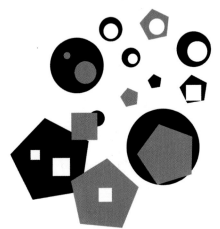

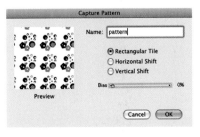

90 Open the *pattern.tif* file. After opening the file, click the *Pattern Selector* icon to reveal the list of patterns. Click in the upper-right corner of the expanded pattern selector and choose the Capture pattern option. When the Capture pattern dialog box appears, name the new pattern pattern and leave all the other settings as they are. Click OK and then click the Pattern selector to expand it. Choose your new pattern from the list. After choosing your pattern, close the file and return to your working file.

91 Ensure that your pattern layer is targeted in the Layers palette and choose the Pattern Pens option from the Brush Category List in the Brush Selector bar. The Variant should remain as you left it last time. However, if it is not, choose the Pattern Chalk option from the Variant list in the Brush Selector bar. If you do not have a large brush size already specified, increase the size of the brush in the Property bar so that it is quite large. Hold down the Alt (or Option) key to temporarily access the Dropper tool. Click a grayish-blue color from the lower right and then paint a small stroke with the current brush category and variant to introduce the pattern in that region. Sample a more neutral color, and this time use the same method in a couple of near regions, twisting the stylus a little as you paint.

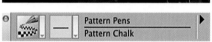

Pattern Pens
Pattern Chalk

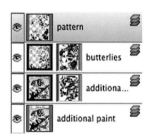

92 Now work your way around the canvas, sampling different colors and painting distorted patterns in a variety of colors in different regions. Experiment with different brush sizes. Also, really concentrate on how the direction in which you paint affects the stroke when working with different pressures. Different directions, pressures, and twists will drastically affect how the pattern is applied in the stroke. Again, don't worry about overdoing it at this point, since we'll be masking the layer next.

93 While the pattern layer is selected, choose Layers > Create Layer Mask from the menu. When the mask appears next to your pattern layer, click it to target it. In the Color palette, select black as the main color. Use the current brush to paint within the mask. Increase and decrease the brush as necessary as you drag it over many of the regions you created previously. The results of masking Pattern Chalk with Pattern Chalk on the same layer can be intricate and very random pattern structures throughout the image. Through this method, any sense of repetition in terms of applied patterns will slowly start to disappear.

94 Although this method introduces intricacy and randomness, it doesn't have the practicality needed to remove specific layer components from view with clear intent. No problem. To address this issue, we simply need to revert back to a tried-and-true method. Again, ensure that the mask is targeted in the Layers palette and then choose the Artists' Oils option from the Brush Category list in the Brush Selector bar. The Variant should still be set to Clumpy Brush. If it is not, make it so. Set the opacity to around 40% in the Property bar and vary brush size as necessary as you paint within the mask. Paint over regions that appear too strong, such as the patterns over the model's face and neck. The more you paint over them, the less visible they become.

95 Open the *pattern1.tif* file. After the file opens, click the Pattern Selector icon in the Content Selectors section of the Tool palette. When the Pattern Selector expands, click the upper-right corner and choose the Capture Pattern option from the list. When the Capture Pattern dialog box appears, leave the settings as they are, but change the name of the pattern to pattern1. Click OK and close the file. Return to your new file and choose your new pattern in the Pattern Selector.

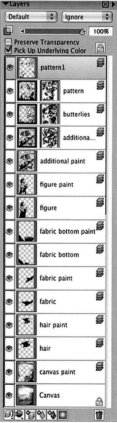

96 In your working file, create a new layer and name it pattern1. Ensure that the new layer is targeted and then select the Pattern Pens option from the Brush Category list in the Brush Selector bar. The Pattern Chalk Variant should still be selected. If it is not, select it. Ensure that you are using a very large brush size in the Property bar. Hold down the Alt (or Option) key and click a light skin-colored region of the model's face. Then move the brush away slightly and click and hold. Do not create a very long stroke. Simply move the stylus a little as you press down. The result will be a swirling application of the pattern. Sample different colors and use this method to add the swirling effect in neighboring regions. Alter the brush size as necessary.

97 Use this method to add a number of swirling patterns in varying sizes and colors on this layer. Sample colors from a variety of regions and carefully consider where you place those colors. If the color placement strays too far from that which already exists in the composition, things could become too chaotic. Increase and decrease the brush size as necessary, and remember, don't worry about overdoing it, since we'll be masking this layer when we're finished. Just be certain that you do not use this pattern to create any long strokes, because the pattern itself is so distinct and recognizable that the repetition within each stroke would be overpowering.

98 Reduce the opacity of the pattern1 layer to 50% in the Layers palette. While the layer is targeted, choose Layers > Duplicate Layer from the menu to duplicate it. Select the duplicate layer and change the Composite Method to overlay at the top of the Layers palette. Target your original pattern1 layer (not the duplicate) in the Layers palette and then choose Layers > Create Layer Mask from the menu to add a mask to it. Click the mask thumbnail in the Layers palette to target it.

177

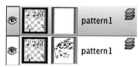

99 Select the Artists' Oils option once again from the Brush Category list in the Brush Selector bar. Ensure that the Clumpy Brush Variant option is selected and then set the main color to black in the Color palette. Use a brush opacity setting of around 40% to paint over areas on this layer within the mask that you feel are too prominent. Even if you completely hide regions on this layer, they will still be faintly visible due to the fact that they exist on the duplicate layer that sits above. When you're satisfied with your masking of this layer, target the duplicate layer above and add a mask to it, too.

PART TWELVE: Blending it all together

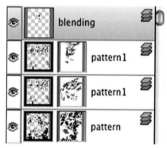

100 Use the same method of painting with the Artists' Oils Clumpy Brush within the mask to hide regions of the duplicate pattern1 layer. When you're satisfied with what you've done, create another new layer at the top of the stack in the Layers palette and name it blending. Ensure that your new layer is targeted and select the Soft Blender Brush option from the Variant list on the Brush Selector bar. Look for a region where the connection of a pattern element connecting with a painted element feels too abrupt. The hair is a good area to find this sort of thing. Alt-click (or Option-click) the underlying color and then paint a small, thin stroke that blends the two distinctly different together. Be mindful of where you begin your stroke and how long you make it. Short, gentle strokes at varying brush sizes and opacity settings that follow the underlying contour will be most effective. Sample color often, and paint a number of strokes to unify the juxtaposed elements on underlying layers.

101 This is exactly same process we used before to add color accents. However, this time we're adding the strokes to add a sense of unity to the composition. By creating sweeping strokes that go across areas that contain patterns as well as smooth, painterly strokes, we can create a feeling of unity rather than that of disconnected collage. Continue this method throughout the image and feel free to add some saturated accents here and there as you go. It might feel like you've painted things, covered them up with stamp elements, and then painted them back in and so on. In some ways this is the case. However, I think if you're going to master the process of painting digitally, you have to embrace these real-world parts of the process. It has been my experience that when painting traditionally, I build up a composition in many stages, and some of what is done at these stages will cover and obscure what was done in previous stages. This is a natural part of the painting process and contributes to the finished result. I think it is important to adopt this ideology when painting digitally as well.

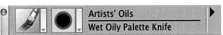

Artists' Oils
Wet Oily Palette Knife

102 Choose the Wet Oily Palette Knife option from the Variant list in the Brush Selector bar. Use the current variant to blend some of your new strokes into underlying layers. Use this tool sparingly and try to simply focus on the adjacent regions to your new strokes. The reason for this is because even though the underlying layers are masked, this brush can pick up the content that is hidden as you paint. This could result in new, unwanted content on this layer. Remember that masking is always an option for this layer as well. If you find it necessary to paint over a region with the Wet Oily Palette Knife that exposes hidden content, you can simply mask the layer and hide this region via the mask. Save your file; you're finished. However, feel free to embellish this file at will, and also note that you can open this file in Photoshop and edit it there as well. All the layers and masks remain intact and exactly as you left them in Painter.

PART THIRTEEN: Final Painter analysis

As you are building up an image in Painter, you can see how the introduction of each new tool, technique, and/or component adds to the whole. However, if you look back afterward, isolating certain layers from the composition will provide insight into what you've done. You can study with clarity the effect of each method and/or tool when it is taken out of the context of the image.

Here's the duplicated additional paint layer. You can clearly see the broken-glass effect achieved via the F-X brush.

Here is the same layer after the mask was applied and it was edited with the Artists' Oils Clumpy Brush.

Here are the butterflies we created with the Pattern Chalk variant. It is impressive what Painter can do with a single image that was manipulated in Photoshop ahead of time.

Again, you can see how using the Artists' Oils to edit the layer's mask helps to blend the layer into the underlying composition, softening the pattern effect.

Here's a look at the layer that contains the strokes made by using the Pattern Chalk with the first shape-based pattern we created in Photoshop.

Editing the layer's mask with the same Pattern Chalk brush creates an interesting and increasingly abstract effect.

The second shape-based pattern we created in Photoshop was more intricate and recognizable. And although it was built up on two separately masked layers, it was very important to create small, swirling strokes to avoid recognition and repetition in the image.

At the end of it all, we reverted to some the very first Artists' Oils variants we used to start off with earlier in the chapter. The ideology is the same as the goal was to blend the underlying imagery. This is an effective method to make things look cohesive, whether at the beginning or the end of the process.

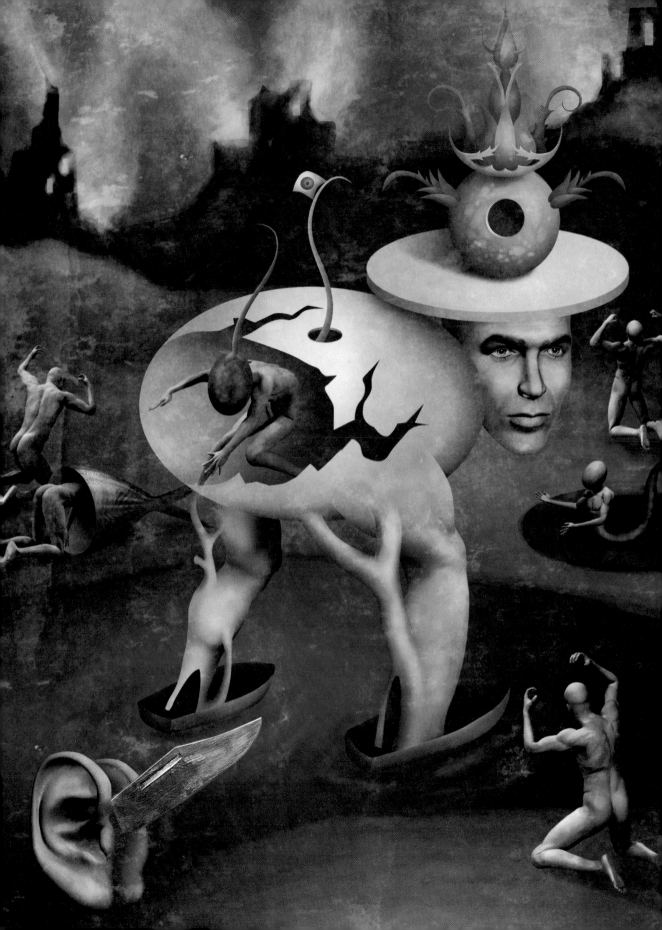

Chapter 5
Create an Old Master
Combining Poser with Photoshop

I n this chapter you'll learn to create a "digital Old Master" inspired by the infamous paintings of Hieronymus Bosch. The image you see before you is the result of combining Photoshop with what Poser has to offer. The third panel of Bosch's triptych *The Garden of Earthly Delights* is our inspiration here. It depicts the hellish results of mankind succumbing to earthy temptations. It is a dark, strange, and ominous piece that shows numerous figures engaged in a rather surreal state of suffering. The fact that there are numerous figures involved makes Poser an ideal application to incorporate into the Photoshop workflow this time around.

Poser is a 3D figure creation tool. As its name suggests, it allows you to pose, create, and render human figures. Actually, Poser will allow you do much more than that. You can animate figures, add clothing, and even create impressively realistic hair. However, for this particular style of artwork, we really only need to make use of its most rudimentary features. But I'm certain that you'll agree, it does an excellent job of allowing us to quickly create nude figures and body parts, which have provided the raw materials for the artwork you see before you.

Many illustrators and digital artists will argue against using Poser. Often they will site the fact that although there are a plethora of options for creating your figures, a Poser "signature appearance" rears its head time and time again, so that the result looks like a Poser work of art rather than being your own work of art. Granted, when you use predefined settings and prefab features within any software package, the results will clearly reveal what you've been doing.

It is important to remember that Poser is not responsible for a certain look within your art; it's how you use Poser that is the determining factor. By avoiding the use of immediately recognizable Poser components such as clothing, hair, and (in many cases) faces themselves, I have created a series of Poser renderings that are more generic in appearance. The result is that the Poser output is a raw material that is built on using Photoshop rather than being the center of attention.

In addition to rendered figures from Poser, other raw materials used here include a couple of simple photographs and a highly textured desktop scan. Basically, each ingredient used to create this illustration is not that impressive on its own. However, it is the method of illustrating and combining these elements in Photoshop that transforms the results from a thrown-together collage into a stunning work of ancient-looking art.

Versions

Photoshop CS4
Poser 8

Requirements and Recommendations

In addition to Photoshop CS4, you'll need a copy of Poser 8 from Smith Micro. If you don't have a copy of Poser 8, a trial version can be downloaded from http://my.smithmicro.com.

What you'll learn in this chapter

Creative Techniques and Working Methods

Working from a single asset

Poser has a lot to offer. It offers a plethora of figures to choose from; what we'll use in this chapter is a fraction of the resources that are available. Don't get me wrong here; I'm not trying to diminish the importance of all the figure assets Poser contains. I simply want to draw your attention to the fact that you can do a lot with very little. In this chapter I'll do this using a single Poser figure for every human figure, or portion thereof, that you see in this illustration. Poser has an inherent flexibility that, when combined with its ease of use, makes it an excellent companion to Photoshop for creating figurative works. Basically, we're going to use the same male figure, over and over again, in this image. We'll use a variety of posing tools, lighting set-ups, camera views, props, and presets to create a diverse array of people and parts within the scene.

Starting from presets

Poser allows you to pose figures any way you like. That being said, it is always easier to start from an existing pose and modify it from there. Poser comes with a massive library of poses, so finding something that comes close to what you're after is never difficult. You can shave hours off your production time by simply sifting through the Pose content in the Library palette. More often than not, you'll find something similar to what you have in mind. Simply start with a preset pose and then modify it from there. After trying this a few times, you'll see the benefit.

Tools, Features, and Functions

Poser cameras

Use the Poser cameras to revolve and rotate around the center of the scene, where the objects and figures are automatically placed when you add them. Rotating the camera only affects how the scene is viewed, not the placement of the object, figures, or their poses. This is a handy way to change your point of view without disturbing the content you painstakingly created.

Memory dots

Poser's memory dots are an excellent feature that allows you preserve the current state of certain things. There are dots to save the way you have configured the user interface as well as camera dots and pose dots. We'll use the latter two throughout the chapter to ensure that no matter what we do, we can revert to a meticulously created pose or customized view.

Project files

All the files needed to follow along with this chapter and create the featured image are available for download on the accompanying Website, in the project files section. If you are not interested in using Poser at all, all the finished renderings are included so that you can follow along with the Photoshop workflow. Or, if you are using Poser yet you want to inspect the actual files used here or don't want to create your own, you can access them from the Website. Visit www.beyondphotoshopthebook.com.

1 Open the *working.psd* file. This file includes a number of paths as well as a green canvas to help get you started. The first thing we need to do is to add some graduated color in the top portion of the background. This will eventually be the sky area. Select the Gradient tool. In the Tool Options bar, select the Foreground to Transparent gradient preset from the gradient picker, and choose the Radial gradient method. Click the foreground color swatch in the Toolbar to access the picker. Select a yellow-ochre color from the picker.

2 Click and drag to create a small radial gradient at the top of the canvas on the Background layer. Repeat this method to create numerous gradients in the top portion of the canvas area. Feel free to alter the opacity of the gradient and use slightly different foreground colors as you see fit. Also, use black as the foreground color to create some gradients around the edges of the canvas. Next, direct your attention to the contents of the Paths palette. Hold down the Control (or Command) key and click the bldgs path to load it as a selection.

3 Click the Create A New Layer button at the bottom of the Layers palette to create a new layer. Press the d key to set the foreground color to black. Ensure that your new layer is targeted in the Layers palette and then press Alt-Delete (or Option-Delete) to fill the current selection with black on the new layer. Now, while the current selection remains active, use the Gradient tool to create a series of gradients in the lower part of the selected area on the new layer. Use a dark red foreground color and the same gradient tool settings you used previously.

Repeat the process

Use this same procedure repeatedly to create the initial background for our hellish scenario.

1 Load the hills path in the Paths palette as a selection. On a new layer, fill the selection with the current dark red foreground color. Create some faint yellow and green-to-transparent gradients within the selection on the new layer.

2 Now load the grass path as a selection. Fill the selection with a lighter green on a new layer. Use the Gradient tool to add radial foreground to transparent gradients, in a variety of colors, into the selected area of your new layer.

3 Load the water path as a selection. Repeat this entire process to create an area of green water and colored gradients on a new layer. Finally, load the shore path and, again, repeat the process using earthy colors within the selection on another new layer.

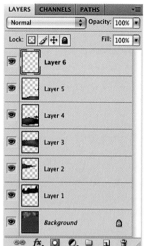

4 Use the Rectangular Marquee tool to draw a rectangular selection to indicate a window within one of the ruined building shapes in the background. Hold down the Shift key and draw a series of additional rectangles, adding them to the selection. Use the Eyedropper tool to click in the sky, sampling the green as the foreground color. Fill the active selection with the new color on yet another new layer. Select the Gradient tool. Add some radial, yellow-to-transparent gradients into the window shapes on this layer.

PART TWO: Creating two-dimensional image components

5 Target the Background layer and then choose Layer > New > Layer From Background from the menu. Name the layer and click OK. Hold down the Shift key and click your top layer. This will target all the layers in the Layers palette. Choose Layer > New > Group From Layers from the menu. This will add all your background layers to a new group, keeping the Layers palette organized. Double-click the name of your group to highlight it and change the name of the group to background. Next, create a new layer and use the Elliptical Marquee tool to draw a large selection border. Select a pink foreground color from the picker and fill the active selection with it.

Layer from background

The only way to add a background layer to a group is to convert it to a normal layer. To do this, you can target the layer and choose the appropriate menu command if you like. However, an even quicker way is to double-click the background layer. This is a shortcut to the new layer options, which allow you to rename and convert the layer. Or, you can simply click the lock icon to the right of your layer thumbnail and drag it into the trash at the bottom of the Layers palette. This step will bypass the layer options and immediately convert your layer. Another method is to right-click (or Control-click) the Background layer's thumbnail and then choose the Layer from Background option from the resulting pop-up menu.

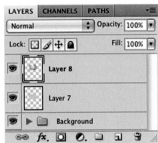

6 Create a new layer and keep the current selection active. Select the Brush tool. Choose a large, soft, round brush preset from the Preset picker and specify a low opacity setting in the Tool Options bar. Use the Brush tool to paint a variety of darker flesh colors, adding shading, on the new layer. You can choose colors from the picker, or Alt-click (or Option-click) anywhere on the canvas to sample an existing color. Paint with a low opacity setting, and create darker regions by building up strokes in the same area.

Crack the egg

Create a crack-shaped selection and fill it will dark shades, to create the inside of the hollow egg shape.

1 Select the Pen tool and ensure that it is set to create paths in the Tool Options bar. With the Add to Path Area option enabled, take your time and carefully draw a closed path that represents a cracked opening in the egg. Load the path as a selection.

2 With the selection active, create a new layer and ensure that it remains targeted in the Layers palette. Set the foreground color to black or a very dark brown. Fill the active selection with your foreground color and select the Gradient tool.

3 Hold down the Alt (or Option) key to temporarily select the Eyedropper tool. Click a light beige color on the canvas to sample it and use it as the current foreground color. Release the Alt (or Option) key. Then select the Gradient tool and drag from the left edge of the selection toward the right to create a light, radial, foreground-to-transparent gradient within the selection. Draw another, smaller gradient using the same method and a lighter color.

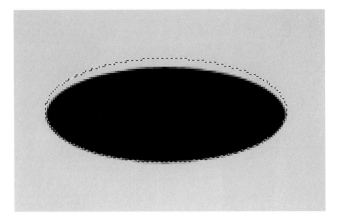

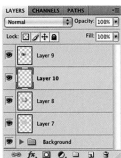

7 Press Control-d (or Command-d) on the keyboard to deactivate the current selection. Use the Elliptical Marquee tool to draw an elliptical selection to represent another, smaller hole. Sample the dark color from the inside of the egg with the Eyedropper tool and fill the new selection with it. Create a new layer and drag it beneath this layer in the Layers palette. Use the Ellipse tool to carefully draw an elliptical selection border that is a little bit larger than the previous one you created. Use the Elliptical Marquee tool to click and drag within the selection border until it lines up with the hole, as you see here.

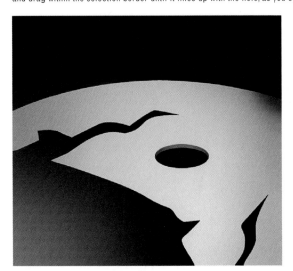

8 Choose a light brown color from the picker and fill the active selection with it on the new layer. Now select the Gradient tool and leave all the tool settings as they were previously. Select a darker brown color from the picker and use the Gradient tool to click and drag inward, from the left and then the right, to create darker, gradient-based shading within the selection. This adds a sense of thickness to the eggshell in this area. Deactivate the selection and select the Pen tool.

ⓘ Transforming selections

In some situations when you are trying to create a very precise selection with a selection marquee tool, no matter how many times you redraw the selection it still won't be quite right. The large elliptical selection created here, used to add dimension to the small hole, is an excellent example of this phenomenon. In an instance like this, you can resize or reshape your selection border by choosing Select > Transform Selection from the menu. The bounding box works just like a Free Transform bounding box, except that rather than transforming your selected contents, it transforms the selection border itself.

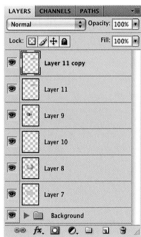

9 Use the Elliptical Marquee tool to draw a large ellipse at the upper right of the egg on the canvas. Create a new layer and drag it to the top of the stack within the Layers palette. Fill your active selection on the new layer with a skin color sampled from the egg. Select the Gradient tool and create a large, radial, foreground-to-transparent gradient within the right side of the selection using a lighter color. Duplicate the layer by dragging it onto the Create A New Layer button at the bottom of the Layers palette. Target the original, underlying layer.

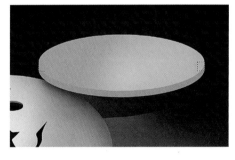

 Accessing the Move tool

When you have a selection tool currently chosen, such as the Elliptical or Rectangular Marquee tool used here, there is a quick way to access the Move tool. Simply hold down the Control (or Command) key and the tool will temporarily switch to the Move tool. Releasing the Control (or Command) key will revert your tool to the original tool.

10 Sample a slightly darker color from within the egg and fill the active selection on the currently targeted layer with it. If you accidentally deactivated the selection, just Control-click (or Command-click) the Layer thumbnail to load it again. You won't see the effects immediately, because the duplicate layer above it obscures this layer. Deactivate the selection and use the Move tool to drag the currently selected layer downward while holding down the Shift key. Drag it down until it begins to create an edge indicating the depth of the platform. Now use the Rectangular Marquee tool to draw two selection borders that cover the areas at the left and right that aren't filled with color and fill them, using the same color.

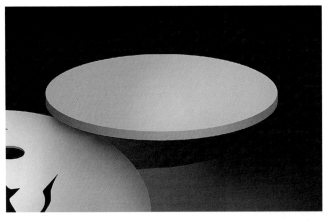

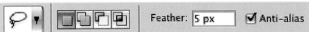

11 Control-click (or Command-click) the current layer thumbnail in the Layers palette to load a selection from the layer's contents. Choose a darker brown foreground color. Use the Gradient tool, with the same settings used previously, to create gradients within the selection. Create one at the left and one at the right to add some depth and shading to the edge of the platform on this layer. Create a new layer and drag it to the top of the stack in the Layers palette. Deactivate the selection and choose the Lasso tool. In the Tool Options bar, set the feather amount to 5 pixels.

 Containing the shadow

When you create this shadow on top of the platform, it could stray beyond the edge of the platform and onto the background. To remedy this problem, Control-click (or Command-click) the Layer thumbnail of the layer that contains the platform top in the Layers palette. This will generate a selection from the contents of the layer. Choose Select > Inverse from the menu to invert the selection. Next, target your first shadow layer and press the Delete key. Then target your duplicate shadow layer and press the Delete key. This will delete any layer content from your shadow layers that strays beyond the confines of the platform.

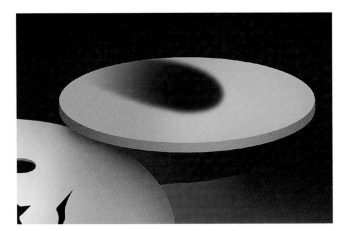

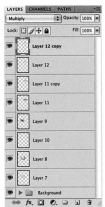

12 Because we'll be placing an object on this platform, we need a shadow to make it look convincing. Use the Lasso tool to draw the shape of the shadow from the center of the platform on a diagonal angle upward to the left. Select the Gradient tool and use it to create a radial gradient from the bottom right of the selection outward. Use the same tool setting and the same foreground color that you used previously. Change the blending mode of the layer to Multiply and then duplicate it to intensify the effect. Deactivate the selection.

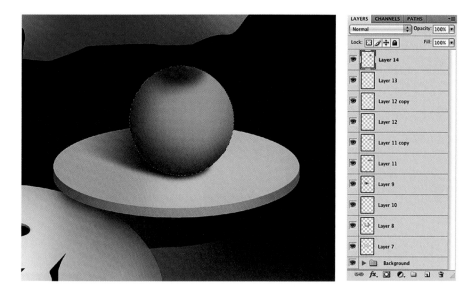

13 Create a new layer. Ensure that it is targeted and residing at the top of the stack in the Layers palette. Hold down the Shift key and create a circular selection border on top of the platform with the Elliptical Marquee tool. Choose a pink foreground color from the picker and fill the active selection with it on the new layer. Select the Brush tool and choose a large, soft, round brush preset. Set the opacity fairly low and select a darker pink color from the picker. Paint some shaded areas around the edge, adding a shadow at the top as well.

Creating organic details

Areas are first defined by path-based selections and then filled with color. Painting within the selection border adds shading and depth.

1 Use the Pen tool to draw a closed path component that resembles a thorny twig. Load it as a selection and fill it on a new layer, using a pink color sampled from the ball. Select the Brush tool.

2 Use a soft, round brush preset to paint shaded areas into the selection on the layer. Use a low opacity setting and a darker pink color. Use the Pen tool to create closed path component that represents a leaf. Load it as a selection and fill it with pink.

3 Paint some shading into the selection and then draw another path component. Load it as a selection, fill it, and paint shading into the selection. Repeat this process until you have created numerous overlapping, shaded leaves on your layer.

14 Use this method of drawing path components, loading selections, filling with color, and painting over the color, to create numerous organic details on the same layer. At the moment, focus on creating details for the left side. When you're finished, deactivate any currently active selections. Duplicate the layer and then choose Edit > Transform > Flip Horizontal from the menu to flip the duplicate layer sideways. Hold down the Shift key and drag the layer contents to the right with the Move tool.

15 Continue to employ what is now becoming a familiar method to create more organic details on a series of layers. Take your time and create a lot of thorny cactus and tulip-like path components. Load them as selections, fill them with color, and shade them using the previous methods. At this point, pay special attention to layer stacking order when you create your components, to create shapes that are clearly in front of or behind other layers. When you're finished, use the Elliptical Marquee tool to draw a circular selection border in the center of the pink ball on the canvas.

Moving contents within the layer

When you create numerous organic details on a single layer, individual details can be moved without affecting the others on the same layer. If you want to move something within a layer, target the layer and draw a selection around the contents of the layer using the Lasso tool or a Marquee tool. Be careful not to include any unwanted details within your selection border. Once you've selected your desired detail on the layer, simply hold down the Control (or Command) key to temporarily access the Move tool. Click and drag within your selection to move the contents within the layer. Go ahead and use this method to edit the contents of your own layers as you see fit.

16 Create a new layer and fill the active selection with a dark pink color. Select the Gradient tool. Again, leave it set to create radial, foreground-to-transparent gradients. Choose a light pink foreground color from the picker and then click and drag, starting at the left edge of the selection, outward, to create a gradient in the left side of the selection on the new layer. Draw another, slightly smaller circular selection and position it so that it reveals the left edge of the larger, gradient-filled circle on this layer. Fill the new selection with a dark red color.

Locking transparency

The reason we've left our selections active while painting is to prevent the paint from straying onto transparent portions of the layer. However, if you want to return to a layer later and paint further after the selection has been deactivated, there is another method you can use, rather than reloading the original selection. Simply target your layer and then enable the Lock Transparency button in the Layers palette. The transparency lock will not allow you to edit any transparent portions of the layer, which allows you to paint within the confines of your layer contents without the assistance of a selection.

17 Add a very subtle gradient inside the current selection using a slightly lighter red and the linear gradient method this time. Deactivate the selection, target all the layers that make up your new object, and add them to a new group in the Layers palette. Use this method of working with paths, selections, filling, and painting to create a flagpole and flag on a new layer. First create the flagpole, then the flag, then create the object on the flag. Carefully create the flagpole path so that the flag looks as though it is rising out of the hole in the egg.

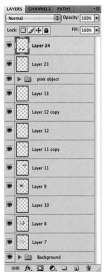

18 As we did previously with the egg shape, the platform, the pink organic object, and the flag, use the same methods to create a couple of boats on a new layer. Your path components will obviously differ, as will your fill colors, brush thickness, opacity, and shading colors, but the basic procedure will remain the same. Create path components. Load the paths as selections. Fill them with color on a new layer and then paint to indicate depth and add shading. In this case, create the bottoms of the boats first, then the inner sides, then the outer sides and backs.

Incorporating photography

Now that you've spent a fair amount of time painting within selection borders, let's incorporate some photographic resources.

1 Open the *knife.psd* file. Use the Move tool to drag the knife into the working file as a new layer. Position the knife in the lower left of the canvas area, where it will eventually be combined with the ears.

2 Open the *fish.psd* file and drag it into your working file as a new layer, too. Position it to the lower left of the egg on the canvas. Drag the layer down in the Layers palette until it rests directly above the background group.

3 Create an elliptical selection. Choose Select > Transform Selection from the menu. Click and drag outside the box to rotate the selection and then press Enter. Fill the selection with gray on a new layer. Add black-and-white, radial, foreground-to-transparent gradients into the selection.

PART THREE: Poser preparation

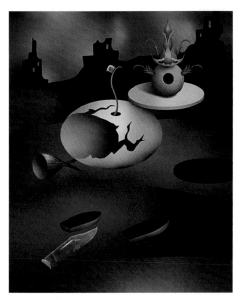

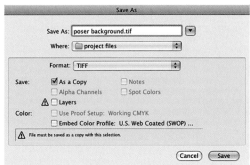

19 We are now at the point in the creation of this illustration that requires us to make the jump to Poser. For those of you who aren't interested in exploring Poser, you can still follow along. The finished Poser renderings are included within the downloadable project files for this chapter. Save a copy of your file with all the layers flattened. It is very important that you save as a copy and do not overwrite the current working file. Save the file in .tiff format and name it *poser background.tif*. Again, save it as a copy so that you do not overwrite your layered file, because we'll be returning to that version later in the chapter.

 Inspiration

I wish I could say that my interest in recreating a Bosch paining was the result of extensive studies in art history or perhaps traveling to Europe to see the original, but that is not true. One day I came across a series of action figures from *The Garden of Earthly Delights* on the Web. I was struck by how well the subject matter translated into such a contemporary, pop-culture medium. After a bit of thinking I got curious about how to create something in a similar vein using contemporary tools. The result of that curiosity is what you see here. However, if you want to check out the action figures, have a look at www.talariaenterprises.com.

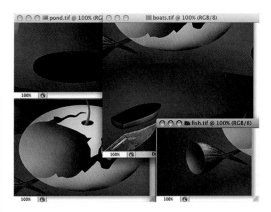

20 Open the *background.tif* file you just created. There are four regions in the image that we'll use as separate backgrounds in Poser to ensure that the models we create will match up in terms of angle and light. Use the Rectangular marquee to select the region that shows the crack in the egg. Copy it and then create a new file. The New options will automatically be set to the Clipboard preset, so just click OK and paste. Flatten the layers and choose Image > Mode > RGB. Then save the file as *egg.tif*. Repeat this process over and over again to save additional images that contain the pond at the right, the fish at the left, and the space above the boats. Name the files in a logical manner using the following names: *pond.tif, fish.tif, boats.tif.*

PART FOUR: Posing against a background image

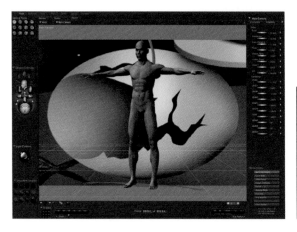

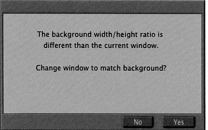

The background width/height ratio is different than the current window.

Change window to match background?

No   Yes

21 Open the Poser file that is included in the downloadable project files. The name of the file is simply *source*. This file contains a single male figure inside the Document window. Choose File > Import > Background Image from the menu and then navigate to your *egg.tif* file that you created earlier. (If you didn't create the background files, worry not; they are included in the downloadable project files as well.) A warning box will appear, informing you that the ratio of the background image is different than that of the Poser file. When asked whether if you'd like to change the aspect ratio of the window to match the background, click yes. You will now see the background image appear in the file.

22 Click the Pose category icon at the top of the Library palette. You will then see a hierarchal list of folders directly below the icon. This list presents a staggering number of options to work from. Click the triangle to the left of the Poser 8 folder to expand it. Then expand the Poser 1-5 folder. Within the Poser 1-5 folder, expand the Poser 5 Poses folder. In that folder you will see two folders containing options for male or female figures. Obviously, expand the Male Poses folder and then expand the Action folder within that. In the Action folder you'll find another folder called Other Actions. Expand the Other Actions folder and then double-click the Jumping 01 pose to apply it to your figure.

23 Now that you've given the figure an initial pose, it is time to alter the Camera controls. If you haven't altered the Camera controls at the left, you are viewing the scene with the Main camera. You will see a large ¾ view of the head at the top of the controls between the two hands. You will also see the name of the camera at the top left of the window. Click and drag the trackball to rotate the camera around the object. Then use the hand icons to move the camera up and down along the Y axis, left and right along the X axis, and forward or backward along the Z axis. Adjust the Camera controls so that the figure more or less belongs in the egg and we are looking down on him slightly.

The Camera controls

From here on, we'll spend a lot of time editing the way the Poser scenes are viewed through the camera. Here is a brief rundown of Camera controls we'll be using often.

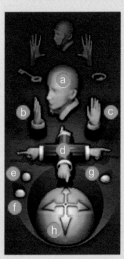

a Click and drag here to select a camera. Right now it is set to the Main camera, but there are a number of other views to choose from.

b All the "hand" icons you see here represent camera plane controls, allowing you to constrain movements to specific axes. The Move YZ control constrains movement along the Y and Z axes, constraining movement to forward/backward and up/down.

c The Move XY control only allows movement, which is up/down as well as left/right. Forward/backward movement is not permitted.

d The Move XZ control only allows for left/right and forward/backward movement. Up/down movement is not permitted.

e Clicking and dragging on this button will scale the scene proportionately within the view.

f You can adjust the focal length of the camera by clicking and dragging here.

g Clicking and dragging the roll icon will allow you to rotate the camera along its own Z axis. Basically, you can rotate the view either clockwise or counter-clockwise.

h The Rotation Trackball allows you to tilt, spin, and rotate along the X, Y, and Z axes all at once as you click and drag.

24 After applying the initial pose to the figure, you'll notice that he is bent forward awkwardly, in an impossible manner. To remove this impossibility, the first step is to impose some realistic limits on what the body is allowed to do in terms of movement. Choose Figure > Use Limits from the menu and you'll immediately see him snap upward. This function makes the body behave naturally, since there is no way a human could bend that far forward. You'll also notice his legs move a little, since they too were arranged in an impossible manner. In the Camera controls, click and drag the large head to switch to the Left camera. Also click and drag the Move XY icon as necessary so that you can see his entire body within the camera view.

Frequently used Editing tools

The Editing tools will allow you to adjust individual body parts in almost any way to create custom poses. Here is a description of the four tools we'll use often throughout this chapter.

a The Rotate tool bends a body part at the joint, allowing you rotate it on any axis, so you can work in three dimensions at once. Select a body part and then drag perpendicular to it to rotate it up or down. Dragging in parallel will rotate the body part forward or backward. All movement depends on your point of view.

b The Twist tool rotates a body part along its length or longest axis. For instance, the head, neck, and torso twist along the figure's spine. For a body part such as the forearm, the axis lies along the length of the arm.

c The Translate/Pull tool closely resembles the Move tool in Photoshop. This is no coincidence, since the Translate/Pull toll allows you to move a selected body part within the camera's view, depending on how you drag. Movement is also dependent on the relationship between the camera position and the figure.

d The Translate In/Out tool allows you to move the selected body part forward or backward within the scene along the Z axis of the camera. Select a body part and drag upward to push it backward or drag downward to pull it forward. Depending on how you move the body part along the Z axis, it will appear larger or smaller.

25 Select the Rotate tool and then click the figure's waist section. Drag to the right slightly to bend the figure forward at the waist. You can always drag back to the left if he is bent too far. Drag up or down if he has shifted from side to side and you want to straighten him. Then select his abdomen and perform a similar operation. Basically, we're trying to achieve a more natural bend in his midsection. Feel free to tweak his waist and abdomen as often as necessary with the Rotate tool until you've achieved a pose similar to what is shown here.

 Selecting body parts

You can select any body part by simply clicking it. You will know that you've selected the body part when it becomes highlighted and the name of the body part is displayed at the top of the camera view in the document window. Sometimes you might find it difficult to select a certain body part by clicking it. In a case like this, simply click the currently selected body part's name at the top of the document window. This will reveal a menu that is called the Current Actor menu. It contains a number of submenus, one of which is body parts. Simply choose the desired body part from the list in the submenu to select it.

26 In the Camera controls, click and drag on the large head to once again select the Main camera. Select the Translate/Pull tool and click the figure's hip to select it. Then pull the selected hip to the left. This will not only move his upper body but also his legs will respond naturally to the movement. Next, select his right foot and use the Translate/Pull tool to pull it to the left, stretching out his right leg slightly. After that, select his chest and pull downward slightly, bending him even further. Continue to use the Translate/Pull and Rotate tools to adjust his chest as well as waist and abdomen. Also use the Rotate tool to adjust each of his feet. Try using the Twist tool to twist waist and abdomen slightly. Then adjust the Camera controls so that your figure looks similar to what is shown here.

PART FIVE: Adding a prop to the scene

27 Click the Props icon at the top of the Library palette. When the folders appear below, expand the Poser 8 folder. Then when the subfolders appear, expand the Primitives folder. Double-click the Ball Primitive to add it to the scene. Now, before you do anything else, ensure that you are happy with the camera view. If you're not, use the Camera controls to alter the camera view so that the figure is situated nicely inside the cracked egg in the background image. When you're happy with the camera view, go to the Memory Dots palette at the bottom left of the Document window. Use the pull-down menu at the top of the palette to set the dots type to Camera. Then click an empty dot. Immediately you'll notice that a full dot appears in its place.

Covering the figure's head
Reposition the ball using a variety of camera views, then return to your desired camera view via the memory dot.

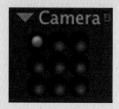

1 Select the top Camera in the Camera controls and then use the Translate/Pull tool to position the ball so that it is in exactly the same region as the figure's head, albeit much lower down by the figure's feet.

2 Now select the Left camera and use the Translate/Pull tool to move the ball up so that it covers the figure's head nicely.

3 Finally, click the camera dot that you just created to revert to your saved camera view. Camera dots are an excellent way to not only preserve your camera view but also to quickly return to it.

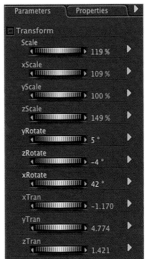

28 Select the ball by either clicking it in the camera view or by choosing Props > ball_1 from the Current Actor menu at the top of the Document window. In the Parameters palette, perform a number of adjustments to alter the size, rotation, and placement of the ball in the scene. The goal is to make the ball look as though it is completely surrounding the figure's head and placing weight on his neck, causing him to bend over. His arms are outstretched to feel around because the ball blinds him. In the Parameters palette are three different sets of dials: Scale, Rotate, and Tran. All three provide options for each axis, but there is also an overall Scale dial that comes in handy for initial adjustments. Have some fun experimenting with different combinations of parameters. Here are the parameters that I used for the ball shown here. Yours might differ slightly, since there is bound to be a slight difference between this and what you've done so far.

PART SIX: Lighting and materials

29 Direct your attention to the Lighting controls, which reside directly beneath the Camera controls at the left side of the interface. In the Lighting controls, you will notice three lights in various positions around a globe. This globe represents the 3D space in your scene. Adjust the positioning of individual lights by clicking and dragging them in the light position indicator. As you move a light, you will see the results immediately in the Document window. You can alter the intensity of individual lights by selecting them and then adjusting the Brightness control. Click the little yellow brightness indicator and drag it to the left or right, depending on whether you want to dim or brighten each light. In this case, dim the brown light at the left and adjust the position of all three lights to resemble what is shown here.

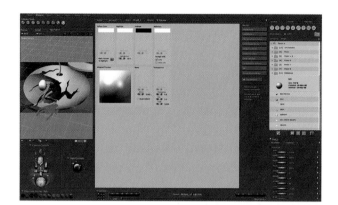

30 Select the orange light at the right and then click the Color icon at the bottom of the light controls to open a standard color picker. Choose a less saturated, brown color so that the skin of the figure feels more natural. Next, click the Material Room tab at the top of the Document window to enter the Material Room and temporarily exit the Pose Room. Because we're going to alter the material of the ball in the scene, choose Props > ball_1 from the Object list at the top of the interface. The simple option is sufficient for what we're doing here and is also the default setting, so leave the tabs alone.

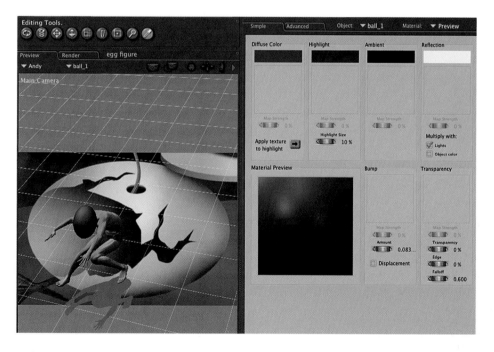

31 Click the Diffuse Color swatch to access the color picker and choose a dark, desaturated, teal-blue color to change the color of the ball. Then click the Highlight color swatch and choose a very dark gray color from the picker, to diminish the brightness of the highlight. Pay attention to the Preview at the left. If you're not satisfied with the results, you can simply click the swatches and try different colors and shades from the color picker until you are happy with your choices.

PART SEVEN: Rendering

Poser workaround 1

If you don't want to create or pose your own figure, or if you want to simply inspect the original Poser file used here, it is included within the downloadable project files for this chapter. The file is called *egg figure.pz3*. Also, if you're not using Poser whatsoever, the rendered file called *egg figure.psd* is included as well.

32 Return to the Pose Room and tweak individual body parts of your figure as you see fit. Here I twisted the chest and abdomen slightly, as well as rotated his right arm a little. When you're satisfied with your pose, choose the Pose option from the pull-down menu at the top of the Memory Dots palette. Then click in an empty space to add a pose dot. Now if you accidentally alter your figure, you can reset it by clicking the pose dot. Next, choose Render > Render from the menu to perform a quick test rendering. If you're not satisfied with something, click the Preview tab at the top of the Document window. Perform any necessary alterations and then do another test rendering. Choose File > Save as from the menu and name your saved file egg figure.

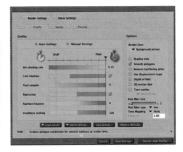

33 Either on the ground in the Camera window or choose Props > Ground from the Current Actor menu. When the ground is selected, click the Properties palette tab beside the Parameters palette tab to make it visible. In the Properties palette, uncheck the Visible option to hide the ground. This will avoid pesky shadows being included within our final rendering. Choose Render > Render settings from the menu. Use the Firefly Auto Settings. The slider will be in the center, between Draft and Final. Grab the slider and drag it all the way to the right to increase the quality to its maximum setting. Then enable the Smooth Polygons option at the right and click the Render Now (Firefly) button. When the rendering is complete, choose File > Export > Image from the menu. Select .psd format and save the file as egg figure.psd.

PART EIGHT: The figure in the fish

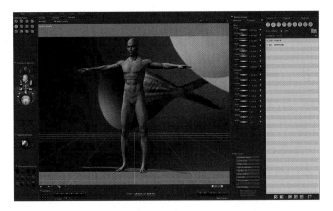

34 Choose File > Open from the menu. If you are prompted to save changes to the *egg figure* file, go ahead and do so. Navigate to the *source* Poser file included in the downloadable project files and open it. If you still see your finished rendering from the *egg figure* file, don't worry about it; simply click the Preview tab at the upper left of the Document window. Choose File > Import > Background Picture from the menu. Choose the *fish.tif* file and click Open. When you're prompted to change the window to match the background, click Yes.

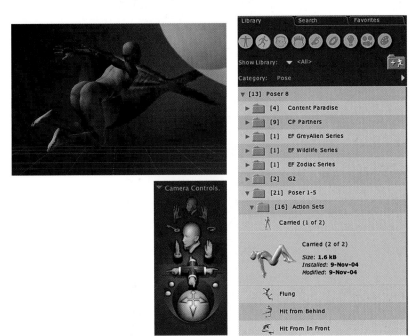

35 Click the Pose icon at the top of the Library palette. When the folders appear below, expand the Poser 8 folder. Then, when all the subfolders appear, expand the Poser 1-5 folder. Inside the Poser 1-5 folder, you'll find an Action Sets folder. Expand it and then double-click the Carried (2 of 2) pose to apply it to the figure. In the Parameters palette, begin adjusting the yRotate, xRotate, and zRotate dials until the figure is rotated in 3D space, so that he looks as though he's going into the fish while kneeling. The pose doesn't have to be perfect at this point; just get started. Then use the camera plane controls to move in closer along the Z axis, making the figure appear larger in the view. Also use the camera plane controls to adjust the positioning along the Y and X axis as necessary.

36 Now spend some time selecting specific body parts and using the editing tools to make the figure look more like he is crawling. Rotate the left and right collars as well as shoulders, to bring his arms down. Then alter the position of his arms via the Translate/ Pull tool. Also use the Translate/Pull tool to alter the way his back arches by selecting and moving his abdomen, waist, and hip. Move his feet to the left a little with the same tool, and then use the Translate In/Out(Z) tool to move his legs apart and bring his right arm forward. After performing these adjustments, choose Figure > Use Limits from the menu. His pose will change, but you can continue to tweak it. Continue in this manner until you like the look of the pose. This is a multistage process and will often require that you revisit certain body parts more than once.

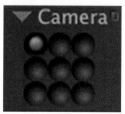

37 Select the Pose option from the pull-down menu at the top of the Memory Dots palette. If you see an existing pose dot left over from last time, Alt-click (or Option-click) it to delete it. When you're happy with the pose of your figure, click in an empty space in the Memory Dots palette to add a pose dot. As before, if you accidentally alter the pose, you can quickly revert by clicking the pose dot. After creating the pose dot, adjust the Camera controls if necessary until you're totally happy with the camera view. Then choose Camera from the pull-down menu at the top of the Memory Dots palette and, again, delete any existing dots. Following that, click in an empty space to add a camera dot, just in case you accidentally shift the Camera controls later on.

38 In the Lighting controls, click the light gray light in the middle. Drag it so that it is almost directly above the globe in the center. Then adjust the left and right lights so that they are both sitting above the top half of the globe on either side. Select the greenish light at the left and change its color to a less saturated grayish-green. Next, select the light at the right; again, change it to a less saturated version of the existing color. When you're happy with the lighting in the scene, press Control-R (or Command-R) or choose Render > Render from the menu to perform a test rendering.

Poser workaround 2

Again, if you don't want to create or pose your own figure, or if you want to simply inspect the original Poser file used here, it is included in the downloadable project files for this chapter. The file is called *fish figure.pz3*. Also, if you're not using Poser whatsoever, the rendered file called *fish figure.psd* is included as well.

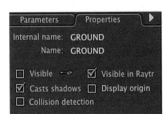

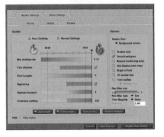

39 Examine the test rendering to see if anything needs tweaking or revising. If it does, click the Preview tab at the top of the Document window and then remedy any concerns you have with the pose or the lighting. As you did previously, choose the ground from Current Actor menu and disable its visibility in the Properties palette. When you're satisfied with everything, press Control-Y (or Command-Y) or choose Render > Render Settings from the menu. In the options for the Firefly Auto Settings, drag the slider all the way to the right to achieve the best render quality. Enable the Smooth Polygons option and then click the Render Now button. When the rendering is complete, choose File > Export > Image from the menu. Select .psd format and save the rendered file as fish figure.psd.

PART NINE: The figure in the pond

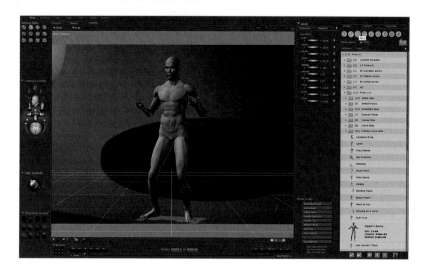

40 Choose File > Open from the menu. If you are prompted to save changes to the *fish figure* file, go ahead and do so. Again, navigate to the *source* Poser file included in the downloadable project files. Open it and, again, don't be alarmed if your finished rendering is still visible in the Render tab. Choose File > Import > Background picture from the menu and import your *pond.tif* file that you created earlier. When you are prompted to change the window to match the background, click Yes. The Pose category should still be displayed in the Library palette. If it isn't, click the Pose icon at the top of the palette. The path through the files is similar to what you used previously: Poser 8 > Poser 1-5. However, collapse the Action Sets folder if it is still expanded and then expand the Creative Pose Sets instead. Double-click the Juggler's stance pose to apply it to the figure.

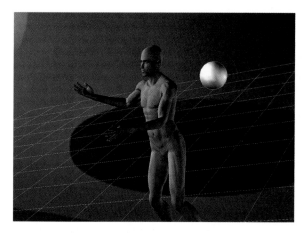

41 As you've done before, use the Editing controls to adjust the pose of the figure. Use the Twist, Rotate, and Translate/Pull tools to adjust his arms, shoulders, hands, abdomen, waist, chest, and head. Select each forearm, one at a time, and increase the xScale in the Parameters palette to 150% so that he has abnormally long forearms. Adjust the Camera controls as well as the pose of your figure until it resembles what is shown here. In the Library palette, click the Props icon at the top and add the same ball primitive you added to the first poser file. You'll need to drag it upward with the Translate/Pull tool to see it in the current camera view.

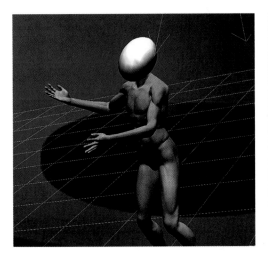

42 Again, as you did with the first figure, use multiple views and the Translate/Pull tool to position the ball over the figure's head. Then use the Parameters palette to adjust the scale, rotation, and translation on varying axes until it looks elongated. It should completely cover his head and look as though it is tilted back. In the Lighting controls, select the left light and then click the Delete Light icon to remove it. Change the color of both lights to a light gray and position them in a similar way to what is shown here. Select the light at the top of the globe, toward the right, and reduce its brightness. Then, in the Parameters palette, set the Shadow amount to 0.

Turning everything gray
Use the Material Room to remove the map from the figure and change him and the ball to a neutral gray color.

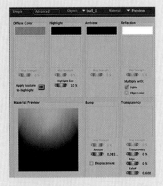

1 Click the Material tab at the top of the Document window to enter the Material Room. From the Object menu at the top, select Andy. Click the Diffuse map to access the Texture Manager. From the menu, choose No texture and click OK.

2 You will immediately see the figure turn white. Next, click the Diffuse Color swatch and then select a gray color from the color picker when it appears.

3 Now select Props > ball_1 from the Object menu. Click the Diffuse Color swatch and choose a similar gray from the color picker. Then click the Highlight swatch and choose an extremely dark gray (almost black) from the color picker.

Beyond Photoshop

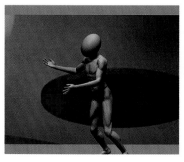

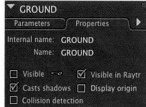

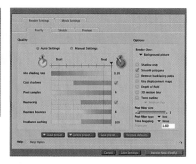

43 Click the Pose tab to return to the Pose Room. Select the ground and disable its visibility in the Properties palette. Press Control-Y (or Command-Y) to access the render settings. Again, in the Firefly Auto Settings, drag the slider all the way to the right. Ensure that you enable the Smooth Polygons option and then click the Render Now button to render the scene. After the rendering is complete, export the image and save it as creature figure.psd. Then choose File > Save As from the menu and save the file as creature figure.pz3.

PART TEN: Creating the legs

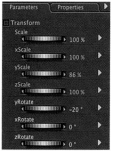

Poser workaround 3

Again, if you don't want to create or pose this figure or if you want to simply inspect the original Poser file used here, it is included in the downloadable project files for this chapter. The file is called *creature figure.pz3*. Also, if you're not using Poser whatsoever, the rendered file called *creature figure.psd* is included as well.

44 Open the source file again and save any changes to the creature figure file when prompted. Import the *boats.tif* file as a background picture. Begin by using the Camera controls to rotate the view so that we are looking at the back of the figure at an angle, and zoom in so that the legs are much bigger. Basically, what we're going to do is make it look like each leg is standing in a boat. The next step is to use the Editing tools to adjust the pose of the figure's legs. Choose Figure > Use Limits from the menu. Use the Translate/Pull tool to move his feet and pull his hip down so that he is sort of squatting with his knees bent and his feet apart. Use the Rotate and Twist tools on different parts of his legs and pelvic region to edit the pose until it resembles what is shown here. Select Body from the Current Actor menu and then reduce the yScale to make him shorter. You might need to adjust the yRotate setting as well.

210

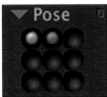

45 This pose will serve as a starting point for the way you will manipulate each leg. In the Memory Dots palette, create a new pose dot. From this starting pose, we'll work on each leg separately. We'll begin with the right leg, pose and manipulate it, then render it. After saving the rendering, we'll use the pose dot to return to the initial pose and repeat the same procedure for the other leg. Bear in mind that you do not have to return to the initial pose if you're comfortable continuing with things the way they are. This is up to you; users' needs will differ, as will each individual Poser file. I simply recommend saving dots at key points in the workflow so that there is something for you to return to if the need arises. One at a time, select and modify the individual components of the right leg: the shin, the thigh, the buttock, and the foot. Select each part and then use the Parameter dials as well as the Editing tools to manipulate it until it resembles what is shown here. When you're happy with the results, add another pose dot for the sake of security. Feel free to use the Camera controls to adjust the view if necessary.

Light and render

When you're finished posing the leg, use what is now becoming a familiar method to adjust the lighting and render the scene.

1 Adjust the lighting controls so that the figure is lit a little more evenly. Select the orange light and change its color to a less saturated brownish-pink color.

2 Select Props > Ground from the Current Actor menu. Then, in the Properties palette, disable the Visible option to hide the ground plane. Choose Render > Render Settings from the menu. Drag the slider all the way to the right. Enable the Smooth Polygons option and click the Render Now button.

3 When the rendering is complete, choose File > Export > Image from the menu. Save the rendered image as legs1.psd. Next, choose File > Save As and save the Poser file in its current state as legs1.pz3.

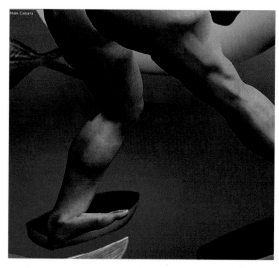

46 After saving the file as *legs1.pz3*, choose File > Save As again, and this time save the file as legs2.pz3. This will prevent accidentally saving over the file you just created. Now, repeat the same procedure you just performed to alter the left leg. Select individual components and use the Editing tools and Parameter dials to alter them. Feel free to adjust the overall pose of the leg and alter the camera view if necessary. Also, you might find it helpful to use the Editing tools to move the other leg out of the way. Don't worry if it gets distorted or weird looking, because remember, there is a pose dot to bring it back into place anytime you like. Again, when you're happy with what you've done, add another pose dot to the Memory Dots palette.

Poser workarounds 4 and 5

Again, if you're interested in seeing the Poser files used here rather than creating your own or are just plain curious, they're included in the downloadable project files for this chapter. They are named *legs1.pz3* and *legs2.pz3*. The rendered versions of these files are there too and are called *legs1.psd* and *legs2.psd*, respectively.

47 Adjust the position of the lights in the Lighting controls so that the darkest shadow is on the figure's inner thigh along the left side of the leg. Feel free to alter the brightness of individual lights as you see fit. Choose Render > Render Settings from the menu to ensure that the Smooth Polygons option is enabled and that the slider has been dragged to the right. If this is not the case, go ahead and reset them. Press the Render Now button to render the scene. Export the finished rendering and save it as legs2.psd. There is no need to hide the ground; it remains hidden. However, you might want to select it from the Current Actor menu and double-check that this is the case in the Properties palette.

PART ELEVEN: Create the face and ear

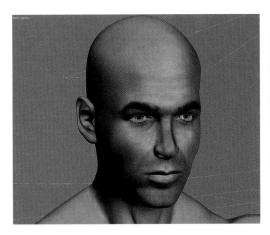

48 Open the Poser *source* file yet again. Save any changes to your *legs2.pz3* file if prompted. Then, in the Camera Controls palette, select Face Camera by clicking the small FaceCam icon at the top of the palette. Then use the Trackball and the Camera Plane controls to rotate and position the face within the view, as shown here. Select the orange light in the Lighting Controls palette and again, change it to a less saturated brownish-pink color. Adjust the position of the lights in a similar manner to what is shown here. Select the light gray light and increase the brightness slightly.

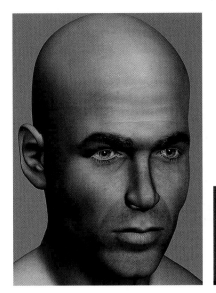

49 When you're satisfied with the current view, go ahead and create a new camera dot in the Memory Dots palette. Also, remember that you can Alt-click (or Option-click) any unwanted dots in the palette to remove them at any point. Choose File > Save As from the menu and save this file as face.pz3. As you've done previously, ensure that the render settings are set to the highest quality and that the Smooth Polygons option is enabled. Render the file and export it. Name the exported file face.psd.

Poser workarounds 6 and 7

The ear and face used in the finished illustration reside within the same Poser file. The file is included in the downloadable project files for this chapter and is called *face.pz3*. There are two camera dots included in the Memory Dots palette. The first will take you to the view of the face; the second will take you to the view of the ear. If you simply want the rendered versions and want to avoid Poser altogether, these files are included as well. The rendered files are called *face.psd* and *ear.psd*.

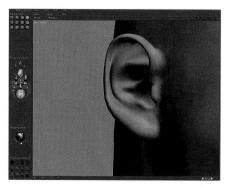

50 In the Camera Controls palette, use the Trackball and the Camera Plane controls to rotate and position the camera view so that the figure's right ear is shown prominently. Try to match this angle as closely as possible because we're going to bring it into the Photoshop file and make it look like it belongs with the knife that resides there already. When you're satisfied with the view, add another camera dot to the Memory Dots palette. In the Lighting Controls palette, adjust the position of the gray light so that it is moved forward on the globe rather than tucked around the side.

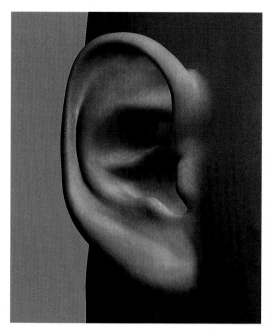

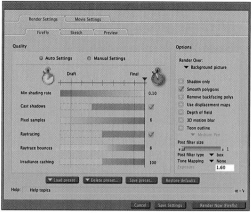

51 Double-check the Render settings to ensure that the slider is all the way to the right, ensuring the best quality. Also, double-check to ensure that the Smooth Polygons option is enabled. Click the Render Now button to render the scene. When it is finished, export the rendered image as ear.psd. Save your face.pz3 file by pressing Control-S (or Command-S).

PART TWELVE: Additional figures

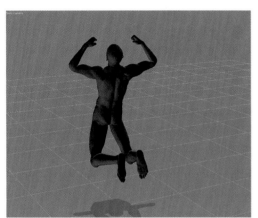

52 Open the Poser *source* file again and, if you are prompted, go ahead and save changes to your *face.pz3* file. Click the Pose icon at the top of the Library palette. When the Poser 8 folder appears below, expand it. Then expand the Universal Poses folder that is contained in the Poser 8 folder. There you'll find an Action folder. Expand that and then expand the Jumping folder within. Double-click the Jumping 04 pose to apply it to the figure. In the Camera Controls palette, use the Trackball and the Camera Plane controls to rotate the view so that we are looking at him from behind and slightly above. Use the Translate/Pull tool to adjust his feet so that they are farther apart and he looks like he is kneeling.

53 Choose Edit > Duplicate 'Andy' from the menu to duplicate the figure. You will notice nothing immediately because the duplicate is placed in the same position as the original. In the Editing Tools palette, click the Translate/Pull tool icon and drag to the right. This will move your figure over to the right. Ensure that your duplicate figure is selected. The Select Figure menu at the upper left should read *figure 1* and not *andy*. If this is not the case, select figure 1 from this menu. Now return to the Library palette. Click the Pose icon if the pose category is not currently displayed. Use the following path to locate the desired pose: Poser 8 > Universal Poses > Action > Comic Book > Hero Pose 03. When you locate Hero Pose 03, double-click it to apply the pose to your duplicate figure.

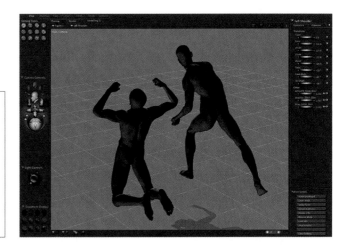

Poser workaround 8

Again, the Poser file used here is available for your use or perusal. It is included in the downloadable project files for this chapter and is called *kneeling1.pz3*. Or, if you're skipping the Poser process entirely and are just following along with the Photoshop portions of this chapter, the accompanying rendering is supplied as well. The rendered image is called *kneeling1.psd*.

54 In the Editing Tools palette, click and drag the Translate/Pull tool to move the figure so that he is to the right of the other figure. Click and drag the Twist tool to twist the figure slightly. Choose Figure > Use Limits from the menu. Use the Translate/Pull and Rotate tools to adjust his pose. Move his left arm down and bend his shoulder. Tilt his head back, and do the same with his waist so that he is more upright.

55 In the Lighting Controls palette, adjust the positioning, the color, and the density of the lights. Basically you want to use less saturated, somewhat neutral colors, and you want the brightest illumination to fall on the scene from the upper left. Keep a light positioned at the upper right as well to define the edges on that side. Select the ground and then disable its visibility in the Properties palette. In the Render Settings, enable the Smooth Polygons option and drag the slider to the right, as you've been doing all along. Render the scene and export the image as kneeling1.psd. Then choose File > Save As from the menu and save the file as kneeling1.pz3.

56 Now, before you do anything else, choose File > Save As from the menu again and save the file as kneeling2.pz3. After saving the file under a new name, select figure 1 and then choose Figure > Delete Figure from the menu. You will be asked if you are sure that you want to delete the figure; answer yes. Use the Rotate, Twist, and Translate/Pull tools to adjust the figure's pose. Move his legs apart, bend his feet, pull his hip down, and bend his waist and each shoulder. In many instances you'll need to use more than one tool to adjust a body part to get it just the way you want it. Also, feel free to temporarily switch to other views if that makes it easier.

57 Tweak the lighting slightly so that there is dark shading behind his right knee and that his left side is brightly lit. Continue to adjust the pose as you see fit. Select his right hand by either clicking it with an Editing tool or choosing Body Parts > Right Hand from the Current Actor menu. Click the + button below the Transform dials in the Parameters palette to reveal the Advanced Hand Controls. Click the Grasp dial and drag to the left to loosen the grasp of his right hand, opening it. Then click the ThumbBend dial and drag to the right to move the thumb out away from the palm of his hand. Repeat this same procedure with the left hand. However, you will need to drag the dials in opposite directions to duplicate the result on his left hand.

 Final Poser workarounds

For the final two Poser figures created
and rendered here, you can access the
original files in the downloadable project
files for this chapter. The Poser files are
called *kneeling2.pz3* and *kneeling3.pz3*. If
you aren't using Poser at all, the finished
renderings are supplied as well. The
rendered files are named *kneeling2.psd* and
kneeling3.psd.

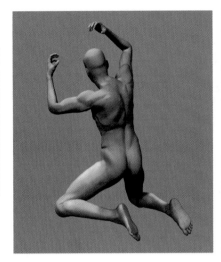

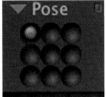

58 When the figure is posed the way you like it and both hands are open, go
ahead and add a pose dot and a camera dot to the Memory Dots palette. Delete any
previously created dots from the palette. Now, the Render Settings should already
be at their highest quality setting and the Smooth Polygons option should still be
selected. The ground should be hidden, too. However, take a moment to double-
check the Render Settings and the visibility of the ground, just to be certain that
everything is fine. When you're satisfied, render the scene and save the rendered
file as kneeling2.psd.

59 Choose File > Save As from the menu.
Save the file in its current state as kneeling.
pz3. Choose Body from the Current Actor menu.
Then click and drag the Twist tool in the Editing
Tools palette to twist the entire figure until you
are seeing it from a similar angle to what is
shown here. Use the Translate/Pull, Twist, and
Rotate tools to manipulate various body parts
until the figure is posed in a similar way to
what is shown here. When you're happy with the
results, add a new pose dot to preserve this
pose, and add a camera dot to preserve the
current view. Delete any previously created dots
from the palette. Save the file and then render
the image using the same render settings as
before. Export the rendered image and name it
kneeling3.psd.

PART THIRTEEN: Bring the rendered figures into Photoshop

⚠ Render dimensions

If you're following along without altering things in Poser, your rendered files should be larger than you require when you bring them into Photoshop. This is fine, because we'll use Free Transform to reduce the size each time. However, if for some reason your renderings are smaller than you require, you'll need to render them at a larger size. Do not increase the size of the smaller renderings or the quality of the imagery will be terrible. You can simply return to your saved files in Poser and increase the size of your renderings by increasing the dimensions. Choose Render > Render Dimensions from the menu and increase the size. Then render your scene again and export it.

60 Quit Poser and return to your working file in Photoshop. Open the *egg figure. psd* file. In the Channels palette, you'll notice an alpha channel. Control-click (or Command-click) the alpha channel's thumbnail to load it as a selection. Do not target the channel, just load it as a selection. The RGB composite channel should remain targeted in the Channels palette. In the image window, use the Move tool to click in the selection border and drag the selected contents into your working file as a new layer. Move the layer above the layer that contains the cracked-egg effect in the Layers palette. Press Control-T (or Command-T) to access Free Transform. Shift-drag a corner point on the bounding box inward to reduce the figure proportionately. Click and drag within the bounding box to position the figure inside the egg. Press the Enter key to apply the transformation.

61 Control-click (or Command-click) the Layer thumbnail of the layer that contains the cracked-egg art, to generate a selection from the contents of that layer. It should be directly beneath your new figure layer. Ensure that your new figure layer is targeted and then, with the current selection active, click the Add Layer Mask button at the bottom of the Layers palette to mask all areas of the layer that fall outside the selection border. Create a new layer and use the methods you used earlier to create a shaded stem that rises out of his head, complete with base leaves. Use the exact same approach you used to create the flag and the pink object.

62 Open the *face.psd* file and load the included alpha channel as a selection. Use the Move tool to drag the selection contents into the working file as a new layer. Drag the layer down, beneath all the egg body layers in the Layers palette. Use Free Transform to resize and position the head under the platform, to the right of the egg. Click the Add Layer Mask button in the Layers palette to mask the layer. Target the mask and select the Brush tool. Use a black foreground color and a hard, round brush tip preset to paint over unwanted regions such as his neck and visible shoulder to mask them. Vary brush size as necessary, but leave the opacity set to 100%.

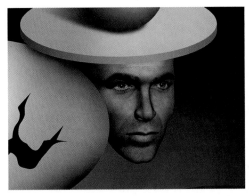

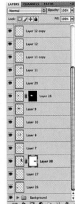

Inside the fish

Now use what are becoming familiar techniques to place a figure inside of the hollow fish, complete with shading.

1 Open the *fish figure.psd* file. Load a selection from the channel and use the Move tool to drag the figure into the working file as a new layer. Position him over the fish as though he is crawling into it. Use Free Transform to adjust the size. Move the layer up or down in the Layers palette so that it sits directly above the layer that contains the hollow fish artwork. Load the layer that contains the hollow fish artwork as a selection.

2 Choose Select > Inverse from the menu to invert the selection. Then choose Layer > Layer Mask > Reveal All from the menu. Target the mask and use the Brush tool to paint with 100% black over the areas you want to hide. Basically, you want to paint over his right arm, shoulder, head, and neck.

3 Create a new layer with a Multiply blending mode and invert the selection. Ensure that you have a large, soft, round brush selected and paint within the selection using black, to add shading on the new layer. Focus on the region where his body meets the edge of the fish at the right. Be sure to use a low brush opacity setting. Deselect.

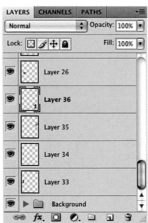

63 Open the *kneeling3.psd* file. Again, load a selection from the channel and drag the figure in as a new layer. This time, drag the layer below the fish layer in the Layers palette. Use Free Transform to resize and position the figure to the left of the fish, slightly behind it. Load a selection from this figure layer's contents and create a new layer with a Multiply blending mode. Paint black inside the selection, as you did previously, to add some shading near the fish within the selection. Deselect and then drag the *kneeling1.psd* and *kneeling2.psd* figures into the working file as new layers. Position them in their appropriate places and adjust their sizes accordingly, using the opening illustration as your guide.

Create a creature

Combine a Poser rendering with a now familiar illustration technique to create an ominous sea creature, complete with tail.

1 Open the *creature figure.psd* file. Load a selection from its alpha channel and drag the selected contents into the file as a new layer. Resize and position the creature over the left side of the pond on the canvas. Use the Lasso tool to draw a selection that surrounds his legs. Press the Delete key and then deselect.

2 Select the Pen tool and draw a closed path component to outline where the creature's tail should be. Load the path as a selection and use the Brush tool to paint gray, sampled from the creature, into the selection. Use a high opacity setting and a large, round brush preset.

3 Reduce the brush size as well as the opacity to paint shading around the tail edges using a darker color sampled from the creature. Continue to sample various shades of gray from the creature and paint them into regions of the tail at varying opacity settings. Vary the brush size as necessary. Take your time to create a convincing effect. Deselect.

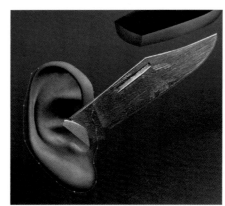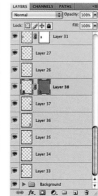

64 Open the *ear.psd* file. Load the alpha channel as a selection and then use the Move tool to drag the contents of the selection into the working file as a new layer. Resize and reposition the ear so that it sits to the left of the knife blade on the canvas. Now, obviously we don't want the partial face at the right. So, to remedy this, select the Pen tool and use it to draw a closed path that carefully traces the edge of the ear and defines its shape at the top, bottom, and right. While the path is targeted in the Paths palette, choose Layer > Vector Mask > Current Path from the menu.

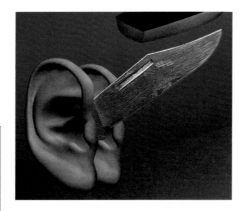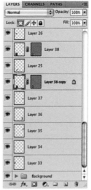

 Transforming your mask

When you enable Free Transform to transform your duplicate ear layer, be certain that the path used in the vector mask is not visible on the canvas area. If this is the case, you'll transform your path within the vector mask instead of the layer and the mask at the same time. If your path is visible, simply click the vector mask in the Layers palette and it will disappear. After the path disappears from the canvas, it is safe to use Free Transform.

65 Find the layer in your file that contains the knife. It will likely be at the top of the stack within the Layers palette. Drag this layer down within the palette until it sits directly beneath your ear layer. Target your ear layer and then duplicate it. Drag the duplicate layer down in the Layers palette beneath the knife layer. Hold down the Shift key and use the Move tool to drag the duplicate ear layer to the right a little. Use Free Transform to reduce the size of the duplicate ear slightly. Enable the transparency lock for this layer.

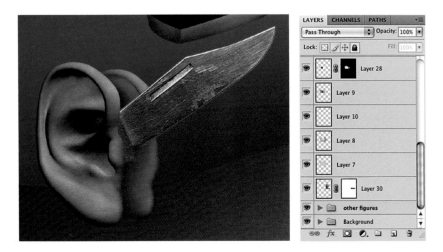

66 Select the Brush tool. Choose a large, soft, round brush preset and a high opacity setting. Paint over the ear on this layer using colors sampled from within the ear. The idea is to gently paint over the detail so that it looks like you're seeing the other side of the ear. Feel free to lower your brush opacity and continue to paint, varying your brush diameter as you go and gently blending the colors together. When you're finished painting, target all the layers that contain the smaller figures. Be sure to include the ear layers, the knife layer, and the fish layers, too. While these layers are targeted, group them and name the group appropriately. Do not include any layers that pertain to the main creature in the center.

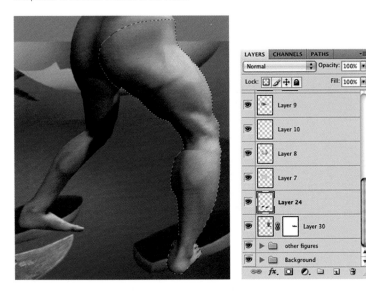

67 In the Layers palette, find your boats layer and drag it down so that it resides beneath the layers that make up the cracked-egg body of the main figure. It is very important that you do this or future layers will overlap other layers incorrectly. Open the *legs1.psd* file. Load a selection from the alpha channel included within the file. Then select the Lasso tool and, while holding down the Alt (or Option) key, draw a closed selection that covers the leg at the left and the area above his hips. This will subtract this region from your existing selection, leaving only the leg at the right selected.

68 Use the Move tool to drag the selected contents into your working file as a new layer. Place the layer above the layers that make up the cracked-egg body of the main figure in the Layers palette. Use Free Transform to resize and position it where the main creature's right leg should go on the canvas so that the ankle is overlapping the outer edge of the boat at the right. Now you'll notice that because we distorted the leg so much in Poser, there is not a smooth contour around the edge. To remedy this, select the Pen tool and draw a closed path to trim the bumpy regions off the edges of the leg as well as the foot where it meets the side of the boat. While the Path is visible on the canvas, choose Layer > Vector Mask > Current Path from the menu.

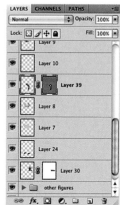

Making the leg look like it belongs there

Soft masking, color adjustments, and painting will make the leg look like it is part of the creature.

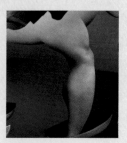

1 Choose Image > Adjustments >Hue/ Saturation from the menu. Now, if you're using your own rendering, the adjustment used here will differ, but basically, adjust the sliders so that the flesh of the leg is a closer match to the egg body.

2 Click the Add Layer Mask button at the bottom of the Layers palette and ensure that the new mask is targeted. Select the Brush tool, choose a large, soft, round-tip preset, and set the foreground color to black. Paint over the top of the leg within the mask, softly blending it into the underlying layers.

3 Now target the layer itself and not the mask. Reduce the opacity and diameter of your current brush. Sample colors from the egg and the leg itself and gently begin to paint over it. Give it a smoother appearance like the egg and use color to enhance the idea that it is part of the egg.

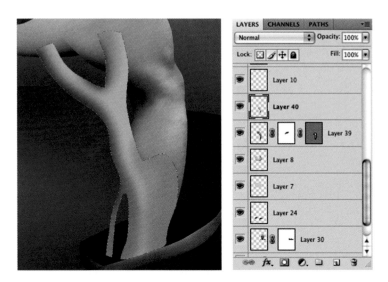

69 Use the Pen tool to carefully create a closed path component that resembles wooden branches attached to his leg, with a doorway at the bottom. Load the path as a selection and fill it on a new layer, using skin color sampled from his leg. Then select the Brush tool and use it, as you've done previously, to paint shaded areas into the selection, blending it nicely into the leg on the layer below. Sample colors from the leg, use varying opacity settings, and vary the size of your soft, round brush preset as necessary. Try to create a sense of depth as you paint.

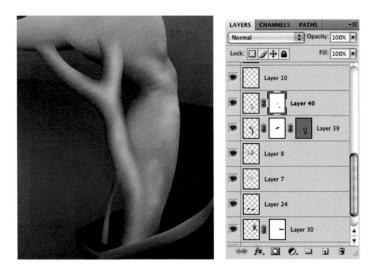

70 Continue to take your time and gently embellish what you've done. Observe the colors at work in the leg and try to mimic that feeling in your branch shape as you add depth and color. When you've got it almost right, reduce the brush diameter and paint some bright, specular highlights on raised regions and then paint some darker, yet very thin, shadows along the edges as necessary. Deselect and add a mask to the layer. Target the mask and use the brush tool to softly paint black over areas of hard edges that you want to blend into his leg on the underlying layer. Concentrate on the top of the branches and the calf area.

71 Open the *legs2.psd* file and load a selection from the alpha channel. As you did previously, Alt-drag (or Option-drag) with the Lasso selection tool to remove the unwanted portions at the top and right from the selection. Use the Move tool to drag the selected leg into the working file as a new layer. Use Free Transform to adjust the size of the leg and position it at the left in its logical place, with the foot overlapping the side of the boat. Drag this layer beneath the layers that make up the cracked-egg body in the Layers palette. As before, use the Pen tool to draw a path that trims the bumpy edges and the foot where it meets the side of the boat. Be certain to create a small doorway in the heel region to match up with the other leg. Add a vector mask to the layer that uses the current path.

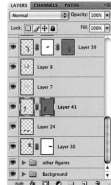

Complete the other leg

Repeat the same procedure so that our creature has a pair of legs to stand on.

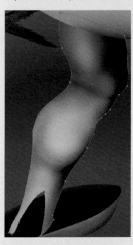
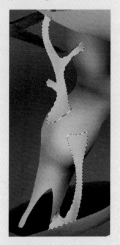
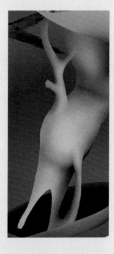

1 Perform a hue/saturation adjustment similar to the one you performed on the previous leg. After that, use the same painting method you used for the other leg to add shading, depth, and, smoothness.

2 Click your vector mask in the Layers palette if the path remains visible to hide it from view. Then use the Pen tool to draw closed shapes similar to the tree-branches structure you created for the other leg. Load a selection from the path and fill it with flesh color on a new layer.

3 Use the Brush tool, as you've done previously, to paint shaded areas into the selection, blending it nicely into the leg on the layer below. Deselect and add a mask to the layer. Target the mask and use the Brush tool to softly paint black over areas of hard edges that you want to blend into his leg on the underlying layer.

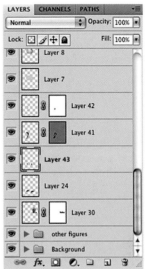

72 Create a new layer and position it directly above the boats layer in the Layers palette. Use the Pen tool to draw two closed path components behind the openings at the bottom of his legs. Load the entire path as a selection. Fill the active selection on your new layer with a dark brown color sampled from the inside of one of the boats. Select the Brush tool and ensure that a large, soft, round brush tip preset is selected. Set the opacity very low and then paint within the selected areas here and there on the current layer, using lighter brown colors sampled from the boats. Deselect when finished.

 Locking image pixels

Another layer lock that you might find useful when you're creating a multilayered illustration such as this is the one located directly to the right of the Lock Transparency button in the Layers palette. This lock, called Lock Image, will lock all the image pixels of the currently targeted layer. Enabling this lock prevents any alterations to the layer by any of the Photoshop paint tools. This is a good lock to enable when you've finished painting on a layer, to prevent accidental alterations later on.

73 Look in the Layers palette and you'll notice that all layers are grouped except those that make up this central creature. If there are any layers that reside above the pink object group, go ahead and drag them beneath it, but other than that preserve their order in the layer hierarchy. Target all these layers and group them. Now take a good look at the image and you might feel that the legs you just added look smooth and illustrated compared to some of the previous figures and body parts you added to the composition. If you think it is necessary, feel free to apply the painting methods we used for the legs to other figures, unifying the feeling overall.

PART FOURTEEN: Painterly effects and surface texture

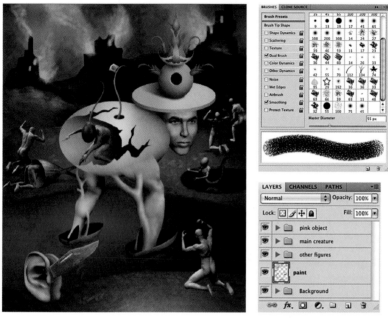

74 Create a new layer and place it directly above your original background layer group in the Layers palette. Ensure that this layer is targeted and select the Brush tool. In the Brushes palette, choose the wet sponge brush tip preset and reduce the diameter. Disable the wet edges option so that the strokes are more solid feeling. Paint a series of small strokes on the new layer using colors sampled from the background. Use low opacity settings and vary the diameter of the brush as you see fit. This is your opportunity to add a bit of texture to the ground, sky, and water as well as make the buildings in the background appear as though they are aflame.

75 Create another new layer and paint over the existing brush strokes on the new layer, using even lower opacity settings, to blend the paint effect. Frequently press down the Alt (and Option) key to temporarily access the Eyedropper tool and sample underlying colors as you go. Create a new layer and position it at the top within the Layers palette. Reduce the brush diameter. Paint brush strokes over different parts of the image, using colors sampled from underlying layers until there are subtle brush strokes all over the surface of the image.

76 Open the *book.psd* file. This is a desktop scan of a very old book cover texture. Hold down the Shift key and use the Move tool to drag the image into your working file as a new layer. Ensure that it is at the top of the stack in the Layers palette. Change the blending mode of the layer to Soft Light and reduce the opacity to 53%. With your new layer targeted, press Control-A (or Command-A) to select the entire layer and copy it by pressing Control-C (or Command-C).

Locking position

If you want to prevent accidentally moving your layers around on the canvas, direct your attention to the Lock Position button in the Layers palette. It is directly to the right of the Lock Image button at the top of the Layers palette. Enabling this lock will still allow you to edit the content of your layer with paint tools. However, you will not be able to move the layer contents until the lock is disabled.

77 In the Channels palette, click the Create New Channel button at the bottom of the palette to create an empty alpha channel. Target the new, empty channel in the Channels palette and paste the copied book texture into the channel by pressing Control-V (or Command-V) on the keyboard. Control-click (or Command-click) the new channel's thumbnail to generate a selection based on the white areas in the channel.

78 Return to the Layers palette and create a new layer. Ensure that your new layer is at the top of the stack within the Layers palette and that your channel-based selection is active. Choose a very light yellow foreground color from the picker. With your new layer targeted, press Alt-Delete (or Option-Delete) on the keyboard to fill the active selection with the new foreground color on the new layer. Deactivate the selection and change the blending mode of the layer to Overlay.

Take a final look at your masterpiece
Examine the tools, techniques, and resources that were necessary to create this stunning and ancient-looking Old Master.

a By creating backgrounds in Photoshop and then importing them into Poser, we were able to render figures using appropriate lighting and angles. That way, when the finished Poser renderings were added to the Photoshop file, they didn't look out of place.

b Although anything can be altered after the fact in Photoshop, we were able to get a head start in Poser by replacing body parts with props, such as this figure's head. In the case of the sea creature to the right, body parts were greatly distorted and the surface color was changed to gray before we rendered the figure.

c By filling path-based selections with color on various layers and then adding highlight and shadow via the Brush or Gradient tools, we can create anything imaginable within Photoshop. Illustrated works can range from the very simple, such as the creature's tail, to the very complicated, such as the organic pink object you see here.

d You don't necessarily have to incorporate entire Poser figures into your composition. Using just a head and a pair of legs, we were able to combine these body parts with Photoshop illustrated elements to create a strange creature as our main point of interest.

e Gently building up paint on a series of layers helps make the composition look more like a real-world painting. Incorporating a desktop scan of old texture helps to give the finished piece the appearance of being centuries old rather than being created in Photoshop.

When you're working with Photoshop and Poser together, there are a myriad of resources you can use. In this chapter, we illustrated components in Photoshop and then combined the rendered figures with them. However, those illustrated components can be easily replaced with Illustrator vector graphics, 3D models, and photographic elements, as shown here.

Here's an example of how a small Poser element can play a large role in the composition. I only used a single hand, but stylistically it melds into the composition nicely because the other elements are rendered 3D models. I don't think it would feel as integrated if I had used photography. Another thing to note is that by altering the colors of the lights in Poser, I was able to employ the same color theme, integrating it further.

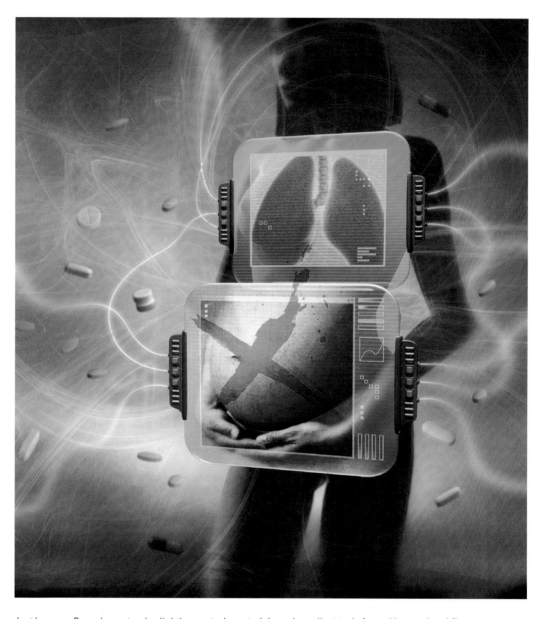

Just because Poser has extensive lighting controls, materials, and excellent tools for making rendered figures appear volumetric, it doesn't mean that you always have to adopt a realistic approach. Here is an example of how Poser was used to simply generate a silhouetted form that matched up nicely with the photographic and 3D elements in the composition.

Chapter 6

The Best of Both Worlds

Combining Cinema 4D with Photoshop

Historically, in the world of digital art and illustration, the general perception was that two-dimensional art and three-dimensional art fell into two separate camps. When I first dabbled in illustration, in the mid-1990s, there seemed to be people who worked in 2D and other people who worked in 3D. Nobody really crossed paths in terms of creating artwork. There was the odd exception, but for me, 3D models showed potential and seemed as valuable a resource as photography when working in Photoshop.

Photography allows us to capture what is around us. There is certainly room to create behind the lens of a camera. However, working with a 3D program allows you to create anything that you can imagine. This lack of limitation in photography is what prompted me to begin working with 3D. However, as a two-dimensional artist, I always had Photoshop integration in mind as I worked. By working in a nonlinear manner, bouncing back and forth between Cinema 4D and Photoshop, compelling results can be achieved. The unified compositions at the end of this process showcase the best of both worlds and result in a uniqueness that exceeds what is commonly perceived as the product of either program on its own.

Versions

Photoshop CS4
Cinema 4D Release 11

Requirements and Recommendations

In addition to Photoshop, you'll need a copy of Cinema 4D. If you don't have a copy of Cinema 4D, a trial version can be downloaded from www.maxon.net.

Model photo: Vincent Lions; Model: Josie Lee; Hair and makeup: Angela Veel

What you'll learn in this chapter

Creative Techniques and Working Methods

A familiar modular approach

When you begin working with Cinema 4D, it will likely feel somewhat foreign if you are new to it or new to 3D in general. However, as you begin to create in Cinema 4D, you will start to notice that it is clearly designed to facilitate a modular, nondestructive, and nonlinear workflow. There is a similarity in logic in working in either Photoshop or Cinema 4D.

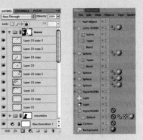

In Photoshop, the Layers palette allows us to construct a file in a way that keeps everything separate. In the Photoshop Layers palette, we have groups that act as containers, layer effects, two different types of masks, blending modes—the list goes on and on. Separate components exist on separate layers and can be edited without affecting original content or other components within the image file. In Cinema 4D, the Object Manager performs a similar task. You can arrange and assemble all the objects in a scene. You can rearrange the hierarchy, assign tags for texture and other attributes, place objects inside deformers or generators in a parent/child relationship—the list goes on and on here as well. Although the components and functions are vastly different from those found in the Photoshop Layers palette, the sensibility of an infinitely flexible workflow remains the same.

An imagery-driven process

You don't need Photoshop CS4 Extended to work along here. We'll be working with imagery that is generated from rendered files when bringing 3D art into Photoshop as 2D files. Because there is no specific need to work with these assets in 3D space or to alter light and texture once they are placed in Photoshop, there is no need to restrict this project to users equipped with the Extended version of Photoshop. This chapter is for everyone who wants to use an image-based approach to bridging the gap between 2D and 3D in Photoshop.

Tools, Features, and Functions

HyperNurbs

HyperNurbs are your best bet when it comes to creating quick and easy organic forms in Cinema 4D. HyperNurbs allow you to interactively subdivide and round your objects with ease.

Render with channels

Simply enabling the alpha channel function in Cinema 4D's Render options will allow you to quickly generate a selection around the perimeter of your objects when you open your renderings in Photoshop. This might seem like a small thing, but it is a monumental time saver.

PART ONE: Building a base in Photoshop

1 In Photoshop, press Control-N (or Command-N) to create a new file. Set the canvas dimensions to 18.75 inches wide by 12 inches high, with a resolution of 72 ppi. Use a CMYK color mode and leave the canvas color set to white. This file will act as the working file for the rest of the chapter. Keep it open at all times because we'll be placing photography and rendered 3D images into it to create the final illustration. From the menu, choose File > Place and navigate to the *face.jpg* file, included in the downloadable project files for this chapter. Click the Place button and then Shift-drag a corner point of the bounding box inward to reduce the size of the placed Smart Object and position it as shown here. When you're happy with the size and placement, press the Enter key.

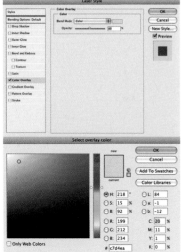

2 Double-click the Smart Object in the Layers palette to open it in a new window. Hold down the Alt (or Option) key and double-click the Background layer in the Smart Object file, to convert it to a standard layer. With the converted layer targeted, choose the Color Overlay option from the Add A Layer Style menu at the bottom of the Layers palette. In the Color Overlay Options, change the Blend mode to Color and reduce the opacity to 49%. Click the color swatch and choose a gray/blue/mauve color from the picker similar to the one shown here. Click OK in the picker, and then OK again in the Layer Styles box.

Project files

All the files needed to follow along with this chapter and create the featured image are available for download on the accompanying Website, in the project files section. Visit www.beyondphotoshopthebook.com.

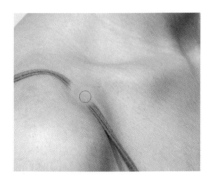

3 Click the Create A New Layer button at the bottom of the Layers palette. Ensure that the new layer is targeted, then select the Clone Stamp tool from the Toolbar. Ensure that you choose the All Layers option from the Sample menu in the Tool Options bar. Select a soft, round brush tip preset from the preset picker and reduce the opacity to 50% to start. Now let's remove the straps from her chest. Zoom in closely on a strap region. Adjust the size of your brush as required so that it is large enough to only cover the strap. Then Alt-click (or Option-click) a region beside the strap to sample it. Then paint over the strap near this region to cover it on the new layer. Use this method repeatedly to gently build up the effect, covering the strap in that region.

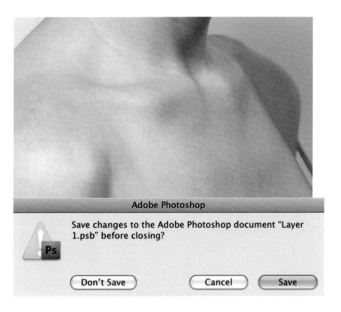

 Tom Bagshaw

My inspiration for this style of imagery is the work of renowned artist Tom Bagshaw. His unique work resides somewhere between realistic painting and graphic design. I love the way he combines two-dimensional and three-dimensional elements in his compositions. Somehow, regardless of the subject, there is always a sense of openness or space in his imagery that I find compelling. View Tom's portfolio at www.mostlywanted.com.

4 Use this method over and over again until both straps are covered in their entirety. Be certain to sample from different regions often and vary the size and opacity of the tool as required. Take your time here; don't be afraid to redo areas that aren't convincing the first time around. Do not worry about the part of her strap that overlaps the background; we'll trim the background later. Right now, just spend your time on removing the straps overlapping her skin. When you're finished, close the file. When prompted, save the changes.

5 In your working file, duplicate the Smart Object by dragging it onto the Create A New Layer button at the bottom of the Layers palette. Change the blending mode of the duplicate layer to Soft Light and reduce its opacity to 69% in the Layers palette.

Stack up adjustments

Build up a few adjustment layers to enhance the contrast and shadows of the stacked Smart Objects below.

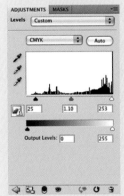

1 Choose the Levels option from the Create New Fill or Adjustment Layer menu at the bottom of the Layers palette to create a new levels adjustment layer. Drag the input slider at the left inward to darken the shadows. Then tweak the midtones as well as the highlights slider at the right to increase the contrast.

2 Next create a selective color layer by choosing selective color from the same menu. In the Adjustments palette, increase the amount of cyan, magenta, and black in the Blacks to deepen the color as shown here.

3 Create another Selective Color adjustment layer; this time, simply increase the black content within the Blacks by 15 to intensify the effect a little more. At this point your file should consist of a couple of stacked Smart Objects with a few Adjustment layers stacked above them.

6 Create a new layer and target it in the Layers palette. Select the Pen tool and ensure that it is set to create Paths in the Tool Options bar. Also ensure that the Add to Path Area operation is enabled before you begin to draw. When you've set everything up properly, carefully draw a path that surrounds her neck and shoulders. Stray away from her eye in the area where her eyelashes overlap the background. Then return to the edge of her head, where her eyebrow and forehead meet the background at the right of the image. Be certain to draw the path well below her hairline; also ensure that it does not include her ear or any hair at the right of the image. It should look something like what is shown here.

 Name the path

Ensure that you double-click your path thumbnail in the Paths palette to name it. It doesn't matter what you name it; you can simply leave it labeled *Path 1*. If you leave the name set to *work path*, it will be overwritten next time you create a path. Be certain to name all paths you create so that you preserve them for use later on.

7 Load the path as a selection by Control-clicking (or Command-clicking) the thumbnail in the Paths palette. Invert the selection by pressing Control-Shift-I (or Command-Shift-I) on the keyboard. Return to your new layer in the Layers palette and select the Gradient tool. Choose the Foreground to Transparent gradient preset from the preset picker in the Tool Options bar and select the Linear method. Leave the opacity set to 100% and then Alt-click (or Option-click) the dark blue/gray region near the bottom of the background in the photograph. Click and drag upward within the new selection on the new layer.

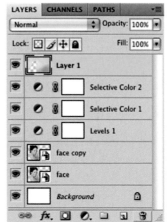

8 Now, Alt-click (or Option-click) in the background of the photograph at the top of the image to sample that color as the current foreground color. Then click and drag downward a little to create a similar gradient effect at the top. After that, switch to the Radial method in the Tool Options bar. Sample colors from within the gradients you just created as well as from the background of the photograph, and repeatedly create numerous new gradients in the rest of the selection on this layer. Alter the opacity and size of the gradients option; also be certain to create a gradient beside her eye that resembles the color that lies outside the selection in that region, to make it believable. Continue like this until the entire selection is filled with smooth gradations of color.

9 Invert the selection and create a new layer. With the inverted selection active, Alt-click (or Option-click) a dark area of skin near her shoulder. Create a radial, foreground to transparent gradient in this area using an opacity setting of 100%. Then sample lighter regions from within the area and add them as necessary, so the gradients you've created look as though they belong. Don't worry about the results looking as 3D as the photograph; we want to also include some juxtaposition between 3D volumetric art and flat 2D art within the image overall. When you're happy with what you've done, press Control-D (or Command-D) to deactivate the selection.

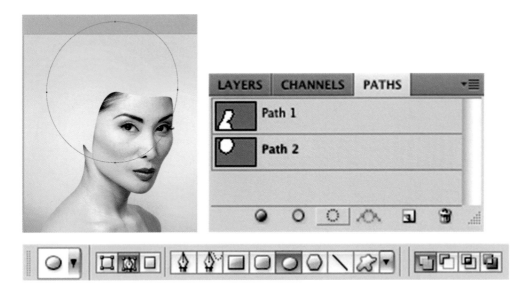

10 Select the Ellipse shape tool and ensure that it is set to create Paths and that the Add To Path Area operation is enabled in the Tool Options bar. Shift-drag to create a perfect circle on the canvas that represents a large afro-like mass at the top of her head. You can position the path as necessary by clicking and dragging it with the Path Selection tool. Also, if you need to resize the path, you can press Control-T (or Command-T) while the path is selected. When the transform bounding box appears, you can Shift-drag a corner point inward or outward to proportionately alter the size. When you're happy with the transformation, press the Enter key to apply it.

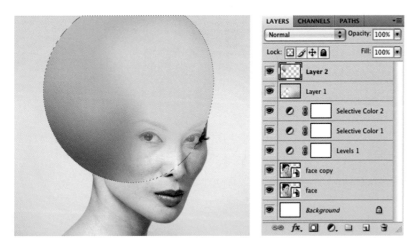

11 Control-click (or Command-click) the ellipse path in the Paths palette to load it as a selection. Return to the current layer in the Layers palette. Select the Gradient tool again and use it within the selection to fill the shape with gradients of colors sampled from neighboring areas of skin on underlying layers. You will use the radial gradient method exclusively, and don't deviate from the foreground to transparent preset or you'll fill the entire selection. Generally, a good working method is to start with darker gradients around the edge, where appropriate, then create lighter, more centralized gradients on top of these. Try to avoid covering the eyes or brows with gradients. However, if this is necessary, that is fine. We will mask the layer next.

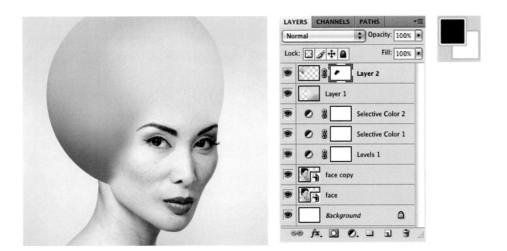

12 Press Control-D (or Command-D) to deactivate the selection, and click the Add Layer Mask button at the bottom of the Layers palette to mask the layer. Target the layer's mask in the Layers palette. By default, when you create a mask and edit it, the foreground color becomes white and the background color becomes black. Press the x key to invert them so that black becomes the foreground color. Use the Gradient tool to create a few small black-to-transparent gradients within the mask, overlapping areas on the canvas where the flesh-colored gradients obscure her eyes and brows.

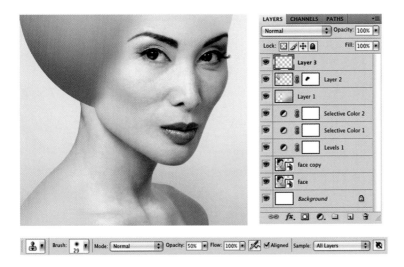

13 Create a new layer and ensure that it is targeted in the Layers palette. Select the Clone Stamp from the Toolbar and ensure that the All Layers method is selected from the Sample menu in the Tool Options bar. Now what we want to remedy at this point are things such as blemishes on her face and bits of stray hair. Use the same method you used previously to clone out her straps within the Smart Object. Find an area and Alt-click (or Option-click) a bit of clean flesh right beside it. Then paint over the offending region. Vary brush sizes and opacity settings as necessary. Sample often, and use a soft-edged brush preset for best results. Again, don't rush this part of the process or you'll regret it later. Do not remove all the details, such as her freckles; these will help the image feel realistic and human after we're done. However, spend a fair bit of time cleaning up stray hairs around the eyebrows and removing any wrinkles from her neck.

14 Now select the Blur tool from the Toolbar. Specify a soft, round brush tip preset and ensure that the strength is set to 100% and that the Sample All Layers option is enabled in the Tool Options bar. Use the Blur tool to paint over regions of her face that could use a little smoothing yet do not need to be replaced. Find regions that are slightly wrinkled or porous. Increase and decrease the strength as necessary and alter the diameter of the brush tip as you go.

15 Create a new Levels adjustment layer by choosing Levels from the Create New Fill or Adjustment Layer menu at the bottom of the Layers palette. In the Adjustments palette, simply drag the middle slider to the right a little to darken the midtones in the image overall. Next, create a new Selective Color layer by choosing the Selective Color option from the same menu at the bottom of the Layers palette. In the Adjustments palette, choose Neutrals from the Colors menu and then increase the amount of cyan and black slightly within the image. Save your file at this point.

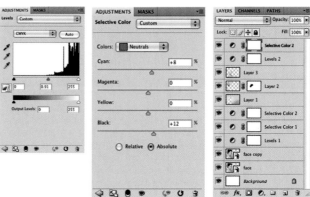

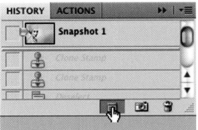

16 In the History palette menu, choose the New Snapshot option. When the new Snapshot dialog box appears, choose the Merged Layers option. Don't worry about the name, it can remain set to *Snapshot 1* because we're going to name the file later when we save it. Click OK. You will see your snapshot appear above the list of history states in the History palette. Depending on how you have the History Options set, there could be another snapshot of your image in its original state. In any case, click the new snapshot at the top of the History palette and then click Create New Document From Current State at the bottom left of the History palette. This will open a document from your snapshot in a new window. The original file remains open in the window behind it.

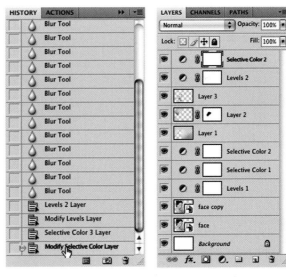

17 In the new snapshot file, select the Crop tool from the Toolbar. Click and drag to draw a rectangular cropping area that surrounds the head but crops out the lower portion of her chest and all the negative space at the right of the image. Press the Enter key to crop the image. Select Image > Mode > RGB from the menu to convert the image to RGB from CMYK. This will help the accuracy of the preview when we get into Cinema 4D. Choose File > Save As from the menu and save the file in .psd format as Background.psd. Close the file and return to your working file in Photoshop. All of the layer will be merged, but don't fret. All you need to do is scroll to the bottom of the History palette and click the very last state at the bottom. This will revert the file to the state it was in right before you merged it. After you click this state, the layers will all become visible in the Layers palette once again.

PART TWO: Getting set up in Cinema 4D

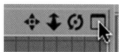

18 Launch Cinema4D. Initially you will only see a single, perspective view in the viewport. To remedy this, click the icon in the upper-right corner of the viewport. This will change the workspace to a four-up view, not only allowing you to see the perspective view but also showing you top, front, and right views at the same time. The first thing we're going to do is bring our *Background.psd* file into the perspective window to use it as a template while creating 3D objects in the scene. Click and hold the Scene Objects button in the top Toolbar to temporarily open the Scene Objects palette. Click the Background Object to create new Background Object within the scene. You will see the Background Object appear in the Object Manager at the right of the interface.

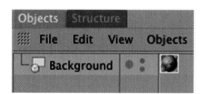

 Not Using Cinema 4D?

If you are following along with the Photoshop portion of this chapter only, you'll find the finished Cinema 4D renderings included in the downloadable project files for this chapter. Simply open them as they are referred to by name in the text and you can follow along with the 3D portions of this chapter.

19 Next, choose File > New Material from the Material Manager menu at the bottom left of the interface to create a new material. Double-click the new material to open the Material Editor. Click Color from the list of options at the left of the Material Editor. In the resulting color options, click the horizontal bar to the right of the Texture option and navigate to the Background.psd file you created. Close the Material Editor window and then drag the material from the Material Manager at the bottom left of the interface directly onto the Background Object in the Object Manager to add it as a texture tag to the object. You will immediately see it appear in the background of the perspective window, but it will be distorted.

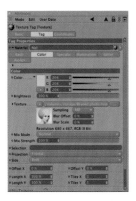 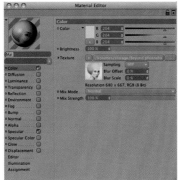

20 To remedy the image distortion, we need to alter the render settings. Before you go to the render settings, however, you should note the exact pixel dimensions of the image in your material. To see the dimensions, you can either double-click the material in the Material Manager to open the Material Editor or, if you double-click the Texture tag in the Object Manager, you'll see the information displayed in the Attributes Manager. The Texture section will display the pixel dimensions directly beneath an image thumbnail. If you're looking in the Material Editor window, ensure that you select the Color option from the left, if it isn't already targeted, and you'll see a very similar display to that which is shown in the Attributes Manager. Make a note of the actual pixel resolution. Yours will likely be a little different than mine.

 Cinema 4D files

If you want to follow along with the project in this chapter, yet the prospect of working with Cinema 4D is daunting or unappealing to you, don't fret; the completed Cinema 4D files are included in the downloadable project files for this chapter. The Cinema 4D files are saved as projects, which include all textures used. The file that contains all the objects we created for the model's face is in a folder named *model 1*. The other file that contains the background elements is in a folder named *model 2*. You can open these files in Cinema 4D and peruse all the elements. You can also render directly from these files if you like.

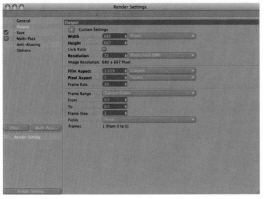

21 Choose Render > Render Settings from the main menu at the top of the interface. In the Render Settings window, click the Output option at the left. In the Height and Width fields, enter the exact pixel dimensions of the image texture in your material. You will immediately see the image displayed in the perspective viewport change to its proper aspect ratio. Close the Render Settings window for the time being. Now that the Background Object has been added to the scene, we can enable or disable the visibility as necessary as we work. Generally, it will only need to be visible from time to time to ensure that the angles of our objects will match up with the perspective of the image.

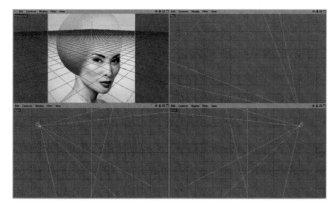

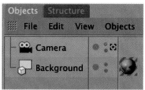

22 Click and hold the Scene Objects button in the top Toolbar to open the Scene Objects palette. Select the Camera object to add a camera to the scene, and then release the mouse button. You'll see a camera immediately appear in the scene. We're not going to use the camera just yet, so for the time being we'll simply hide it. In the Object Manager, double-click the top visibility dot to the right of your camera object. The dot will turn red, and although the object continues to exist in the Object Manager, it will be hidden from view.

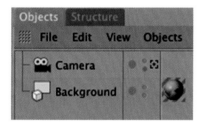

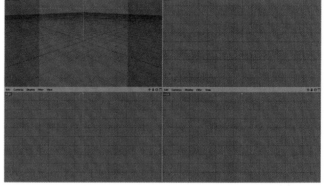

 Toggling views

Using the function keys from F1 through to F5 will allow you quickly toggle through the main views in the viewport. These are the four views that are present when you are viewing four at a time. F1 shows the perspective view, F2 shows the top view, F3 shows the right view, F5 shows the front view, and F5 takes you back to a four-up view.

23 Now that we're editing the visibility of objects within the scene, we should direct our attention to the Background Object as well. Begin by double-clicking the bottom visibility button to the right of the Background Object. It will turn red, but it will remain visible in the scene. This actually hides the visibility of the object when the scene is rendered. Although we have quite a bit of modeling ahead of us, now is as good a time as any to hide it in future renderings. Remember, this Background Object is going to be used only as a guide; we don't want it visible in the finished art. Also, it is less visually distracting to simply hide the Background Object from view when it is not being used. To do this, simply double-click the top Visibility button to the right of the Background Object in the Object Manager. Now that you've hidden both objects within the scene, it will appear empty, but it is not.

PART THREE: Working with 3D shapes

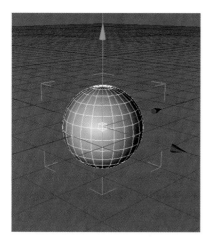

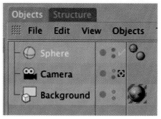

24 Click and hold the Primitive Object button in the top Toolbar to open the Primitive Object palette. Select the Sphere Object and immediately you'll see a Sphere Object appear in the viewport as well as in the Object Managers. In the perspective panel of the viewport, click the icon in the upper right to view the perspective panel only. We'll edit the Sphere in a single pane only for the time being so that we can view it much larger as we work. For what we're going to do, we do not need the other three panes visible just yet. We can always switch to a four-up view again at any point by clicking the same icon in the upper right.

25 Now, although we are starting with a sphere, we're really going to alter the geometry of this shape so that it becomes something else altogether. This shape will surround the left eye in the Photoshop image. Bear that in mind while you're working, but don't dwell on matching it up perfectly just yet. First we'll create a compelling object, and then we'll align it nicely afterward. Click the Make Object Editable button in the Toolbar at the left. Then choose the Polygon tool from the Toolbar at the left. Click a polygon near the left side of the sphere to select it and then use the axis handles to move it away from the rest of the object, stretching it out. Try this again with another polygon to a lesser degree.

26 After moving some individual polygons, click the Point Tool button in the Toolbar at the left. This will allow you to select and edit individual points on the shape. Now, as you did previously with individual polygons, select individual points and then use the axis handles to move them around, modifying the shape even further. After experimenting with moving individual points, click the Edge Tool button in the Toolbar at the left. This will allow you to select individual edges and then move them around in the same manner.

A bigger impact

By combining a Selection tool with the Polygon tool, we can alter the object drastically by moving a series of points at once.

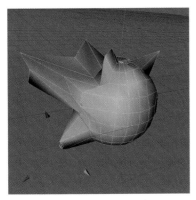

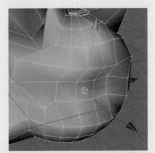

1 Click and hold the Live Selection button in the top Toolbar to reveal the Selection palette. Select the Lasso option when the palette appears. Next, click the Point Tool button in the Toolbar at the left.

2 Click and drag over the area near the front of the sphere. This action will select all the points in your selected area. When the axis handles appear, drag the red one, the X, toward the back of the scene.

3 Use this same method to select only the innermost four points within this cluster of modified points and drag them even further back along the X axis. This will create a smaller, deeper recessed area within the shape.

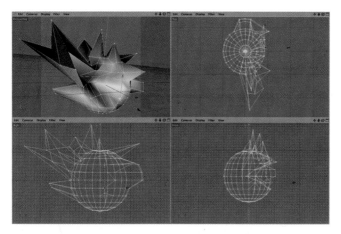

27 Have some fun editing the shape using these methods. Feel free to tweak points, polygons, and edges as you see fit. Also feel free to use the navigational icons in the upper-right side of the image to rotate, reposition, and zoom in or out of the view as you work. Clicking the far-right navigational icon will revert the interface to a four-up view. You will likely find it beneficial to work on your shape in views other than just the perspective view. This will give you a better grasp of the way the shape appears in 3D space and provides more control while editing. To work in a different view, simply click inside that panel and continue to edit the shape.

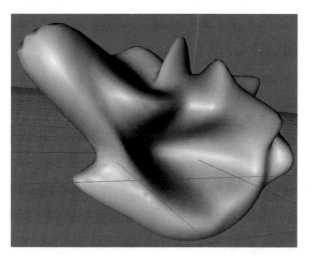

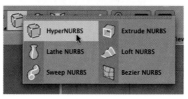

28 Click and hold the HyperNurbs Object button in the top Toolbar to open the Nurbs Object palette. Select the HyperNurbs object to add this object to the scene. In the Object Manager, drag it to the top of the hierarchy if it is not already there. Then, in the Object Manager, drag the sphere object onto the HyperNurbs object. This will make the sphere object a child of the HyperNurbs object. The HyperNurbs object will gently smooth out all the sharp edges of your manipulated sphere object, giving it a more organic appearance.

A nondestructive workflow

Always remember that files are constructed in a modular and editable manner in Cinema 4D. This means that although you have placed your manipulated sphere inside a HyperNurbs object, you can still edit the sphere independently of the Nurbs object, and vice versa. Think of it as a similar procedure to placing a layer inside a group in Photoshop. While the group contains the layer and has an effect on it, the layer can be edited on its own; the same holds true with the group. Furthermore, you can remove a layer from a group at any point in Photoshop. This is also true for the sphere object within the HyperNurbs object in Cinema 4D and holds true for any child/parent relationship within the Object Manager.

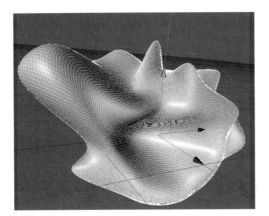

29 One thing you will notice is that portions of the surface will look somewhat jagged and still show subtle polygonal edges, even after the advent of the HyperNurbs object. To remedy this, click the HyperNurbs object in the Object Manager to select it. Then, in the Object tab of the Attributes manager below, increase the Subdivision Editor and the Subdivision Renderer to 4 in each case. In this instance it worked fine. You might find that a different setting works better for you. However, don't increase it beyond what is necessary, since more subdivisions consume more memory and can slow the rendering process and viewport navigation.

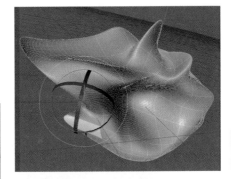

 Scaling, moving, dragging

In case you haven't noticed, the Scale, Move, and Rotate tools come into play often while you're working in Cinema 4D. When you select an object and any of these tools, you'll notice that the X, Y, and Z axes are each represented by a single color. Using one axis only allows you to constrain what you're doing to that particular axis. With the Move tool, simply click and drag an arrowhead at the end of an axis. With the Rotate tool, simply click and drag one of the bands. Select the colored band that corresponds to the desired axis. Scaling works in the same manner, but you need to click and drag a box rather than an arrow or band. Clicking and dragging the object, not an axis, with any tool will affect all axes.

30 Now click the Sphere object in the Object Manager. Simply selecting it here makes it active; you can edit it further without dragging it out of the HyperNurbs object. This is a fine example of the modular approach of Cinema 4D that I keep going on and on about. Click the Polygon tool from the Toolbar at the left, then choose the Move tool from the Toolbar at the top. Click any polygon to select it. Previously, when we selected a polygon, point, or edge, we moved it within the scene, thus reshaping the object. However, this time we're going to take the manipulation of this object a step further. This time when you select a polygon, try then selecting the Rotate or Scale tool from the top Toolbar. Rotate and/or scale the selected polygon using the controls as they appear. Use this method on a number of different polygons until you're happy with the resulting shape.

31 If necessary, click the upper-right navigational icon to switch to a single-pane view in the viewport. Choose Cameras > Scene Cameras > Camera from the menu to view the scene using the camera we created earlier. The angle and scale will change as you switch views. In the Object Manager, click the top Visibility button to the right of the Background object. This will remove the red dot and make it visible once again in the viewport. Use the navigational icons at the right to rotate, zoom, and reposition the scene within this camera view so that the angle of the object matches up nicely with the angle of the background image. Also, feel free to select your object in the Object Manager and then use the Scale and/or Rotate tools to adjust its actual size and position within the scene.

Creating a surface texture

Now we'll create a new material to map onto the current object and subsequent objects in the scene.

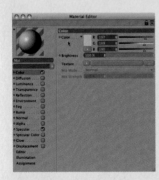

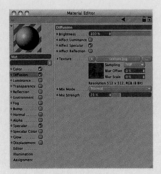

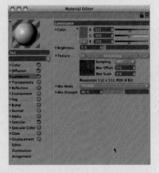

1 Choose File > New Material from the Materials Manager menu. Double-click the new material thumbnail to open the Material Editor. In the Color channel, change the RGB color values to 197, 189, and 190.

2 Click the Diffusion channel at the left, directly underneath Color, and enable it by clicking the check box. Click the horizontal bar to the right of Texture in the diffusion options. Select the texture.jpg file from within the downloadable project files. Scale down the Mix strength to 21%.

3 Click the Luminance channel beneath Diffusion and enable the corresponding check box. Set the RGB color to 115, 109, 109. Set the Brightness to 5%. Again, click the horizontal bar to the right of Texture and navigate to the same texture.jpg file. Reduce the Mix Strength to 46%.

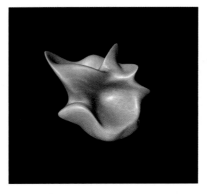

32 Close the Material Editor and add the material to the object by dragging the material thumbnail either from the Materials Manager onto it in the viewport or directly onto the object in the Object Manager. Regardless of how you actually do this, you'll notice a texture tag appear to the right of your object in the Object Manager. Click the texture tag in the Object Manager and then direct your attention to the Attributes Manager beneath it. You'll notice that by default, the projection is set to UVW Mapping, which looks pretty good. However, if you do a quick test rendering by pressing Control-R (or Command-R), it is likely that the texture will create the appearance of a vertical seam on the surface of the object. To remedy this, increase the Offset X value slightly and then do another quick test rendering. If it is fine, leave it as is. If it's not, increase the offset and try it again. In this case, a 5% offset was fine.

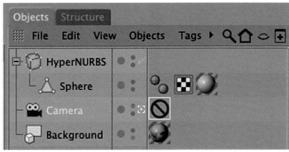

33 We've spent a fair amount of time so far positioning our object in the scene and using the background image as a reference. Right now, in our camera view, things are looking exactly as we want them to. So now would be a good time to lock the camera, so to speak. The way to do this in Cinema 4D is to add a protection tag to the camera. First, click the camera in the Object Manager and then choose Tags > Cinema 4D Tags > Protection from the Object Manager menu. You'll see the protection tag added to the camera in the Object Manager. This will prevent you from altering the camera, helping maintain consistency later on as we begin to render image files.

PART FOUR: Lighting the scene

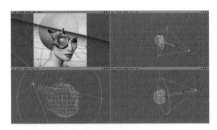

34 Click and hold the Scene Objects button in the top Toolbar. Select the Spotlight Object and release the mouse button to create a new spotlight within the scene. Click the upper-right navigational button to switch to a four-up view if you aren't there already. Select the spotlight in the Object Manager and then use the Move and Rotate tools from the top Toolbar to reposition the light so that it is shining down slightly on the object and a little to the left of it. It is likely that you'll need to perform the rotations and movements in more than a single pane in the viewport to get it right. Also, you'll see a large circular shape, indicating the outer edge of the light. Click one of the points of this circle and drag outward to adjust the outer angle, which makes the beam of light appear wider.

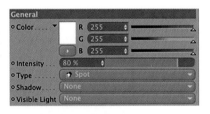

35 Click the spotlight in the Object Manager. Once you've selected the spotlight, direct your attention to the General tab of the Attributes Manager. Here, reduce the intensity of the light to about 80%. Next, click and hold the Scene Objects button to reveal the Scene Objects palette and then select the Light object to add an omni light to the scene. This light will be used as a fill light to lighten the shadows. Again, use the various panels in the four-up view to position the light so that it fills some of the darker shadow regions with a bit of light. While the light is selected in the Object Manager, reduce its intensity to around 23% in the General tab of the Attributes Manager.

PART FIVE: Rendering the scene

36 Ensure that your Camera view is the active view in the viewport. Choose Render > Render Settings from the menu. You can leave the setting in the General category set to Full Render. In the Output category, the size will be set to the same size as your Background object. Enable the Lock Ratio check box. After that, increase the size by an inch or so in either the height or width field so that the rendered output is a little larger yet remains proportionately accurate. Enable the Save check box at the left and click Save to enter the Save category. In the Regular Image settings, enable the Save check box. Then choose a path for the saved file by clicking the ... button. Specify a destination for the rendered file and name it rendering1. Set the format to TIFF (PSD Layers) and the depth to 8 Bit/Channel. Enable the Alpha Channel check box as well as the 24-bit dithering option. Close the Render Settings and then choose Render > Render To Picture Viewer from the menu.

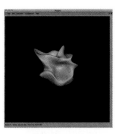

Render larger

I suggest rendering things a bit larger than actual size. This way, if you want the components to appear a little larger within the Photoshop file afterward, you'll have the resolution you need. It is never a problem to reduce the size a little in Photoshop, but I advise against scaling anything larger than the actual resolution allows.

37 The file will immediately be rendered to the Picture Viewer. Don't worry about saving the file; it is automatically saved after rendering as per your specifications in the Save section of the Render settings. Go ahead and look in the file directory within the operating system of your computer to verify that the rendered file was indeed placed in the destination that you specified. If, for any reason, your file does not appear in your specified destination, you can choose File > Save Picture As from the Picture Viewer menu and specify a location to save the rendered image. When you're satisfied that the rendered file is where you want it be, go ahead and close the Picture Viewer.

PART SIX: Repeating the process

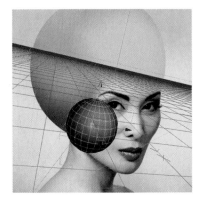
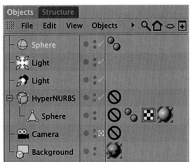

38 In the Object Manager, click the Sphere, and then Control-click (or Control-click) on the HyperNurbs object to select them both. Choose Tags > Cinema4D Tags > Protection from the Object Manager menu to lock them both by adding protection tags to them. Next, click twice on each of the visibility dots to the right of the HyperNurbs object in the Object Manager until they both appear red, hiding the object from view as well as preventing it from rendering. We are finished with this object, but we might as well leave it in the file in case we need to access it later for something else. Create a new Sphere object in the Camera view and position it over her cheek at the left of the image.

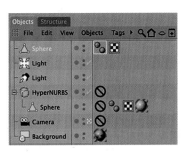

39 Click the Make Object Editable button in the left Toolbar to make the sphere editable and then begin to edit the shape as you did previously with the other sphere. Click the Point tool, the Edge tool, or the Polygon tool to select a polygon, point, or edge of the object and then move it around within the scene via the Move tool in the top Toolbar. Basically, we want to create another shape to overlay her cheek in the Photoshop composition. We'll follow a similar process to that used to alter the previous shape, beginning by altering the actual geometry of the shape.

40 After altering the geometry a little, create a new HyperNurbs object, just as you did last time. Then, in the Object Manager, drag the sphere into it. Ensure that the sphere is selected in the Object Manager and then continue to edit the geometry of the shape using the methods you used previously. Remember that you can do some interesting things by using the Rotate and Scale tools in the top Toolbar to modify polygons or sides. Also, remember that you can select a number of points, edges, or polygons on the shape by using the Lasso tool from the top Toolbar. Then you can modify the selected points as a group. When you think your shape is looking interesting, preview it with the other shape in the scene to gain an understanding of the relationship between the two in the composition. Click once on the top Visibility dot to the right of the hidden HyperNurbs object in the Object Manager to make it visible.

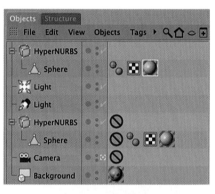

41 If you're happy with the visual relationship between the objects, double-click the same Visibility dot to hide it again. If not, continue to alter your current object as necessary until you're satisfied. Next, drag the most recent material you created onto the object in either the Object Manager or the viewport. After adding the material to the object, click the Texture tag in the Object Manager and try experimenting with some different projection settings in the Attributes Manager below. Each time you change the projection, do a quick render by clicking the Render Active View button in the top Toolbar. For the shape I created, the default UVW Mapping projection worked just fine. However, no two shapes will be alike, and you might find that a different projection works better for you. Or you could find that even though you are using UVW mapping, you might need to edit the offset amount, the way we did with the previous object.

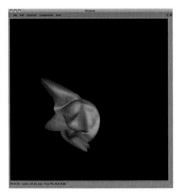

42 Choose Render > Render Settings from the menu. You can leave everything set up as it was previously, except for the Save category. Go to the Save setting and then click the … button to the right of the Path option. When prompted, change the name of the finished file to rendering2. Leave the destination the same so that it ends up in the same place as your first rendering. Close the render settings and then choose Render > Render to Picture Viewer from the menu. After the rendering is complete, go ahead and close the Picture Viewer window. This file will automatically be saved alongside your previous rendering.

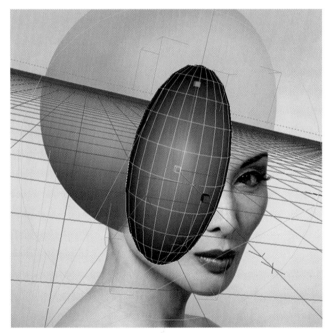

43 Now, as you did with the previous object, double-click both of the Visibility dots to the right of your HyperNurbs object in the Object Manager. This hides it from view in the viewport and ensures that it does not appear in any future renderings. The object is still there, it's just not visible. Now create another Sphere object. While the sphere is selected, click the Object Tool button in the Toolbar at the left. Then, in the Coordinates Manager, double the Y size in relation to the X and Z sizes.

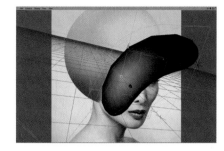

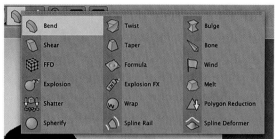

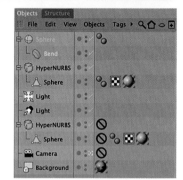

44 Click and hold the Deformers button in the top Toolbar to access the Deformers palette. Select the Bend deformer and then release the mouse button to create a new Bend deformer. In the Object Manager, drag the Bend deformer onto the modified Sphere to make the deformer a child of the sphere. Select the Bend deformer in the Object Manager and then, in the perspective viewport, click and drag the orange handle at the top of the deformer. Drag upward and the sphere will bend to the right. Keep dragging until it looks something like what is shown here.

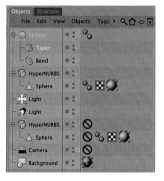

45 Now click the Deformers button again, and this time specify a Taper deformer from the palette to add it to the scene. Drag this deformer onto the Sphere object in the Object Manager to make it a child of the sphere, just as you did previously with the Bend deformer. Select the Taper deformer in the Object Manager and then click and drag the orange handle at the top in perspective viewport to taper the sphere. Drag downward until the sphere begins to resemble what is shown here.

46 You will notice that the resulting sphere is not smooth and that there are jagged, polygonal edges visible. To remedy this, select the Sphere in the Object Manager. After the sphere is selected, increase the number of segments until it appears smooth in the Attributes Manager. Also, try playing with the Radius setting until you see the ideal shape begin to present itself. While the Sphere itself is selected, use the Move, Rotate, and Scale tools in the top Toolbar to position it nicely over her eye at the right of the image.

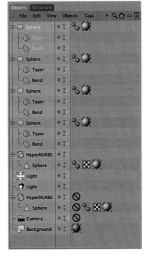

Expanding/collapsing

In the Object Manager, you'll notice that the available space fills up quickly as you continually add objects to your scene. However, each parent object has a small box to the left of it within the Object Manager; if the children of this parent are visible, clicking this icon will collapse the object, hiding the children from view. If you want to expand a parent object that is collapsed, simply click the same icon to expand it, revealing the children contained within.

47 Now drag the same material from the Materials Manager onto the object in either the viewport or the Object Manager to add a Texture tag to it. Control-click (or Control-click) the sphere in the Object Manager and drag it upward to duplicate it. With the duplicate selected, use the Move, Rotate, and Scale tools in the top Toolbar to reposition, rotate, and resize it within the scene. Create more duplicates of the object using this method. Then, enable the visibility of your two original HyperNurbs objects to aid in positioning the new objects. It doesn't matter whether the new objects are touching the older HyperNurbs objects; we'll be hiding the visibility of the HyperNurbs objects again shortly.

Selecting points

Sometimes it can be difficult to select a specific point on a spline object, especially when the points are very close together. Try zooming in very close; or, if the same point remains selected no matter what, it can be easier to click the background so that no single point is selected, then click the point you want to select. Alternatively, you can press Alt-d (or Option-d) to hide the axis handles. If the handles are hidden, executing the same command will reveal them.

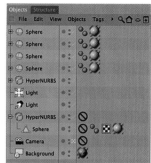

48 Hide the visibility of the HyperNurbs objects when you're happy with the placement of your duplicated objects in the scene. Also, you can edit the deformers that are children of your spheres at any point. To edit the effect of a deformer, simply select it in the Object Manager and then click and drag the orange handle that appears in the viewport. Next, choose Render > Render Settings from the menu. Again, in the Save options, click the ... button in the Path field and then name the file rendering3. Next, choose Render > Render To Picture Viewer from the menu, to render the scene in its current state. After rendering, close the Picture Viewer and then double-click both Visibility dots to right of each sphere object in the Object Manager, to hide them from view and prevent them from appearing in future renderings.

PART SEVEN: Working with spline objects

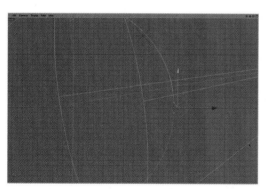

49 Click the top-right navigational icon in the view port to switch back to a four-up view. Click and hold the Spline Object button in the top Toolbar to reveal the Spline Object palette. Select the Circle option and release the mouse button to create a circular spline object within the scene. To edit the spline, click the Make Object Editable button and then select the Point tool from the Toolbar at the left. Select the Front viewport. Zoom in on the right side of the circle using the navigational buttons at the upper right. Control-click (or Control-click) just above and just below the point at the right to create two additional points on the spline. Then select the original point between the two and drag it slightly to the right.

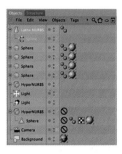

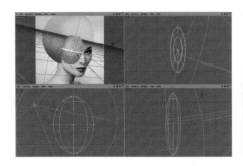

50 Click the HyperNurbs button in the top Toolbar and select Lathe Nurbs from the palette to create a new Lathe Nurbs object. In the Object Manager, drag the spline object onto the new Lathe Nurbs object to make the spline a child of the Lathe Nurbs object. Immediately, you will see the results of the Lathe Nurbs object. Next, click the Object tool in the left Toolbar and then select the Scale tool from the top Toolbar. Click and drag the X, Y, and Z handles in the view port separately, to reshape the object until it resembles what is shown here. Examine all the views, not just the camera view. The Front and Top views especially provide a clear view of the shape after scaling.

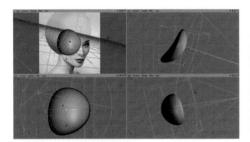

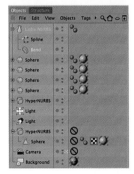

51 Click the Deformers button in the top Toolbar and select the Bend deformer. In the Object Manager, place the Bend deformer inside the Lathe Nurbs object and drag it beneath the spline object. Select the Rotate tool in the top Toolbar. Rotate the X axis by about −95 degrees and the Z axis by about 90 degrees. Next, click the Object tool in the left Toolbar and then select the Scale tool from the top Toolbar. Resize the Bend deformer so that it fits around the object a little tighter. Now, click and drag the orange handle to bend the spline. Here, you can see the effect that the rotated and scaled Bend deformer has on my shape. For your reference, I am showing you the object properties of my Bend deformer in the Attributes Manager. Also, here's a view of the exact size and rotation in the Coordinates Manager. If you plan to type these values in, be sure that you have the Object tool selected when you do it. It is fine if your attributes and coordinates differ from these, as long as your shape begins to resemble the one shown here. I have changed the Display in each viewport to Gouraud shading so that you can see the effect clearly.

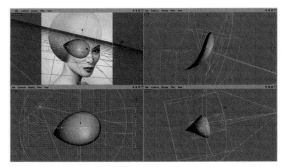

52 Again, click the Deformer button in the top Toolbar and select the Taper deformer from the Deformer palette. Select the Rotate tool from the top Toolbar and rotate the Taper deformer 90 degrees along the Y axis. As you did previously while working on the Bend deformer, click the Object tool if it is not currently active, and then select the Scale tool in the top Toolbar. Scale the X, Y, and Z axes separately so that the Taper deformer fits nicely around your shape. Click and drag the orange handle to taper the object. Here again is a glimpse of the size and rotation of the deformer in the Coordinates Manager as well as the object properties of the Taper in the Attributes Manager. Again, it is fine if yours differs slightly, just try to create something that resembles what is shown here.

Embrace the nondestructive

When editing Taper and Bend deformations that are applied to this particular spline object, you'll notice that hierarchy plays an important role. Try moving them up or down in the Object Manager, changing their place within the object hierarchy. You'll notice that this changes the final result of both deformers as it applies to the spline. However, you must ensure that they remain beneath the spline. Also, an important thing to point out is that you may edit a deformer and then apply another, only to find yourself tweaking them both here and there to achieve an optimal result. I find this back-and-forth process an intuitive way to work, reminiscent of the process of painting, to a degree.

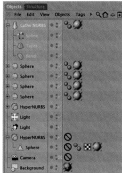

53 Drag the material onto the Lathe Nurbs object in either the viewport or the Object Manager to add it as a Texture tag. You can play with other Projection options in the Tag Properties within the Attributes Manager. In the case of this object I have created here, the default UVW mapping seems fine. However, yours may differ slightly, so feel free to offset or try another mapping option that suits your shape. In the Object Manager, click the Visibility dot to the right of each sphere and the Nurbs object that is hidden from view. Use these as a guide for placing your new shape so that it falls in the lower region of the back of her head. Use the Move and Rotate tools from the Toolbar at the top to rotate and reposition the object as necessary.

54 Ensure that the Lathe Nurbs object is selected in the Object Manager. Then click and hold the Second Generators button in the top Toolbar to reveal the Second Generators palette. Choose the Instance option to create an instance of the Lathe Nurbs object. Use the Move and Rotate tools to rotate and position the object within the scene. The instance will automatically be placed in the same location as the original, so you'll need to move it to where you want it. At this point we're only concerned with how the objects are positioned and how they relate to each other visually within the Camera view. It doesn't really matter if they appear to be all over the place in other views. This artwork is destined to be rendered and then placed in a 2D composition in Photoshop, so a proper relationship within 3D space is not really important.

55 Control-click (or Control-click) on the Instance object in the Object Manager and drag it upward to create a duplicate of it. Use the Move and Rotate tools to reposition the duplicate instance within the camera view. Repeat this process a number of times until you've created a nice layered effect of these instances that fits nicely into the empty area at the back of her head. Also, note that you can use the Object tool at any point to scale an individual instance, altering its proportion.

 Why instances?

An instance is a duplicate of an object. The thing that makes an instance unique is that it lacks its own geometry and simply refers back to the original shape for this data. It is there in the scene, but the file size is much smaller because you're not duplicating the same geometry over and over again. Also, any edits you perform to the original object are immediately updated in all the instances of that object.

56 Now try adding some other duplicates of the instances at different locations within the scene. Just ensure that they do not touch or overlap the existing ones. These are there just in case we want to scatter some more around as singular objects or clusters of objects while compositing in Photoshop. There is a chance that we will never use these, but I always feel that it is very easy to create a little extra while you're at it. Anything you don't want after rendering can be deleted or masked in the final composition. When you're satisfied with what you scattered around, click and hold the Generators button in the top Toolbar and choose Null Object.

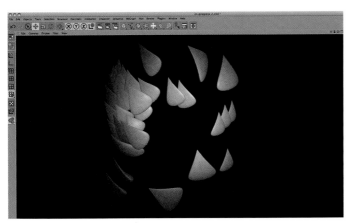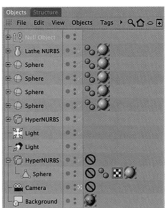

57 Click the very bottom instance object in the Object Manager and then Shift-click the very top instance object in the Object Manager, to select all the instances. Drag the selected instances onto the Null object you just created to contain them all somewhere. Then collapse the Null object in the Object Manager to instigate a bit of order within the Object Manager. When you're creating duplicate after duplicate as we've done here, it doesn't take long to fill the Object Manager with dozens of objects, making it an effort to wade through later. Think of a Null object in Cinema 4D as the equivalent to a Layer Group in Photoshop. It is a nice tool that lets you contain things in the area of the interface that allows you to organize the content. Click once on the Render Active View button to test your rendering in the Camera view.

58 Choose Render > Render Settings from the menu. Click Save at the left to access the Save options. Click the ... button in the Path options. Change the name of the rendered file to rendering4. Close the Render settings and then choose Render > Render To Picture Viewer from the menu. After the file is rendered, close the Picture Viewer. Save and close your file.

PART EIGHT: Returning to Photoshop

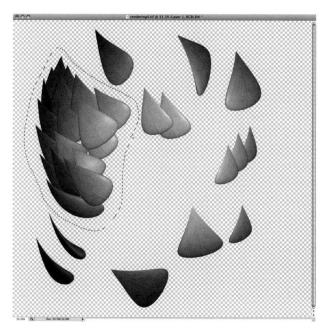

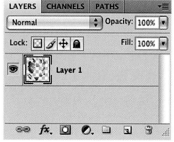

59 Return to your working file in Photoshop. If it is not open, go ahead and open it. Keep your working file open and then open the *rendering4.tif* file. In the *rendering4.tif* file, locate the alpha channel entitled *Alpha 1* in the Channels palette. Control-click (or Command-click) on the Channel's thumbnail to load the channel as a selection. Return to the Layers palette and press Control-J (or Command-J) to copy the selected contents to a new layer. Then drag the Background layer onto the Trash icon at the bottom right of the Layers palette. Use the Lasso tool to draw a closed selection around the large cluster of objects at the left.

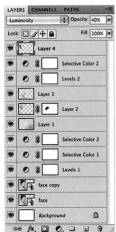

60 Use the Move tool to click inside the selected area and drag the contents of the selection into your working file as a new layer. Drag your new layer to the top of the stack if it isn't already there in the Layers palette. Press Control-T (or Command-T) to activate the Free Transform operation. When the bounding box surrounds your layer contents, Shift-drag a corner point to adjust the size proportionately and move it into place over the back of her head. When you're happy with the placement, change the blending mode of the layer to luminosity and reduce the opacity to 40%. Control-click (or Command-click) the Layer thumbnail to load a selection from the contents of the layer.

61 While the selection is active, choose the Solid Color option from the list in the Create New Fill or Adjustment Layer menu at the bottom of the Layers palette. When the picker appears, choose a region of slightly darker flesh by clicking it in the image window. Click OK to close the picker, then drag the layer beneath the underlying layer in the Layers palette so that you can see your objects once again. Duplicate the top layer by dragging it onto the Create A New Layer button at the bottom of the Layers palette. Change the blending mode of the duplicate layer to Hard light and reduce the opacity to 11%. Now duplicate this newly copied layer and change its blending mode to Overlay. Increase the opacity of this layer to 100%. After increasing the opacity of the layer, duplicate it one more time, but leave the opacity and blending mode alone afterward.

62 Control-click (or Command-click) the current layer's thumbnail to load a selection from the contents. While the selection is active, choose the Hue/Saturation option from the list within the Create New Fill or Adjustment Layer menu at the bottom of the Layers palette. In the Adjustments palette, adjust the hue and saturation sliders to enhance the pinkish hue and increase the saturation. Depending on the color of your underlying solid color layer, your hue and saturation adjustment values may vary slightly from these.

Brighter highlights
Use a channel-based selection to enhance lighter regions of the underlying object.

1 Target any of the layers beneath the Hue/Saturation adjustment layer in the Layers palette that contains your rendered object. Press Control-A (or Command-A) to select all. Press Control-C (or Command-C) to copy, and then Control-click (or Command-click) the targeted layer's thumbnail to generate a selection from its contents.

2 While the selection is active, click the Create New Channel button at the bottom of the Channels palette. Target your new channel in the Channels palette and then press Control-V (or Command-V) to paste the copied layer contents into the active selection within the new alpha channel.

3 Load a selection from the contents of the channel by Control-clicking (or Command-clicking) the channel's thumbnail. Return to the Layers palette and, while the current selection is active, create a new solid color layer. When the picker appears, specify a light pink color and click OK. After that, drag the solid color layer to the top of the stack in the Layers palette.

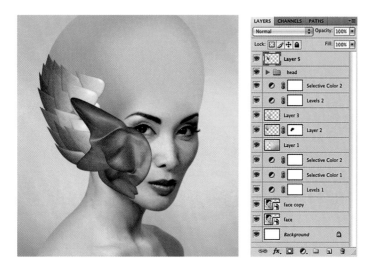

63 At this moment, you should have your top layer targeted in the Layers palette. Hold down the Shift key and then click the darker pink solid color layer you created earlier. This will select both solid color layers as well as all layers in between. Press Control-G (or Command-G) to group them. Double-click the name of the group in the Layers palette to highlight it and then change the name of the group to head. Open the *rendering2.tif* file. As you did before, load a selection from the included alpha channel. Then simply use the Move tool to click the selected image component and drag it into your working file as a new layer. Use Free Transform to adjust the size and position it over her cheek area.

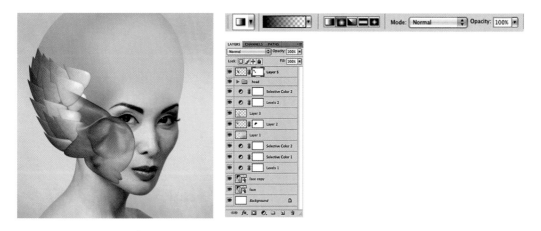

64 Click the Add Layer Mask button at the bottom of the Layers palette to mask the layer. Target the mask in the Layers palette and select the Gradient tool from the Toolbar. Specify a black foreground color and then choose the Foreground to Transparent gradient preset from the preset picker in the Tool Options bar. Select the Radial method in the Tool Options bar and then carefully create a few small, black-to-transparent, radial gradients within the mask to gently fade certain regions of the layer contents.

 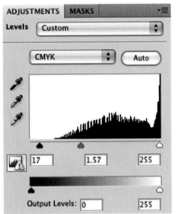

65 Duplicate the current layer and change the blending mode to Hard light. Right-click (or Control-click) the layer's Mask thumbnail in the Layers palette. When the pop-up menu appears, choose the Delete Layer Mask option to remove the mask from this layer. Control-click (or Command-click) the Layer thumbnail to load a selection from the contents, then choose Levels from the list of options in the Create New Fill or Adjustment Layer menu at the bottom of the Layers palette. Adjust the input level sliders in the Adjustments palette, similar to what is shown here, to lighten the midtones and deepen the shadows.

66 Control-click (or Command-click) the Levels adjustment layer mask thumbnail to load a selection from it. While the selection is active, create a new Selective Color layer, as you've done previously. This will create a Selective color layer that is masked by the active selection. In the Adjustments palette, select Neutrals from the list of colors and then edit the CMYK sliders, removing mainly cyan and black by about 10% or so. Then, select Blacks from the list of colors and increase the magenta, yellow, and black somewhat evenly. Then increase the amount of cyan slightly.

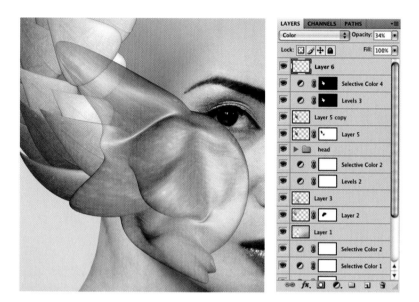

67 Now load a selection from the Selective Color layer's mask. While the selection is active, create a new layer and ensure that it is targeted. Change the blending mode of the layer to Color and select the Gradient tool. Right now you want to introduce some Foreground to Transparent, Radial gradients into areas of the selection that could use some more pink in them. Sample areas of her skin and then click and drag over the necessary regions. You don't want the result to be too drastic, however, so try reducing the opacity of the layer after the fact to something rather low. Yours will likely differ slightly, but the opacity setting I settled on was 34%. Ensure that you keep this selection active.

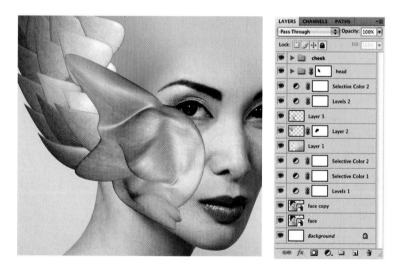

68 While the selection is active, target the head group beneath your current series of layers in the Layers palette. Choose Layer > Layer Mask > Reveal All from the menu. Target the new layer mask and create some Black to Transparent, Radial gradients within the selection to hide regions that are visible through the above layers. Press Control-D (or Command-D) to deactivate the selection. Next, target all the layers above the current group and group them as well. Name the new group cheek.

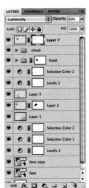

69 Open the *rendering1.tif* file. Load a selection from the alpha channel in the file and then use the Move tool to drag the selected contents of the rendered image into your working file as a new layer. Again, use Free Transform to adjust the size and positioning. Feel free to Rotate as well if necessary. When you've carefully positioned the rendered object over her eye at the left of the image, press the Enter key to apply the transformation. Add a mask to the layer and use the Gradient tool to create a small Black to Transparent gradient within the mask to hide the area at the lower left where the object overlaps the one below. Change the blending mode of the layer to Luminosity and reduce the opacity to 69%.

Altering the rendered object

Use a duplicate alongside an adjustment and fill layer to make the object look as though it belongs on her face.

1 Duplicate the layer and change the blending mode of the duplicate layer to Soft light. Then duplicate this newly duplicated layer as well so that there are two duplicate layers.

2 Control-click (or Command-click) the Layer thumbnail (not the mask) to load a selection from the layer's contents. With the selection active, create a new Selective Color layer. In the Adjustments palette, slightly increase the amount of yellow and magenta while decreasing the amount of cyan in the Neutrals.

3 Control-click (or Command-click) the layer's mask to load it as a selection and then create a new solid color layer. Select a light yellow color from the picker and click OK. Change the blending mode for this solid color layer to Darken so that it only affects the underlying highlights.

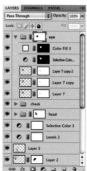

70 Target all the layers and adjustment layers that sit above the cheek group in the Layers palette and group them. Change the name of the group to eye. Add a mask to the group and then use the Gradient tool to create some Radial, Black to Transparent gradients in the mask to hide the regions of the group in areas that overlap her eye. Next, expand the group and Control-click (or Command-click) any Layer thumbnail or Adjustment Layer mask thumbnail to generate a selection around the perimeter of the shape.

Blending the cheek object
Use a tried-and-true method to carefully blend the cheek object into her face.

1 While the selection is active, target the cheek group in the Layers palette and then choose Layer > Layer Mask > Reveal All from the menu. Select the Gradient tool and set the foreground color to black.

2 Use the Radial method to create some Foreground to Transparent gradients within the selection on the currently targeted layer's mask. Create some gradients that cover the top edge of the cheek group, yet be careful to not totally obscure the detail at the lower left in the selection.

3 Next, deactivate the selection and then create some gradients in the area where the object overlaps her face at the right. You really want to gently mask out the hard edge here as well as blend the lower portion into her jaw.

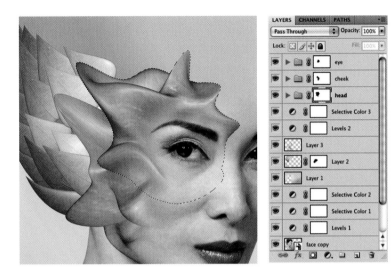

71 Return to one of the layers within your eye group and load a selection from the contents again by Control-clicking (or Command-clicking) it. While the selection is active, target the head group's mask in the Layers palette. Set the current foreground color to black, if it isn't already, and then press Alt-Delete (or Option-Delete) on the keyboard to fill the active selection with black within the currently targeted mask. This will hide the overlap in the upper-left region of the eye shape.

72 Deactivate the current selection and return to the open *rendering4.tif* file. Use the Lasso to draw a selection around a single object. Now you can see why we scattered some duplicate objects around. Although we won't use them all, the advantage is that there are plenty of options to choose from. Use the Lasso to draw a selection around the piece at the upper right. After creating a closed selection around it, choose Edit > Transform > Flip Horizontal from the menu. After flipping it, use the Move tool to drag the selected contents into the working file as a new layer. Drag this layer to the top of the stack if it isn't there already. Use Free Transform to adjust the size and rotation as well as position it just to the left of her cheek area.

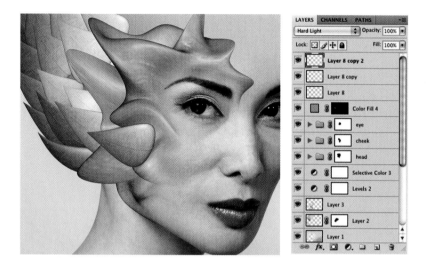

73 Change the blending mode of the layer to Luminosity. Control-click (or Command-click) the layer's thumbnail to load a selection from the contents. While the selection is active, create a new solid color layer. While the picker is open, run the Eyedropper over a medium-pink region and click to sample it. Click OK and then drag the solid color layer beneath the previous layer in the Layers palette. Now duplicate the top layer and change the blending mode of the layer to Screen. Reduce the opacity of the layer to 53%. Duplicate this layer as well, then change the blending mode to Hard light and increase the opacity to 100%.

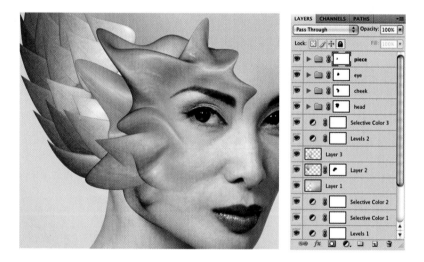

74 Again, Control-click (or Command-click) the layer's thumbnail to load a selection from the contents. While the selection is active, create a new Hue/Saturation adjustment layer. In the Adjustments palette, adjust the Hue to +37, decrease the Saturation by 16, and increase the Lightness by 10. Target all these layers and group them. Rename the group piece. Add a mask to the group and then use the Gradient tool to create some small, Radial, Black to Transparent gradients in the mask. Create the gradients in the region where the right side of the shape overlaps the cheek details to blend it in nicely.

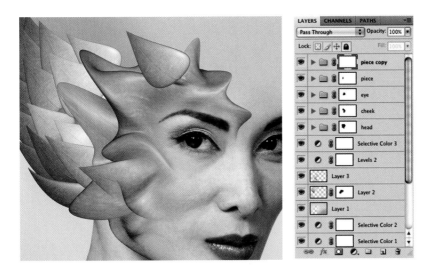

75 Duplicate the group by dragging it onto the Create A New Layer button at the bottom of the Layers palette. With the duplicate group targeted (not the mask), press Control-T (or Command-T) to enter Free Transform. When the bounding box appears, click and drag outside it to rotate the group. Then click and drag inside the box to reposition the contents of the group so that it is overlapping the top of the object that surrounds her eye. Target the Layer mask and set the foreground color to White, if it isn't already. Then press Alt-Delete (or Option-Delete) to fill the mask with white, revealing the entire group.

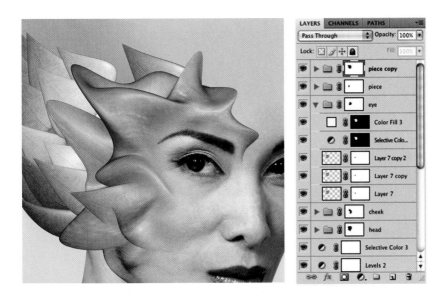

76 Expand the Eye group in the Layers palette and then Control-click (or Command-click) one of the layers to generate a selection that outlines the shape. With the selection active, target the mask of your Piece Copy group in the Layers palette. The background color should be set to Black. If it is not, press the x key until it is. Then press Control-Delete (or Command-Delete) to fill the active selection with black within the currently targeted mask, hiding the contents of the group in this area. Deactivate the selection.

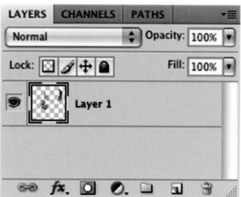

77 Open the *rendering3.tif* file. Load a selection from the alpha channel contained within the file. While the selection is active, return to the Layers palette and press Control-J (or Command-J) to copy the selected contents to a new layer. Drag the background layer onto the Trash icon at the bottom of the Layers palette to delete it. Use the Lasso tool to draw a closed selection around only the large shape at the bottom left. You might need to zoom in close to do this. Be careful not to include any portions of the other shapes.

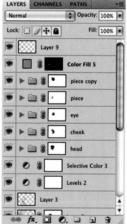

78 Use the Move tool to drag the selected contents into your working file as a new layer. As before, use Free Transform to position, resize, and rotate the contents of the selection as required. Position it near the lower left of her cheek in the image window. Change the blending mode of the layer to Luminosity and reduce the opacity to 52%. Control-click (or Command-click) the Layer thumbnail to load a selection from the contents of the layer. While the selection is active, create a new solid color layer. When the picker opens, move the mouse over a pink region of the image and click to sample that color. Click OK and then drag the new solid color layer beneath the Object layer in the Layers palette.

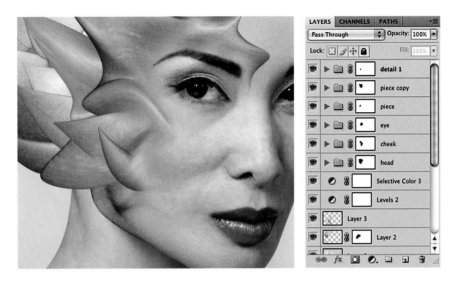

79 Target the top layer and duplicate it. Change the blending mode of the duplicate layer to Overlay and increase the opacity to 100%. While this layer is targeted, hold down the Shift key and click the solid color layer you just created. This will select all three layers that make up this object. When the three layers are selected, press Control-G (or Command-G) to group them. Name the group detail 1. Add a mask to the group and select the Gradient tool. Select a black foreground color and then introduce some Radial, Black to Transparent gradients into the mask to fade the right side of the grouped object into the background.

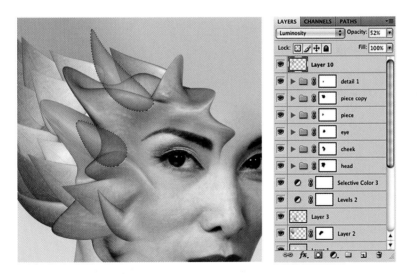

80 Return to the open *rendering3.tif* file. Use the Lasso to draw a selection around the two objects directly above the object you selected previously. Next, use the Move tool to drag the selected contents into your working file as a new layer. Ensure that your new layer is at the top of the stack in the Layers palette and then use Free Transform to adjust size and rotation and to position the objects similarly to what is shown here. Change the blending mode of the layer to Luminosity and reduce the opacity to 52%. Control-click (or Command-click) the Layer thumbnail to load a selection from the contents.

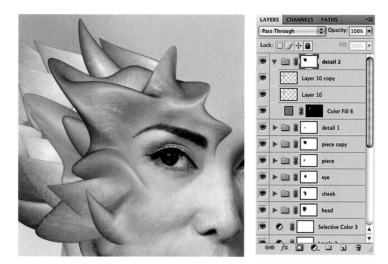

81 While the selection is active, create a new solid color layer with a pink fill color, as you've done previously numerous times. Then drag the solid color layer beneath the layer that contains the rendered objects in the Layers palette. Duplicate your top layer, then change the blending mode of the duplicate layer to Overlay and increase the opacity to 100%. Target these three layers and then press Control-G (or Command-G) to group them. Change the name of the group to detail 2. Control-click (or Command-click) the Piece Copy group's layer mask to load it as a selection. While the selection is active, ensure that you have the new detail 2 group targeted in the Layers palette and then click the Add Layer mask button at the bottom of the palette.

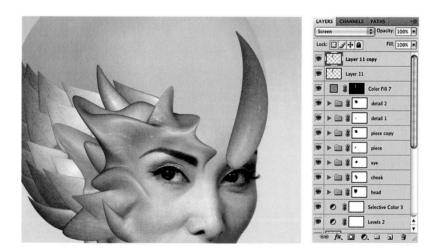

82 Now, return to the *rendering3.tif* file and use the Lasso tool to draw a selection around the object at the upper right. Drag it into your working file as a new layer and change the blending mode to Luminosity. Use Free Transform to increase the vertical size as well as rotate and position the object at the edge of her forehead. Create a selection from the contents of the layer by Control-clicking (or Command-clicking) the thumbnail in the Layers palette. Then as you've done numerous times already, create a solid color layer with a pink fill and drag it beneath the layer with the rendered object on it. After that, duplicate the top layer that contains the rendered object and change the blending mode of the duplicate layer to Screen.

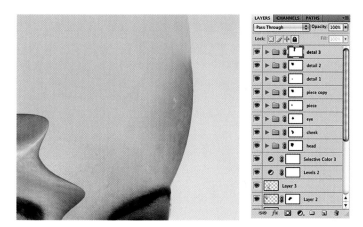

83 Target these three new layers and group them. Name the group detail 3 and add a mask to the group. Target the mask and then create some Radial, Black to Transparent gradients within the mask to blend the top, left, and bottom of the edges into the underlying layers so that it looks like it belongs at the right edge of her forehead. Take your time and create numerous small gradients along the left side to blend it without hiding too much of the content at the right.

PART NINE: Adding tribal designs

84 Select the Pen tool and ensure that it is set to create Paths in the Tool Options bar. Now take your time and carefully draw a nice tribal design that will represent the right edge of the piece overlapping her eye. Start drawing in the brow area and work your way down, creating a nice design beside her nose, onto her cheek, and finally tracing the line of her jaw. Work your way back along her jawline until you reach the point where it intersects with a protruding shape. Then you can simply close the path by creating a few points and working your way back to the starting point. The right edge of the path is not important. Really focus on creating interesting detail on the left edge and carefully edit the points and curves with the Direct Selection tool as necessary until you're 100% satisfied with the path.

85 Control-click (or Command-click) your new Path thumbnail in the Paths palette to load it as a selection. Return to the Layers palette and create a new layer. Change the blending mode of the new layer to Multiply and select the Gradient tool. As before, ensure that the radial method is specified and the Foreground to Transparent preset is selected in the Tool Options bar. Hold down the Alt (or Option) key and click on a dark pink region to sample the color. Release the Alt (or Option) key and repeatedly click and drag within the selection border along the right edge and bottom to add some gradients in this area, gently darkening it. Feel free to use different colors and to vary the opacity of the Gradient tool as you work.

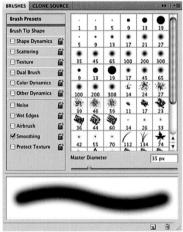

86 While the current selection remains active, create a new layer and ensure that the new layer is targeted. Change the blending mode of the layer to Multiply and sample a darker color from within the image. Alt-click (or Option-click) a darker purple region over her eye or within her lips. Next, select the Brush tool and make the Brushes palette visible by clicking the Toggle the Brushes Panel button in the Tool Options bar. Choose a soft, round preset and disable any dynamic functions so that the stroke is even. Reduce the opacity of the brush to around 20% and then paint along the edge within the selection in a few select places. This will add a sense of depth to the tribal design. Deactivate the selection.

87 Use the Pen tool to draw a path over her other brow area. Use the same procedure to load a selection from, and then add a series of gradients into the selection on a new layer with a Multiply blending mode. While the selection is active, again use the previous method to brush some darker regions into the selection on yet another layer. Repeat the process to add some tribal detail below here eye on her other cheek and also on her neck and shoulder. When you're finished, group all the layers that make up this tribal detail and name the group tribal. Save your file.

PART TEN: Create a mountain range

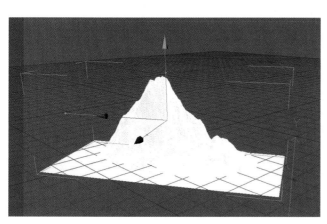

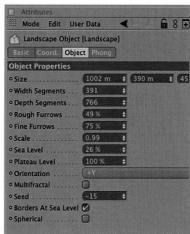

88 Return to Cinema 4D and create a new file. Click and hold the Primitive Objects button in the top Toolbar. When the Primitive Objects palette appears, select the Landscape object. Ensure that the new landscape object is selected in the viewport and then direct your attention to the Attributes Manager. In the Attributes Manager, substantially alter the default attributes of the object. Have some fun experimenting here and considerably altering the Landscape object. Regardless of what you do here, ensure that you add a considerable amount of width and depth segments so that the object appears detailed and smooth when you render it.

89 Now, before we get too involved in creating the mountain range, let's set up the viewport and render settings so we're working to the exact same scale as the working file in Photoshop. Use the navigational icons at the top right of the viewport to rotate the scene, zoom out, and then position things so that the mountain is at the far left. Next, choose Render > Render Settings from the menu. In the Output section, set the width to 18.75 inches and the height to 12 inches. Set the resolution to 72 pixels per inch and then click the Save option at the left. In the Save options, click the ... button to the right of the Path option. Name the file mountain and specify a destination for the rendering. Ensure that the Alpha Channel option is enabled and then close the Render Settings.

90 Create another Landscape object and again have some fun editing the object in the Attributes Manager. Try to make it distinctly different from the previous object, yet be certain to ensure that you specify a lot of height and width segments so that the render is smooth and detailed. Use the Move and Rotate tools in the top Toolbar to position the new object next to the previous one within the scene. When you're happy with the result, continue to create more Landscape objects. Edit their individual attributes to make them unique, and position them in the scene so that they are neatly lined up in a row.

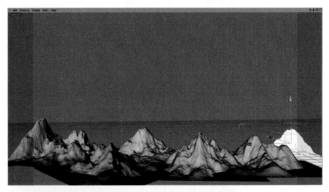

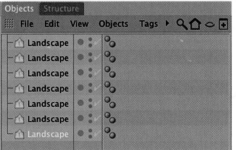

91 Click and hold the Scene Objects button in the top Toolbar. When the Scene Objects palette appears, select the Spotlight object to create a new spotlight within the scene. Use the Move tool to position the light at the left of the scene; then use the Rotate tool to point it at the mountain. Click the navigational icon at the upper right to access a four-up view. Feel free to use any of the available views to position the light exactly where you want it. When you're satisfied, select the Perspective view and then click the same navigational icon to hide the other three views. In the Perspective view, click and drag an orange handle on the circle to adjust the width if necessary. In the Attributes Manager, reduce the intensity to around 84%.

92 In the Object Manager, Control-click (or Control-click)and drag the Light upward to duplicate it. Use the Move tool to drag the duplicate light to the right in the Perspective view so that it illuminates the central portion of the mountain range. Reduce the intensity of this light to around 52%. Now Control-click-drag (or Control-click-drag) this light upward in the Object Manager to duplicate it as well. Use the Move tool to move this newly duplicated light to the right side in the perspective view. Considerably increase the intensity of this light. Select individual lights as necessary and use the Rotate tool to adjust their aim if needed.

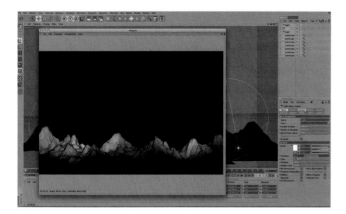

93 Click the Render Active View button in the top Toolbar to preview your rendering. This will give you an indication of how your lights are working to illuminate your scene evenly. Bear in mind that the values for intensity I stated earlier were for my file. Depending on the spatial relationship between your lights and the objects, you might need to increase or decrease the intensity of individual lights. When you're satisfied with the illumination, choose Render > Render To Picture Viewer from the menu. After the rendering is complete, close the Picture Viewer and return to your working file in Photoshop.

94 Now create a new Hue/Saturation adjustment layer at the top of the stack in the Layers palette. Open the *mountain.tif* file. In the Adjustments palette, adjust the Hue to +19 and increase the Saturation by 43. In the Channels palette, locate the alpha channel within the file. Control-click (or Command-click) the Alpha Channel thumbnail to load it as a selection. Return to the Layers palette and, while the selection is active, hold down the Shift key as you drag the contents of the selection into your working file with the Move tool. It will be added to the file as a new layer. It is likely that your rendered mountains, like mine, have left some empty spaces beneath the mountain range. To remedy this, ensure that the layer containing the mountains is targeted and then select the Brush tool.

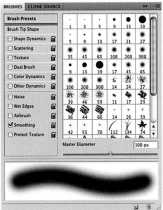

95 In the Brushes palette, select a large, soft, round preset. Disable any shape dynamics applied to the preset. Alt-click (or Option-click) one of the darkest black regions at the bottom of the mountains, to sample the color. Ensure that the opacity of your brush is set to 100% in the Tool Options bar and then use the brush to paint over all the empty spaces beneath your mountains on the current layer. Change the blending mode of the layer to Overlay and then duplicate it. Control-click (or Command-click) the Layer thumbnail in the Layers palette to load a selection from the contents.

A mountainous group
Building an environment is as simple as stacking up layers inside a carefully masked group.

1 While the selection is active, create a new solid color layer with a blue fill color. Ensure that it is lighter than the blue at the bottom of the mountains. Change the blending mode of the solid color layer to Lighten so that it only brightens darker regions beneath it.

2 Target these three layers in the Layers palette. Press Control-G (or Command-G) to group them. Name the new group mountains and ensure that it is targeted in the Layers palette. Use the Move tool to Shift-drag the group down a little on canvas.

3 Control-click (or Command-click) the first path you created in the Paths palette. This is the one that traces her neck and shoulders. When the path-based selection appears, return to the Layers palette. Ensure that the new *mountains* group is targeted and then choose Layer > Layer Mask > Hide Selection from the menu.

PART ELEVEN: Creating some 3D leaves

96 Save your working file and open the *leaf.psd* file. Choose Select > Color Range from the menu. When the Color Range options appear, click anywhere on the white background in the image window. Then drag the fuzziness slider all the way to the right to ensure that anything remotely white in the image will be included in the resulting selection. Click OK to select the white range of color in the image. Invert the selection by pressing Control-Shift-I (or Command-Shift-I).

Trim and prepare

Creating and adding an alpha channel will allow us to trim our image when we bring it onto Cinema 4D.

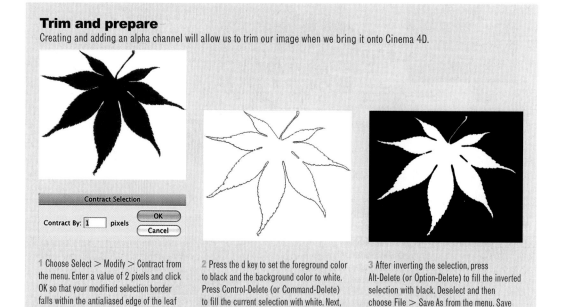

1 Choose Select > Modify > Contract from the menu. Enter a value of 2 pixels and click OK so that your modified selection border falls within the antialiased edge of the leaf in the image.

2 Press the d key to set the foreground color to black and the background color to white. Press Control-Delete (or Command-Delete) to fill the current selection with white. Next, press Control-Shift-I (or Command-Shift-I) to invert the selection.

3 After inverting the selection, press Alt-Delete (or Option-Delete) to fill the inverted selection with black. Deselect and then choose File > Save As from the menu. Save the modified image as alpha.psd and close the file.

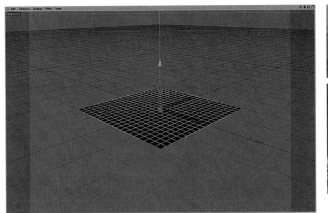

97 Return to Cinema 4D and create a new file. Click and hold the Primitive Objects button in the top Toolbar. Select the Plane object from the Primitive Objects palette when it appears. A 2D plane will appear in the scene. While the plane is selected, choose File > New from the Materials Manager menu to create a new material. When the new thumbnail appears in the Materials Manager, double-click it to access the Material Editor.

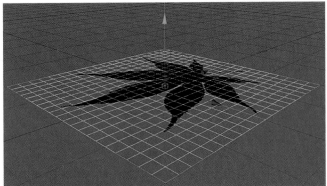

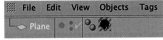

98 In the Color channel of the Material Editor, click the … button to the right of the texture option. Navigate to the leaf.psd file included with the downloadable project files and click Open. Enable the Alpha channel at the left and then click it to access the Alpha options. In the Alpha channel of the Material Editor, click the … button to the right of the Texture option. Navigate to the alpha.psd file you created previously and click Open. Close the Material Editor and then drag the Material thumbnail from the Material Manager onto the plane in the viewport or the Object Manager. This will apply the material to your object, and you'll see a Texture tag appear beside the plane in the Object Manager.

99 Select the Rotate tool from the top Toolbar and rotate the plane object so that it is standing rather than laying flat within the scene. Click and hold the Deformers button in the top Toolbar to access the Deformers palette. Select the Bend deformer. In the Object Manager, drag the Bend deformer onto the Plane object to make it a child of that object. In the viewport, click and drag the orange handle to bend the object. You can rotate or move the deformer at any time, and this will affect the way it deforms the object. Also, you might want to scale a single axis of the deformer. To do this, click the Object Tool button at the left and then select the Scale tool from the top Toolbar. Use the Scale tool to click and drag the colored box for the desired axis, to scale it independently of the others.

100 It is important to embrace the nondestructive nature of Cinema 4D as you're working. Freely edit various aspects of the Bend deformer. Try experimenting with different rotations, nonproportionate scaling operations, bend amount, and movements. After you're satisfied, create another Bend deformer and drag it onto the Plane object on the Object Manager. Now that this deformer is a child of the object, too, go ahead and alter the bend amount, adjust the rotation, and even move or scale the deformer as you see fit. Take note of how both deformers work to alter the plane. Remember, they can be edited independently of each other at any point.

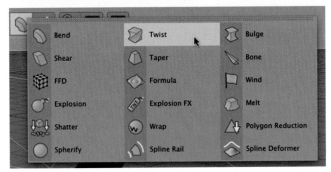

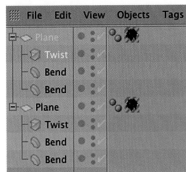

101 Click and hold the Deformers button again in the top Toolbar. This time, select a Twist deformer from the Deformers palette. As you did previously with the Bend deformers, make it a child of the plane object and then adjust the orange handle to twist its parent object. Also Rotate, Scale, and/or Move your Twist deformer within the scene to edit its effect on the parent. When you're happy with the results of the Twist deformer, Control-click (or Control-click)the parent and drag upward in the Object Manager to duplicate it. Use the Move tool to reposition the duplicate object within the scene. Click the children of the duplicated plane in the Object Manager and edit them to make the duplicate leaf slightly different from the original.

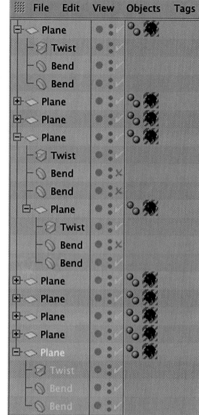

102 Use the navigational controls at the upper right of the viewport to zoom out considerably and rotate the view as well. Create a vast number of duplicates within the scene. Scatter them around, but try to ensure that they do not overlap each other within the Perspective view. Take some time and edit the individual deformers within some of the duplicates. You can disable some of the deformers entirely by clicking the green checkmarks next to them in the Object Manager. The green checkmark will turn to a red *x*, switching the deformer off until you click the x again to enable it. Continue until you're satisfied that you have achieved a diverse scattering of shapes.

103 Choose Render > Render Settings from the menu. In the Output section, set the width to 14 inches, set the height to 10 inches, and set the resolution to 72 pixels per inch. In the Save section, click the ... button to the right of the Path option. Specify a destination and name the file rendering5.tif. Ensure that the Alpha Channel option is selected and then close the Render Settings window. Choose Render > Render to Picture Viewer from the menu. When the rendering is complete, quit Cinema 4D and return to your working file in Photoshop.

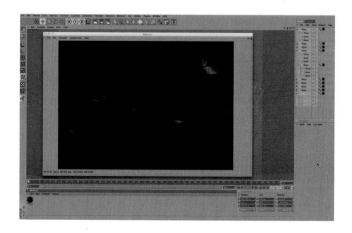

PART TWELVE: Create a textural effect from the leaves

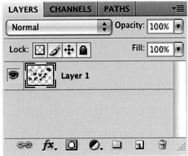

104 In Photoshop, open the *rendering5.tif* file. In the Channels palette, Control-click (or Command-click) the Alpha channel included in the file to load it as a selection. Return to the Layers palette and press Control-J (or Command-J) to copy the selected contents to a new layer. Drag the background layer onto the Trash icon at the bottom of the Layers palette to delete it. Use the Lasso tool to draw a rough selection.

105 Use the Move tool to drag the selected contents into your working file as a new layer. Change the blending mode to Hard light and reduce the opacity to 50%. Press Control-U (or Command-U) to perform a Hue/Saturation adjustment to the new layer. Reduce the Saturation by 68%, increase the Lightness by 10, and then press Control-T (or Command-T) to access Free Transform. Rotate, Resize, and Reposition the layer contents so that the two leaves are more or less upside down and extending beyond the top of the canvas. Press Enter to apply the transformation and then use the Move tool to Alt-drag (or Option-drag) the leaves to the lower left behind her head, duplicating the layer. Perform a Hue/Saturation adjustment to slightly reduce the saturation of the leaves on this layer.

106 Return to the *rendering5.tif* file and deactivate the current selection. Use the Move tool to drag the contents of the entire layer into the working file as a new layer. Activate Free Transform and rotate the leaves as well as adjust their size. You want the leaves to, more or less, surround her head at the left of the canvas. Press the Enter key to apply the transformation and then change the blending mode of the layer to Screen. Reduce the opacity of the layer to 90%.

Building up the texture

Continue to stack up layers while repositioning and altering blending options, to build up the leafy texture overall.

1 Duplicate the layer and use Free Transform to adjust the size and rotation as you move it lower down and toward the left of the canvas. Reduce the layer opacity to 60%.

2 Duplicate the current layer. Use the Move tool to position the newest duplicated layer higher and to the right of the canvas. Reduce the opacity of this layer to 40%. Return to the *rendering5.tif* file.

3 Use the Lasso tool to select leaves, one at a time, and drag them into the working file as new layers. Position each layer with the Move tool. When you're happy with the result, target all these individual leaf layers and merge them by pressing Control-E (or Command-E).

107 Press Control-U (or Command-U) to perform a Hue/Saturation adjustment. Reduce the saturation considerably until the leaves appear to be almost gray. Reduce the opacity of the layer to 33%. This will add some subtle, dark leaves to the composition. Next, have some fun scattering some more lighter leaves around. Begin by duplicating the current layer. Change the blending mode of the duplicate layer to Screen and increase the opacity of the layer to 55%. Use Free Transform to resize, rotate, and reposition the contents of the layer. Next, duplicate this layer and reposition the contents on the canvas area. Repeat this process one more time, and that should be sufficient.

108 In the Layers palette, target all the layers that make up the leafy pattern and group them by pressing Control-G (or Command-G). Add a mask to the group and select the Gradient tool. Use the Foreground to Transparent preset and select the Radial method in the Tool Options bar. Set the foreground color to Black and then create a series of gradients in the mask to gently hide leaves that overlap her head, face, and shoulders or that appear too prominent within the scene. Feel free to tweak as you see fit from this point on. The file is constructed in a modular manner so that you can directly alter individual components without adversely affecting other parts of the composition.

Here is another example of separate 3D rendered work that was combined in Photoshop. The nanotech robot was a separate rendering from the cellular material in the background. Some of the texture details, such as the light and buttons, were embellished after the fact using Photoshop's paint tools.

In these two images, you can see the benefits of experimenting with the incorporation of texture and photographic elements as well. The top image uses a simple stormy sky photo to set the mood. However, the image below relies on photographed elements for the wings of the main creature. It also has some tactile surface texture applied to it to make it feel more natural.

7

Chapter 7

Sculpting Raw Materials

Combining ZBrush with Photoshop

When I first caught wind of ZBrush, I didn't believe it would actually work. It promised something that all of us who dabble in 3D from time to time wanted, but deep down we knew it couldn't really be possible. As a 2D artist, I always found 3D software unintuitive on some level. I just want to be an artist and not get bogged down with tools or caught up in the process. I want to work intuitively, and until I tried using ZBrush I thought that intuitive 3D was a myth.

ZBrush is an amazingly powerful tool. Perhaps equally important, it is incredibly intuitive. This is a 3D application made for artists. It is likely that first-time users will grumble about the interface and how foreign it feels. Granted, it is different from what you're accustomed to when working with Adobe software. But when you come to grips with it, you'll see that it is a truly effective design, and the software is a true joy to work with. ZBrush is an endless labyrinth of features and functions that will seriously blow your mind. In this chapter, we'll scratch the surface of what is possible, using ZBrush to create raw sculpted components. We'll then take all those components into Photoshop and build a stunning textural illustration.

Versions	Requirements and Recommendations
Photoshop CS4 ZBrush 3.2	In addition to Photoshop, you'll need to download the 30-day trial version or purchase a copy of ZBrush. ZBrush is available from www.pixologic.com. And while ZBrush works with a mouse, it is infinitely beneficial to use a pressure-sensitive tablet to take full advantage of the intuitive control that ZBrush can offer.

What you'll learn in this chapter

Creative Techniques and Working Methods

Learn the relationship between height and value

Something of interest when making the jump from 2D to 3D is the way that 2D grayscale value can translate into a displacement, or height information, in a 3D program. The alpha functionality within ZBrush is a perfect example of this. Alphas are used with brushes in ZBrush, much like brush tips are used with brushes in Photoshop. In Photoshop, the grayscale data that makes up the brush tip controls how paint is deposited within the stroke. Areas of black deposit 100% of the paint. Areas of white deposit no paint. And areas of gray deposit amounts of paint relative to their black percentages. In ZBrush, the grayscale data within an alpha is used to determine the height at which an area is displaced when you paint over it. Areas of white are 100% displaced. Areas of black are not displaced at all. Areas of gray displace based on the percentage of white within the grayscale value. To put it into perspective, try to think of how alpha channels work in Photoshop. The logic is quite similar, yet instead of displacement, white determines the degree of selection in an alpha channel.

  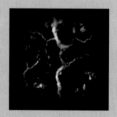

Tools, Features, and Functions

Blending modes and opacity

Apart from the act of building all the components, a major ingredient in the visual success of this image is how everything blends together when you stack it all up in the Layers palette. When you move into the Photoshop compilation portion in the latter part of this chapter, you'll go through the process of combining different blending modes and opacity settings until it feels like second nature.

Masks

Equally important as the way the layers blend together is what exactly is revealed on each layer. In this chapter, you'll learn to methodically mask layers in a variety of diverse ways, yielding impressive results along the way.

PART ONE: Preparing alphas for ZBrush

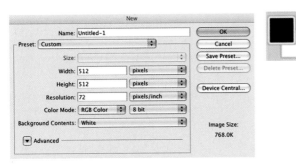

Project files

All the files needed to follow along with this chapter and create the featured image are available for download on the accompanying Website, in the project files section. Visit www.beyondphotoshopthebook.com.

1 Before we begin sculpting in ZBrush, we'll create a few images to be used as alphas. An alpha in ZBrush is similar to a custom brush tip in Photoshop. Well, sort of. Except rather than depositing paint, it controls how displacements occur as you paint. Confused? Don't worry if it doesn't entirely make sense to you right now. All will become clear as you work your way through this chapter. To get started, create a new file in Photoshop that is 512 pixels by 512 pixels at 72 ppi, RGB mode. The color of the canvas doesn't matter, so go ahead and leave it set to white. Press the d key to set the foreground and background colors to their default settings of black and white.

Skipping ahead

If you decide that you do not want to complete the ZBrush portion of this project and simply want to get on with the comprehensive Photoshop work, you can skip ahead to Part 5 of this chapter and begin there. However, it would be beneficial to read through the initial stages of the project as well to gain insight into the entire process.

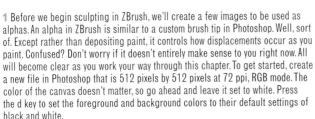

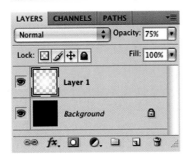

2 Fill the background with black by pressing Alt-Delete (Option-Delete) on the keyboard. Click the Create a New Layer button in the Layers palette. With the new layer targeted, select the Gradient tool from the Toolbar. Press the x key to invert the foreground and background colors so that white is now the foreground color. In the Tool Options bar, select the Foreground to Transparent preset from the Gradient picker and select the Radial method. Leave the opacity set to 100 and then click the center of the canvas and drag outward, almost to the edge. Reduce the opacity of the layer to 75%.

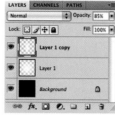

 Alphas available

If you don't want to create your own alphas or are not happy with the outcome, worry not. The alphas created in Part 1 are also included in the downloadable project files for this chapter. Feel free to use them if you prefer; the names are the same as those specified in Part 1.

3 Duplicate the layer by dragging it onto the Create a New Layer icon at the bottom of the Layers palette and press Control-T (or Command-T) to access Free Transform. When the bounding box appears, hold down the Alt (or Option) key as you click the left or right center handle and drag inward. When you've significantly scaled the gradient horizontally, press the Enter key to apply the transformation. Increase the opacity of the current layer to 85% and then select Layer > Flatten Image from the menu. Choose File > Save As to save the image as a .psd file. Name the file bump.psd.

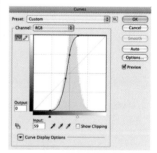

4 Open the *cement1.jpg* file. Choose Image > Adjustments > Black and White from the menu. The goal is to convert this image to grayscale and maximize the contrast at the same time. From the preset menu, choose the infrared option as your starting point. Then drag the Yellows slider to the right until it reads 300. Click OK and then press Control-M (or Command-M) to make a Curves adjustment. The first thing you'll need to do in the Curves dialog is to drag the left and right input level sliders at the bottom of the curve closer to the center. Then click the actual curve itself to add a couple of additional points. Move the points around until your curve starts to look like the one shown here. Basically, all you're trying to do is maximize the contrast overall.

5 Press Control-I (or Command-I) to invert the image. Then choose Filter > Blur . Gaussian Blur from the menu. Specify an amount that blurs the image just enough to remove the small, noisy, and sharp bits but still preserves the inverted cracks. Click OK and select the Rectangular Marquee tool. Hold down the Shift key to constrain the aspect ration to a perfect square. Then click and drag to select a region of the image that contains some interesting details.

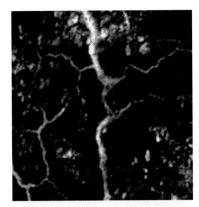

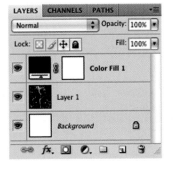

6 Press Control-C (or Command-C) to copy the selected contents, and then press Control-N (or Command-N) to create a new file. Do not close the *cement1.jpg* file yet. In the new file dialog box, ensure that the Preset menu is set to Clipboard and click OK. Then press Control-V (or Command-V) to paste the copied image in as a new layer. If you want to enhance the contrast further, go ahead and perform another Curves adjustment. Choose the solid color option from the Create New Fill or Adjustment Layer menu at the bottom of the Layers palette. When the picker appears, choose a black color and click OK. Do not be alarmed when the entire image is obscured by black. We will remedy that next.

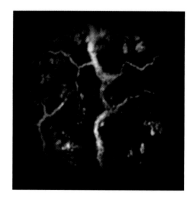

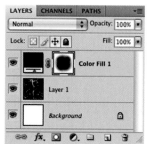

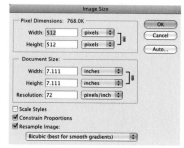

7 Target the new solid color layer's mask in the Layers palette and select the Gradient tool. Press the x key to set the foreground color to black. In the Tool Options bar, choose the Foreground to Transparent preset and enable the Radial method. With the opacity still set to 100%, click and drag from the center out, within the layers mask, to reveal the imagery beneath. Click and drag to create additional gradients within the mask as you deem necessary. Simply ensure that there is some solid black at each edge of the canvas. Flatten the image and then choose Image > Image Size from the menu. Alter the dimensions so that the image is 512 pixels by 512 pixels at a resolution of 72 ppi. Save the image as a .psd file and name it cement1.psd.

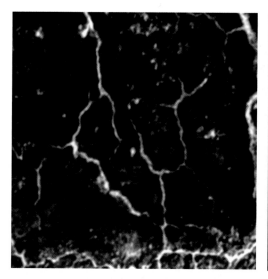

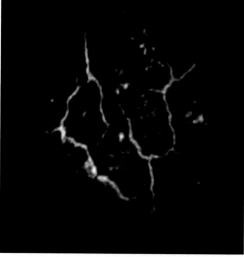

8 Return to the open *cement1.jpg* file and draw another square selection around a different region of detail. This time, because this is the last alpha we'll create from this file, we can simply crop the image instead of copying and pasting. Choose Image > Crop from the menu to crop the file to your selection border. Again, feel free to perform another curve adjustment or any other tonal adjustment if you feel it is needed. Next, create a solid black layer and mask it using the exact same method you used previously. When you're happy with the result, flatten the image and adjust the image size so this file is also 512 by 512 at 72 ppi. Save the file as a .psd file and name it cement2.psd.

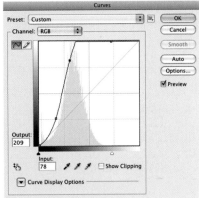

9 Open the *cement2.jpg* file. Just as you did with the previous image, choose Image > Adjustments > Black and White from the menu. From the Preset menu choose the High Contrast Red Filter option. This is good for an initial conversion, but again, you'll need to press Control-M (or Command-M) to make a Curves adjustment. This time, drag the highlight input level slider at the bottom left considerably to the right. Then add a couple of points to the curve by clicking it. Drag the points to edit the curve until it begins to look like the one shown here, greatly increasing the contrast and brightening light areas.

Creating another alpha
Follow the same procedure one more time to create another alpha destined for ZBrush.

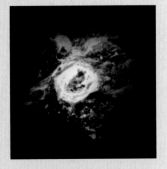

1 Press Control-I (or Command-I) to invert the image, then choose Filter > Blur > Gaussian Blur from the menu. Enter a small amount to reduce the sharpness and remove some minute details from the image.

2 Use the Rectangular marquee tool to click and drag while holding down the Shift key to create a square selection around a region of interesting detail. Try to get the round, white detail near the center. Select Image > Crop from the menu and then use Image > Image Size to change the image to 512 pixels by 512 pixels at 72 ppi.

3 Create a new, black, solid color layer and then edit the mask by adding Black to Transparent gradients into the mask. Gently reveal the underlying layer this way, ensuring that there is solid black at every edge. Flatten the layers and save the file as cement3.psd.

PART TWO: Sculpting in ZBrush

 Getting familiar with ZBrush

Although I'll walk you through each step of the ZBrush process as it pertains to the creation of this chapter's artwork, you might want to do a little brushing up on your own. The Pixologic Website has some excellent training videos in its Education section. The online training is free and easy to follow. ZBrush is capable of so many things. What I'm showing you in this chapter simply scratches the surface of what can be achieved.

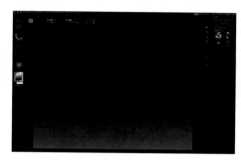

10 After you've downloaded and installed the 30-day trial version of ZBrush from the Pixologic Website, go ahead and launch it. Depending on the version you're using and the way things are configured on your machine, it is likely you'll immediately be confronted with a script that asks you what you want to do. Although the script offers a number of tools to start with, simply press the Esc key to make it go away. This will give you a blank canvas to begin with. Chances are that the Tool palette already appears in the Tray at the right, as shown here. If it doesn't, click the Tool button and then click the icon in the upper left of the palette, and it will be placed in the tray. Next, click the Transform button at the top to reveal the Transform palette, and use the aforementioned method to add it into the Tray on the right.

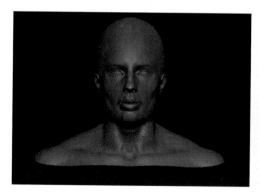

11 In the Tool palette, click the Load tool button and navigate to the *head.ztl* file that is included with the project files for this chapter. The head tool will immediately appear in the Tool palette, automatically becoming the currently selected tool. For this reason, you'll notice a subpalette appear beneath the Tool palette. If this list appears daunting or overwhelming, worry not; we're not going to delve into anything too complicated here. We're simply going to use ZBrush to sculpt some raw materials to be incorporated into a Photoshop composition later on. Click and drag the canvas while the Head tool is selected to place the head mesh on the canvas. Holding down the Shift key as you drag will assist in constraining the rotation of the mesh.

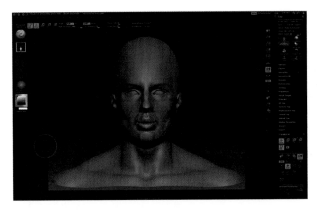

12 Click the Edit button in the upper right. Then, to the immediate left of the tray at the right, click and drag the Rotate button while holding down the Shift key to ensure that you're viewing the mesh straight on. Then click the Frame button to fill the canvas area with the mesh. Also, you can use the Scale, Move, and Rotate buttons in the same click-and-drag manner to position or resize the mesh on the canvas at any point, provided that the Edit button remains enabled. Press Control-D (or Command-D) a couple of times to subdivide the mesh, increasing the polygon count and thus smoothing the surface.

13 The tray at the right can get cluttered fast, so click the word Tool above the Tool palette to collapse it while we're not using it. You can expand it anytime by simply clicking in the same region. Next, click the Activate Symmetry button in the Transform palette. Ensure that the > X < and > M < buttons are enabled. This will ensure that any sculpting we do to one side of the head will be mirrored on the other. Click the Brush button at the left and select the Standard sculpting brush. Then, beneath that, click the Stroke button and select the Freehand stroke.

Dropping to the canvas

One thing that takes some getting used to in ZBrush is that a 3D mesh can be dropped to the canvas, making it no longer editable in 3D space. For that reason it is essential that you keep the Edit button enabled as you work. However, if you ever find that you cannot edit or reposition your mesh, worry not; all is never lost in ZBrush. Your tool in its most recent state is always available in the Tool palette. You simply need to select it, then click and drag the canvas to create a new, editable instance of the mesh. But don't forget to immediately enable the Edit button. If the previous mesh that has been dropped to the canvas is visible while you're working with your new mesh, you can clear the canvas by pressing Control-N (or Command-N).

On canvas controls

While you're working in ZBrush, you can quickly resize your brush on the canvas by pressing the s key. A pop-up slider will appear that you can drag to resize your current brush. Or, if you want access to a myriad of other tools and functions on the canvas as you work, simply hold down the Spacebar. A box will appear containing almost everything you need to work with in ZBrush: brushes, alphas, navigation controls, tool sliders, and much more.

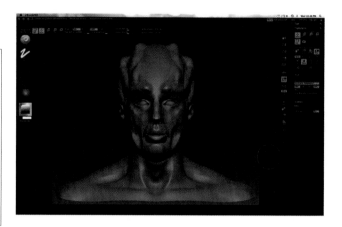

14 Begin by painting a few vertical strokes on the forehead, near the sides of the head. Then try painting some horizontal strokes over the eyebrows to swell the brow. Then add some more vertical strokes to the side of the head, and so on. Next, try holding down the Alt (or Option) key while painting. This creates the opposite effect, resulting in recessed areas rather than raised areas. Try creating recessed regions below the cheekbones, in the temple areas, and on the neck where appropriate.

15 A couple of things that affect sculpting are Draw Size, which is essentially the brush size, and Z Intensity. Z Intensity controls how aggressively the brush behaves when displacing the mesh. The default setting is 25, which is quite aggressive. Try reducing this for a more subtle effect. Sliders for these controls are always available directly above the canvas.

Smooth results

Some brushes, such as the Snake Hook or Inflate, can have quite a drastic effect, and I find that the results are best when such brushes are used with moderation. However, another thing that I've found is that the best results are achieved by using a multiple brush strategy. For instance, if I perform a Snake Hook operation, I'll modify it with the Move Brush using low Z Intensity. Then finally I'll smooth it out with the Smooth Brush at a very high Z Intensity. The general idea is to perform a task that makes a noticeable difference on the mesh, then carefully integrate it again so that it looks natural.

16 ZBrush has a myriad of Brush and Stroke options. Try some different brushes and also try varying the Strokes as you work with them. The first time you use ZBrush, all these options will seem a little daunting. An important thing to remember is that when you select a brush, stroke, or any tool in ZBrush, you can access a brief description of the tool and its behavior by holding down the Control (or Command) key. These descriptions are very helpful when it comes to deciding what you're going to use and how you're going to go about it. Continue to reshape the head, using large Draw Sizes and low Zintensity settings. Some of the brushes I used to get the general shape you see here were the Clay, Move, Inflate, and Standard options. To smooth the mesh a little more, press Control-D (or Command-D) once.

17 Try using the Snake Hook brush with a small Draw Size to pull minute sections of the mesh outward. Using the Dots or Freehand strokes works well with this tool. Do not overdo it with the Snake Hook brush or you can quickly make a mess of your mesh. Here you can see that I used the Snake Hook brush to create a pointed-ear effect and extend a point from the bottom of his chin. Remember that you can rotate your mesh as you work as well as alter its position and size on the canvas by using the buttons to the left of the tray at the right side. At the top of this stack of buttons are some very useful tools for navigating the canvas as well.

PART THREE: Putting your alphas to use

Saving your tool

After spending some time sculpting the initial tool, it will become something else entirely. To access this tool at a later date, you'll need to save it. If you simply save the document in ZBrush, the tool is dropped to the canvas and not saved as an actual tool. Upon saving, you can decide whether to save the tool or the document, or you can click the Save As button in the Tool palette.

18 Now that the head is deformed into something completely different, it is time to add some interesting surface details by integrating the alphas you created previously into the ZBrush sculpting process. First, choose the Standard Brush and the Dots Stroke. Click the Alpha button beneath the Stroke button and, when the floating palette of Alphas appears, click the Import button in the bottom-left corner and then navigate to the *bump.psd* file you created previously. Once you load the file, it will appear in the list of user alphas in the Alphas palette. Select this alpha and then paint a few strokes on your model. Adjust Z Intensity and Draw Size as required. Gently build up some things that resemble veins as well as create some sharper ridges on existing raised areas. Press Control-D (or Command-D) to subdivide the mesh again.

Standard VS Displace

You'll notice that I have you performing displacements with the Standard brush here, which works fine for this purpose. However, when pushing the mesh, the Standard Brush favors the screen orientation. If you are a 3D purist, you might want to consider using the Displace brush instead. The main difference is that the Displace brush will push the mesh according to the direction of the actual surface, helping preserve the underlying detail. For what we're doing here, the difference is negligible, so it's your call.

19 Load the *cement1.psd* as an alpha using the method mentioned previously. Then select the DragRect stroke. Click and drag the central orb of the head a couple of times using a Z Intensity of around 10 or so. The DragRect is different from the Freehand or Dots strokes in that it places the alpha once each time you click and drag, with the size determined by the distance of your drag. To blend in this effect a little, choose the Smooth Brush and the Dots Stroke. Set the Z Intensity to something quite low, around 10 or 12. Then gently paint over the raised regions you just created to soften them a little.

20 Load the remaining alphas that you created previously using the aforementioned method. Select the Standard Brush and the Dots stroke. Select the *cement2.psd* alpha and set the Z Intensity to 10. Use a rather large Draw Size and then paint short strokes over the surface of the mesh to add a gentle distress to areas of the creature's skin. Remember that you can also carve into the surface by holding down the Alt (or Option) key as you paint.

21 Keep the brush set to Standard and the stroke set to Dots, but now select the cement3 alpha. Because this alpha has a large, prominent white lump in the center, it is ideally suited to creating discernable masses on the surface of the mesh. It will create bulbous, round extrusions, so paint very short strokes over areas such as ridges or sharp, raised points that already exist on the mesh. Use varying Draw Sizes and a Z Intensity of around 25 to make prominent details on the mesh.

 Does yours look different?

I can appreciate that as a Photoshop user you might find the process of sculpting in ZBrush quite challenging. There is a strong possibility that at this point you're getting very frustrated because your mesh doesn't really match up to the one shown here. Worry not; you can follow along with my mesh if you like. You can load my mesh just as you loaded the initial Head tool earlier in the chapter. My mesh is included with the downloadable project files and is called *headsculpt.ZTL*. Remember to drop your current mesh to the canvas by *un*clicking the Edit button, and then clear the canvas by pressing Control-N (or Command-N) first.

The Shift key

While you're working with the Standard brush, the Displace brush, or any 3D sculpting brush for that matter, you can quickly switch to the Smooth brush by holding down the Shift key as you work. Switching back to your previous brush is as simple as letting go of the Shift key.

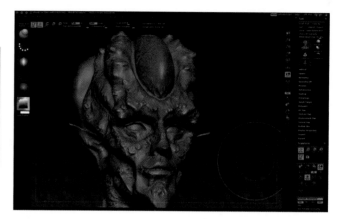

22 Select the Smooth brush and choose either the Freehand or the Dots stroke. Click the Alpha button and choose the Alpha Off option. Then, with varying Z Intensity and varying Draw Sizes, paint short, light strokes over areas that appear too coarse or sharp. This will ensure that they blend nicely into the surface. Have some fun experimenting with other brushes. Try using the Magnify brush with the Dots stroke and your Bump alpha. This will help to swell bulbous areas out from the mesh surface. Using a large Draw Size is perfect for regions like the orb on his forehead or the smooth area at the back of the head.

A mouse won't cut it

Although it is theoretically possible to use a mouse to sculpt in ZBrush, it is nearly impossible to achieve the same result that comes from using a pressure-sensitive tablet. Your tablet doesn't need to be anything fancy or impressive. For this chapter I used a little Wacom Bamboo tablet; the sense of control and flawless interactivity that it provides is essential to the sculpting process. Simply put, if you're using a mouse, your sculpting won't be as refined as what you see here.

23 Feel free to continue in this manner until you're satisfied with the surface texture and sculpted regions of the head. Now let's try one last brush. Select the Tracks3 brush. You'll notice that when you select this brush, the stroke is set to Dots and a default alpha is already selected. As you click and drag with this tool, you'll notice that tracks are deposited in the stroke. The alpha that is used results in an effect similar to the underside of an octopus tentacle. Add a few of these tracks, but not too many; it can quickly become overwhelming. Be certain to vary the Draw Size and Z Intensity along the way. When you're finished, press Control-D (or Command-D) to subdivide the mesh one last time. Use the Smooth brush as you did previously to soften any areas that appear too sharp.

24 Deactivate the Edit button so that your tool is dropped to the canvas. Then press Control-N (or Command-N) to clear the canvas. Don't fret; your tool is not gone forever, it is still there in the Tool palette. If you're using your own tool, go ahead and select it in the Tool palette. If you're using the tool included with the downloadable project files, go ahead and load it. Click the Load Tool button in the Tool palette and navigate to the *headsculpt.ZTL* file to load it. The newly loaded tool will be the active tool. Click the Document button at the top of the interface to view the Document palette. Drag the Height slider to the right until the height reaches 1600 pixels; the Width will self-adjust proportionately. Then click Resize to change the size of the canvas. You'll need to click and drag upward a number of times on the Zoom button to zoom out and bring the entire canvas back into view.

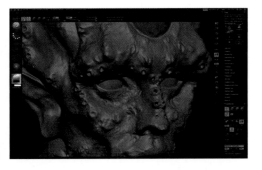

25 Your tool is already selected, so clicking and dragging the canvas will add the a new mesh to the canvas. Before you do anything else, enable the Edit button by clicking it. Then use the Move, Scale, and Rotate buttons to get your mesh looking exactly the way you want it on the canvas. When you're satisfied with everything, click the AAHalf button just below the Scroll, Zoom, and Actual buttons for navigating and viewing the canvas. Immediately, the screen will change considerably. Your display might not look exactly like what you see here, but the effect will be the same. Do not scale or rotate the mesh or mess with the Zoom button; the canvas is simply scaled down by 50%, and any areas that extend beyond the viewable area are still there. Just sit tight for a moment and leave things as they are.

 The AAHalf button

Pressing the AAHalf button in ZBrush will display your document at exactly half its size. When this AAHalf is enabled, ZBrush will antialias the image, smoothing any jagged edges. When you export an image with AAHalf enabled, it is reduced to half the size of the original. However, when you know that AAHalf will be employed at the export stage, before you begin you can simply create a document that is twice the size of what you require.

PART FOUR: Changing materials and exporting images

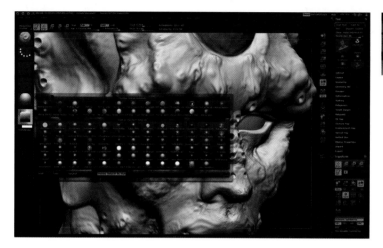

26 Click the Document button once again to reveal the Document palette. In the Document palette, click the Export button to export the canvas as an image file. Name the file Head Red and ensure that you export as a .psd file. We included the word *red* in the filename to refer to the material applied. We haven't talked about materials until now because we've been busy sculpting; the MatCap Red Wax material is the default material when you're working in ZBrush. Because we'll be compositing these images in Photoshop later, we want to have a number of duplicate images that employ different materials each time. Click the Material button to reveal all the included materials. Now select the MatCap White Cavity material. Export an image file after changing the material and name it White Cavity.psd.

Exporting a variety of resources

Creating a number of images with varying materials is as easy as simply changing a single variable and exporting repeatedly.

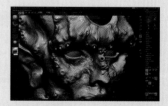

1 Now change the material to MatCap Pearl Cavity and export the image as a .psd named Head Pearl.psd. Next, select the MatCap Gorilla material and then export the image as Head Gorilla.psd.

2 Choose MatCap WedClay01 next, then export the image as Head Clay.psd. After that, choose the MatCap GreenRoma material and then export the image as Head Roma.psd.

3 For the next one, choose MatCap Skin004. Export the image as Head Skin.psd. Finally, for the last material, choose BasicMaterial2 and export the image as Head Basic.psd.

27 Zoom out a little by clicking and dragging upward on the Zoom button until you can see the entire canvas. At this point we'll create an image that we can place in an alpha channel, which will eventually become a selection in Photoshop. This will save us time isolating each figure from the background as we composite the images across a stack of layers. In the Document palette, set the Range to 0. Then select a black color from the color box at the left. After doing that, go back to the Document palette and click the Back button. This turns the entire background black. Select the Flat Color material and then select a white color from the color box to make the mesh appear as solid white against the black background. To export the image so that it lines up with the rest, you must first click the AAHalf button. Then export the image and save it as Head Channel.psd.

PART FIVE: Building the composition in Photoshop

28 Quit Zbrush and don't bother saving changes to the document when prompted. It doesn't really matter because we've saved the tool, and saving the document drops the mesh to the canvas anyway; so even if we did open the document later, the mesh wouldn't be editable in its current position on the canvas. Open the *background.jpg* file in Photoshop. This simple photograph will act as the initial backdrop for our figure. However, things are going to change considerably, and this simple image will form the basis for an immersive and textural environment for our creature to inhabit within the finished illustration.

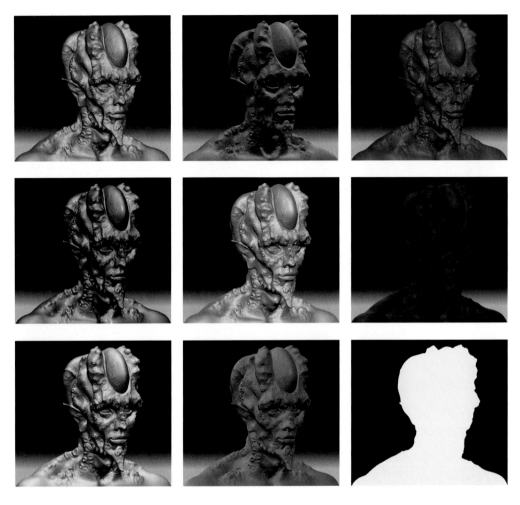

Here's a look at all the AAHalf rendered images that were exported from ZBrush. The first eight offer abundant variety due to the diverse materials that were applied to the mesh, whereas the last image will be used to create a common selection border. Some offer sharp highlights, some flat surfaces, some darker or lighter values overall, and some offer differences in terms of shadows. The important thing to note at this point is that diversity is a great asset for what we're going to do next. Each image will be used on layers, with blending modes chosen specifically to enhance unique traits. As the composition begins to build up across a multitude of layers, all the blending modes will work together to create something entirely new from the diverse individual components.

PART SIX: Create a textured background

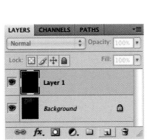
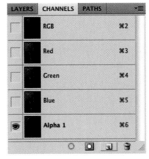

29 Open the *rusty.jpg* file. Use the Move tool to click the image and then drag it into the *background.jpg* file while holding down the Shift key. Holding down the Shift key will ensure accurate positioning and is something you'll need to keep on top of when I mention it as we progress through the chapter. The file will be added to the *background.jpg* file as a new layer. Change the blending mode to Luminosity. With the newly pasted layer targeted in the Layers palette, press Control-A (or Command-A) to select the contents of the entire layer and then press Control-C (or Command-C) to copy it. At the bottom of the Channels palette, click the Create New Channel button. Target the new channel in the Channels palette and press Control-V (or Command-V) to paste the copied image into the channel.

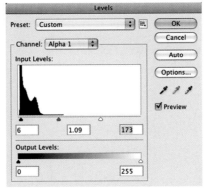
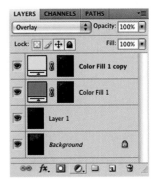

30 Press Control-L (or Command-L) to perform a Levels adjustment within the channel. Drag the Input Levels sliders to enhance the contrast as shown here. Control-click (or Command-click) the Channel thumbnail to load it as a selection and then return to the Layers palette. With the top layer targeted and the current selection active, create a new solid color layer by choosing the Solid Color option from the Create New Fill or Adjustment Layer menu at the bottom of the Layers palette. When the picker appears, choose a medium green color and click OK. Your new solid color layer will be automatically masked by the active selection. Change the blending mode of the layer to Overlay. Drag the solid color layer onto the Create New Layer button to duplicate it. Then, double-click the duplicate layer's thumbnail to access the picker. This time, choose a lighter green color and click OK.

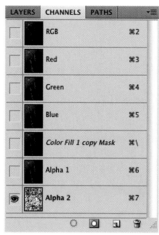
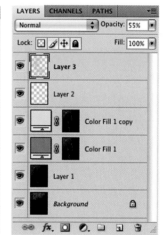

31 Open the *glass.jpg* file. Select all and copy. Create another new alpha channel in your working file and paste the copied glass image into it. Load the channel as a selection by Control-clicking (or Command-clicking) the channel's thumbnail. With the new selection active, click the Create A New Layer button at the bottom of the Layers palette to create a new layer at the top of the stack. Select the Gradient tool and choose the Foreground to Transparent gradient preset from the Gradient picker in the Tool Options bar. Select the Radial method and set the opacity to 100 in the Tool Options bar as well. Next, click the foreground color swatch to access the picker. Select a light green color and click OK. Click and drag within the active selection on the new layer to create a few large gradients on the new layer. Press Control-D (or Command-D) to deactivate the selection. Reduce the opacity of the layer if necessary.

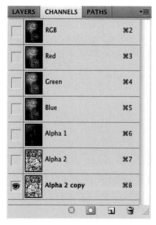
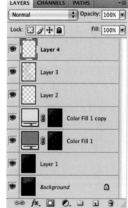

32 Go back to the Channels palette and drag the newest alpha channel onto the Create New Channel button to duplicate it. With the duplicate channel targeted, select Edit > Transform > Flip Horizontal from the menu. After flipping the channel, load it as a selection. With the selection active, create a new layer in the Layers palette. Ensure that you still have the Gradient tool selected with the previous preset and options in place. Choose a lighter green color from the picker and then create a few gradients within the selection on the new layer in the upper-left region of the canvas. When you're satisfied, deactivate the selection.

PART SEVEN: Stack up the exported images

33 Keep your working file open for the time being. We're going to abandon it for the next procedure. However, we'll return to it shortly. In any case, now is a good time to save what you've done so far. After saving your working file, open all the .psd files that you exported from ZBrush. If you skipped the part about working with ZBrush earlier in this chapter, these files are included among the downloadable project files. Begin with the *Head Red.psd* file; we'll use this image as the base of the stack, and this file will act as our head working file. Next, find the *Head Pearl.psd* file. Use the Move tool to click the Head Pearl image and drag it into the *Head Red.psd* while holding down the Shift key. Reduce the opacity of the new layer to 32%.

Continue building
Just keep dragging in different image files, varying the way they blend.

1 Now drag the image from the *Head Gorilla.psd* file into the head working file while holding down the Shift key. Change the layer blending mode to Color and reduce the opacity to 53%.

2 Again, Shift-drag the *Head Clay.psd* image file from its original file into the head working file as a new layer. Change the blending mode to Luminosity and reduce the opacity to 70%.

3 Next, drag the *Head Skin. psd* image into the head working file while holding down the Shift key. Change the blending mode to Overlay and reduce the opacity of the layer to 70% as well.

Viewing a mask

If you want to view any layer mask as a grayscale image on the canvas, simply Alt-click (or Option-click) the Mask thumbnail in the Layers palette. When you're finished viewing it and you want to see your image on the canvas once again, simply Alt-click (or Option-click) it again to hide it.

34 Duplicate the top layer and change the blending mode to Soft Light. Click the Add Layer Mask button at the bottom of the Layers palette to mask the duplicate layer and then target the new mask. Select the Gradient tool and select the Foreground to Transparent method in the Tool Options bar. Select the Radial method in the Tool Options bar as well and then press the x key to set the current foreground color to black. Click and drag within the mask to create few Black to Transparent Radial gradients. Create the gradients over the areas of his horn-like protrusion in the foreground as well as his raised cheek areas to lessen the shiny effect in those regions.

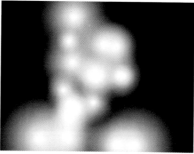

35 Duplicate Layer 2, which contains the *Head gorilla.psd* image, and then drag the duplicate to the top of the stack in the Layers palette. Change the blending mode of the layer to Multiply and reduce the opacity to 49%. Choose Layer > Layer Mask > Hide All to mask the layer, hiding it entirely for now. Select the Gradient tool and ensure that the mask is targeted in the Layers palette. Use the same Gradient tool settings you used previously, and if the foreground color is not currently white, press the D key. Create a series of White to Transparent, Radial gradients that cover most of the figure except for his chin, nose, lips, and horn at the right of the canvas. Here's a preview of how the mask looks at this stage.

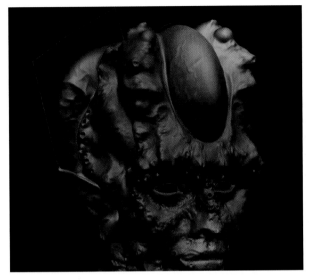

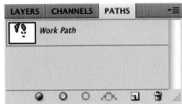

36 Select the Pen tool and ensure that it is set to create paths in the Tool Options bar and that the Subtract From Path Area operation is enabled. Carefully draw a path component that outlines a single eye, returning to your first point to close the path component. Then draw another around his other eye. Draw another around his teeth and yet another around the orb in his forehead. Finally, draw one carefully between the fleshy area at the back of his head and the raised region above his ear. For the rest of this path component, you can stray out onto the background; it won't matter later on. Control-click (or Command-click) anywhere on the canvas where there is no path component. This will temporarily change the Pen tool to the Direct Selection tool, and clicking will ensure that no single Path component is selected.

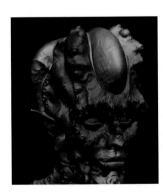

37 Ensure that the path itself is targeted in the Paths palette, yet no single path component within the path is selected. If the path is targeted, it will remain visible on the canvas. Return to the Layers palette and the top layer should still be targeted. If for any reason it is not, click it in the Layers palette. Once you're sure it is targeted, click the Add Vector Mask button at the bottom of the Layers palette. This will add a vector mask to the already masked layer, making use of the current path and hiding the regions of the layer that reside within your closed path components.

ⓘ Which mask am I adding?

When you target an unmasked layer and click the Add Layer Mask button at the bottom of the palette, it will automatically add a standard layer mask. However, if your layer already has a layer mask applied to it, this button then becomes the Add Vector Mask button. Clicking the Add Vector Mask button will, as it clearly states, add a vector mask to your layer. Now you can add a vector mask using this button without having a standard layer mask already applied to the layer. Simply hold down Control+Alt (or Command+Option) and click the button. This will add a vector mask to the layer.

 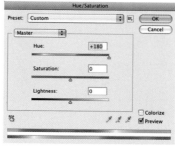 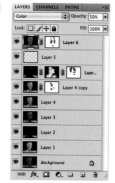

38 Now drag the *Head Roma.psd* into the head working file as a new layer. Remember to hold down the Shift key as you drag it with the Move tool. Press Control-U (or Command-U) to make a Hue/Saturation adjustment to this layer's contents. Drag the Hue slider to 180 and click OK. Change the blending mode of the layer to Color and reduce the opacity to 50%. Add a layer mask and then use the Gradient tool within the mask to hide certain regions of the layer. Create some Black to Transparent, Radial gradients within the mask over his cheeks, chin, and horn-like ridges.

 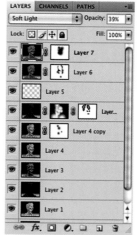 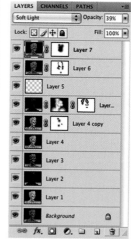

39 Drag another instance of the *Head Roma.psd* into the head working file as a new layer while holding down the Shift key. This time do not bother altering the hue of the layer. Change the blending mode to Soft Light and then reduce the opacity to 39%. Add a layer mask and use the methods employed previously to create a series of Black to Transparent, Radial gradients within the mask, focusing on the lower region of the orb and his nose. When you're finished, target the layer and not the mask in the Layers palette. Select all and copy. Then click the Create New Channel button in the Channels palette and paste the copied art into the new channel. After pasting, press Control-D (or Command-D) to deactivate the selection and then return to the Layers palette. Don't worry, we'll return to this new channel soon enough.

40 Make another duplicate of Layer 2—the layer that contains the *Head Gorilla.psd* artwork. Drag the duplicate layer to the top of the stack in the Layers palette and change the blending mode to Multiply. Reduce the opacity of the layer to 21% and select the Pen tool. Ensure that it is set to create paths and enable the Add to Path Area operation in the Tool Options bar. Carefully draw a closed path that meticulously traces the line between the figure's jawline and lower ear, dividing that area from the neck and shoulders. Then continue to draw the lower part of the path, covering the neck and shoulders and closing the path. Ensure that this path is targeted in the Paths palette and then Control+Alt-click (or Command+Option-click) the Add Layer Mask button to add a vector mask to the layer using the currently selected path.

41 Now click the Add Layer Mask button again to add a standard layer mask. Ensure that the mask is targeted in the Layers palette and select the Gradient tool. Use the same methods as before to create some Black to Transparent, Radial gradients within the mask. Concentrate on his neck area. Hold down the Control (or Command) key and click the Vector Mask thumbnail in the Layers palette to generate a selection from the layer mask. With the selection active, create a new layer and press the D key to set the foreground color to black. Then create some Radial, Black to Transparent gradients within this selection on the new layer. Concentrate on darkening his shoulders.

Hide/show the selection

If you find that the selection border is in your way as you're working, simply press Control-H (or Command-H) to hide it. It will still be there, but the marching ants will disappear. Typing the same keyboard command will make it reappear as well. This is one of those things I do so often that it feels like second nature as I work. I don't even think about it. I find that hiding the selection border allows me to better focus on the image.

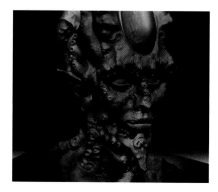

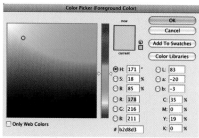

42 In the Channels palette, Control-click (or Command-click) the alpha channel you created previously to load it as a selection. Then create a new layer at the top of the stack in the Layers palette. With your new layer targeted, select the Brush tool and select a soft, round brush preset. Click the foreground swatch in the Toolbar to access the picker. Choose a very light greenish-blue color from the picker and click OK. Use varying sizes and also vary the brush opacity between 20% and 50% as you paint within the selection on the new layer. Focus on adding the light green color into areas such as the suction cups and other raised details of his face. Be careful not to overdo it.

Continue painting
Build up effects by painting within the same selection while varying color and layer blending methods.

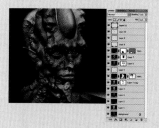

1 Keep the current selection active and create a new layer. Select a bluish-purple color from the picker and use the same brush to paint within the selection on the new layer. Set the opacity to 50% and build up strokes under his eyes, around his lips, and in the recessed areas of his cheeks and temples.

2 Change the blending mode to Color and then create another new layer while the current selection remains active. Ensure that the new layer is targeted, and select a very light green foreground color from the picker. Begin to paint over some of the raised areas of his face with the current brush settings. Also work on other regions, such as the inside of his ear.

3 Continue to paint in regions that require lightening. Remember to vary brush size and opacity as necessary. To enhance the effect of this layer, change the blending mode to screen and duplicate it. Reduce the opacity of the duplicate layer to 20% so that the effect is not overwhelming, and press Control-D (or Command-D) to deactivate the selection.

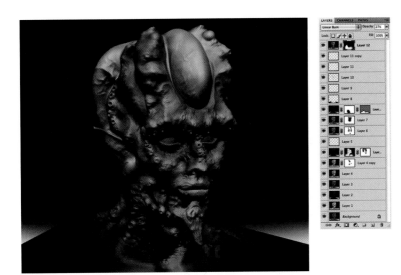

43 Use the Move tool to drag the *Head Basic.psd* image into the working file as a new layer while holding down the Shift key to ensure proper positioning. Change the layer's blending mode to Linear Burn and then reduce the opacity of the layer to 27%. Add a mask to the layer and use Radial, Black to Transparent gradients to mask almost all the layer content except for the area that covers his shoulders.

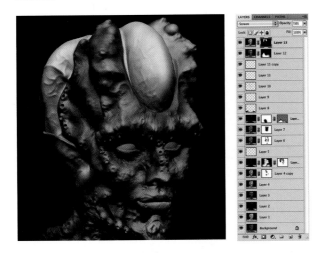

44 Next, use the Move tool to Shift-drag the *Head Cavity.psd* image into the head working file as a new layer. Change the blending mode of the layer to Screen and then reduce the opacity to 58%. Ensure that this new layer remains targeted while you Control-click (or Command-click) the Layer 2 copy layer's Vector Mask thumbnail to load it as a selection. Invert the selection by pressing Control-Shift-I (or Command-Shift-I). After the selection is inverted, click the Add Layer Mask button at the bottom of the Layers palette. This will mask all the areas on the layer that lie outside the selection border.

 Can't find Layer 2 copy?

You might have named your layer something different, and that is fine. You can easily find the layer referred to here because it contains the head with the gorilla material applied to it and it is the first layer to which you applied a vector mask.

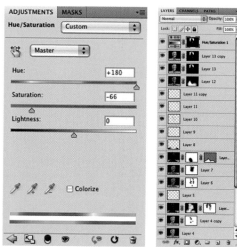

45 Duplicate the layer and change the blending mode to Overlay. Reduce the opacity of the duplicate layer to 23%. Control-click (or Command-click) the duplicate layer's Mask thumbnail in the Layers palette to load it as a selection. While the selection is active, choose the Hue/Saturation option from the Create New Fill or Adjustment Layer menu at the bottom of the Layers palette. In the Adjustments palette, adjust the hue to +180 and decrease the saturation by 66.

 Creating adjustment layers

You'll notice as you work through this book that I always tend to create new fill and adjustment layers by using the menu available at the bottom of the Layer palette. However, if the main menu appeals to you more, you can always create a new fill or adjustment layer via the New Fill Layer or New Adjustment Layer submenus within the Layer menu in the menu bar.

46 Control-click (or Command-click) the adjustment layer's mask to load it as a selection. Create a new layer and select the Gradient tool. Ensure that the Foreground to Transparent option is enabled and that the Radial method is selected in the Tool Options bar. Hold down the Alt (or Option) key to temporarily access the Eyedropper tool. Click in one of the lightest regions of the central orb of his forehead to set the foreground color to the color of that region. Ensure that the new layer is targeted and that the current selection is active. Click and drag within the selection border over each eye to create a couple of small radial gradients. Click from the eyelid down so that these gradients are strongest at the top each eye. Use this same method to create a few smaller gradients within the selection over his teeth on the new layer as well. Change the blending mode of the layer to Overlay.

 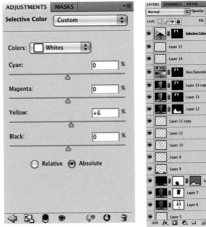

47 Create a new layer and then introduce a couple of smaller gradients into the active selection at the bottom of his eyes on the new layer. This will help make his eyes appear as though they are glowing. While the selection is still active, choose the Selective Color option from the Create New Fill or Adjustment Layer menu at the bottom of the Layers palette to create a Selective Color layer. In the Adjustments panel, choose whites from the Colors menu and increase the yellow content by 6.

Adding texture

Remedy the plastic feeling of this 3D model by adding a desktop scan as surface texture.

1 Open the *texture.jpg* file. Use the Move tool to drag it into the working file as a new layer while holding down the Shift key. Change the blending mode of this new layer to Soft Light.

2 Duplicate the layer and change the blending mode of the duplicate layer to Overlay. Reduce the opacity of the layer to 29% and add a layer mask. Use a soft, round brush and a black foreground color to paint over raised areas of the figure within the mask, thus hiding the texture in these areas. Vary brush size and opacity as necessary.

3 Duplicate this layer and change the blending mode to Color Dodge. Reduce the opacity of the layer to 10%. This will brighten the underlying image using unmasked areas of the layer. If certain areas seem too prominent or not prominent enough, feel free to edit the mask further.

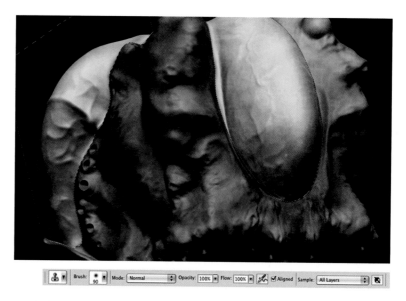

48 Load a selection from any of your masks that reveal only the head lobes, eyes, and teeth. This can be the Selective Color layer, the Hue/Saturation layer, or either of the two image layers that meet this requirement. Select the Clone Stamp tool and create a new layer. Ensure that the new layer is targeted and that the selection is currently active. In the Tool Options bar, choose All Layers from the Sample menu. Zoom in closely on the creature's head lobes and you'll see a few regions that need repairing before we go any further. Areas of concern are the bright area at the left of the frontal lobe and other bright areas where the back lobe meets the darker purple part of his head.

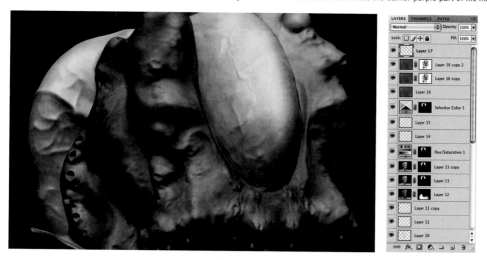

49 What you need to do now is find an area in need of repair and then Alt-click (or Option-click) in the neighboring area to sample it. Then paint over the area in need of repair with the newly sampled region. The best results will be achieved by sampling often and very close to areas in need of repair, since we'll as painting in small strokes. In some cases you'll be literally stamping instead of painting, merely clicking once instead of clicking and dragging. Use a soft round brush tip preset and vary the size as required. I recommend leaving the opacity set at 100 to ensure that the results do not appear too soft compared to the rest of the image. Deselect.

PART EIGHT: Putting the composition together

50 Hold down the Alt (or Option) key and double-click the background layer in the Layers palette to convert it to a standard layer. Target the new layer, which will be called Layer 0. Then hold down the Shift key and click the top layer in the Layers palette as well. This will target all the layers in the palette. Press Control-G (or Command-G) to group them. Next, find the *Head Channel.psd* file. Select all and copy. Return to your head working file and create a new channel in the Channels palette. Paste the copied art into the channel and then Control-click (or Command-click) the channel's thumbnail to load it as a selection. While the selection is active, target your new group in the Layers palette and click the Add Layer Mask button to mask the group.

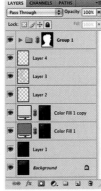

51 Now you should still have your working file open. Remember, the file that contained the multilayered background that we created in Part 5? I know that a lot has happened since then, so if you closed it, open it up again. Now, in the Layers palette, drag the group from your head working file into the working file that contains the background that you created previously. Move the group to the top of the stack in the Layers palette if necessary and use the Move tool to reposition the visible artwork on the canvas.

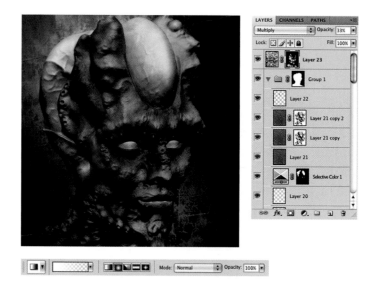

52 Load a selection from the alpha channel that contains the contents of the *glass.jpg* file that you created earlier. While the selection is active, create a new layer and set the foreground color to black by pressing the d key. Then press Alt-Delete (or Option-Delete) to fill the selection on the new layer with black. Deselect and change the blending mode of the layer to Multiply. Reduce the opacity of the layer to 33%. Now hold down the Alt (or Option) key and click the Add Layer Mask button at the bottom of the Layers palette to add a mask to the layer, which is completely filled with black, thus hiding the contents of the entire layer. Select the Gradient tool and set the current foreground color to white. Ensure that the Foreground to Transparent preset is selected and that the Radial method is chosen in the Tool Options bar. Click and drag within the mask to reveal sections of the layer.

 Renamed layers?

When you drag your group into the working file, take a look inside the group and you'll notice that the numbers within the names of your layers are increased. Don't worry, everything is fine. It is just that Photoshop CS4 is smart enough to find all layers that have not been named and then rename them sequentially. Only the names are affected; the layers themselves and the hierarchy do not change. Also, if you have done something differently along the way, such as skipping a layer or combining layers, your numbered layers will not match up exactly with those shown here. Again, don't fret, simply obey the spirit of this chapter and focus more on getting the techniques down so that your image resembles the one shown here.

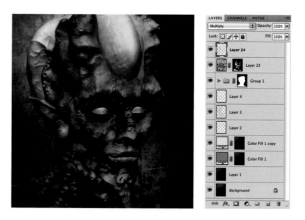

53 Create a new layer and change the blending mode of the layer to Multiply. Load the same channel as a selection once again. Select the Brush tool and then temporarily switch to the Eyedropper tool by holding down the Alt (or Option) key. Click an area of deep red or burgundy within the image to sample that color and then release the Alt (or Option) key. Use a large, soft, round brush tip and varying opacity settings as you paint within the selection, over regions of similar color to emphasize it.

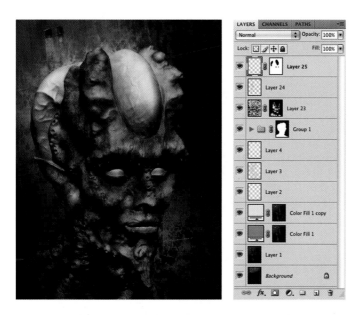

54 Click the foreground color swatch in the Toolbar to access the picker. Select a somewhat luminous light blue color and click OK. Invert your currently active selection and create a new layer. Paint with the same brush, albeit a lower opacity setting, within the inverted selection, over raised regions of the creature's head. This will help create the illusion of textured highlights. Deselect and expand the group that contains the head layers. Control-click (or Command-click) a Mask thumbnail that reveals just the head lobes, eyes, and teeth to load a selection from the mask. This could easily be the mask attached to the Selective Color layer or the Hue/Saturation layer. When the selection loads, hold down the Control-Alt-Shift (or Command-Option-Shift) keys while you click the Groups Mask thumbnail in the Layers palette. This will perform an intersection and chop away the area of your selection that lies outside his head. Hold down the Alt (or Option) key and click the Add Layer Mask button.

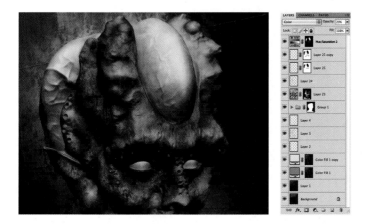

55 Duplicate the layer and change the blending mode of the duplicate layer to Soft Light. Load a selection from the layer's mask and then invert the selection. With the inverted selection active, create a new Hue/Saturation adjustment layer. In the Adjustments panel, enable the Colorize option. Then set the hue to 75 and the saturation to 74. Next, in the Layers palette, change the blending mode of the adjustment layer to Color and reduce the opacity to 29%.

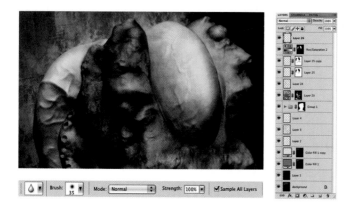

56 Select the Blur tool. Set the Strength to 100 and enable the Sample All Layers option in the Tool Options bar. Create a new layer and ensure that it is targeted in the Layers palette. Paint with the Blur tool over any areas that appear too harsh or sharp to soften them. This will help integrate the creature into the environment as well as make sure that areas such as his eyes and head lobes don't look like they were pasted on after the fact. Use a soft, round tip and vary the size as necessary. Also, feel free to use the Clone Stamp tool to perform any minor repairs you deem necessary on this layer. Think of this as the final repairs layer before we begin embellishing the image and adding texture overall.

PART NINE: Surface texture and embellishments

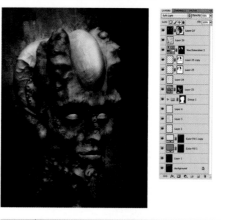

 Not-so-white highlights

You'll notice in nearly every instance where I create highlights that I never use solid white. I always use a light version of some sort of color. The reasoning for this is basic observation. In the real world, highlights are rarely pure white, so creating pure white highlights in an image just looks fake. The result is simply too harsh, and if you want to brighten highlights further, using color gives you room to continue; white does not.

57 Open the *wall.jpg* file. Select all and copy. Paste it into the working file as a new layer and change the blending mode of the layer to Soft Light. Reduce the opacity of the layer to 43% and then click the Add Layer Mask button to create an empty layer mask. Target the new mask in the Layers palette and select the Gradient tool. Set the foreground color to black. In the Tool Options bar, ensure that the Foreground to Transparent gradient preset is selected and the Radial method is selected. Create a number of gradients within the mask that hide the texture primarily over regions of the creature's face.

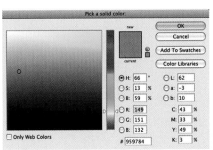

58 Target the new layer instead of the mask in the Layers palette. It is very important that you click the Layer thumbnail and not the Mask thumbnail for this to work properly. Once you have the layer targeted, select all and copy. Then, in the Channels palette, create a new alpha channel and paste the copied art into it. Load the channel as a selection and return to the Layers palette. While the selection is active, select the Solid Color option from the Create New Fill or Adjustment Layer menu at the bottom of the Layers palette to create a new, masked, solid color layer. When the picker appears, run the mouse pointer over a medium green color in the creature's frontal lobe and click OK.

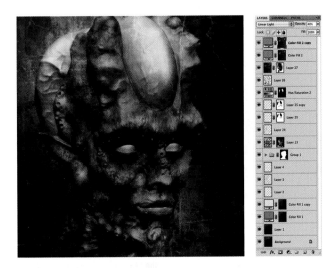

59 Change the blending mode of the new solid color layer to Linear Dodge (Add) and reduce the opacity to 40%. Duplicate the layer and then change the blending mode of the duplicate layer to Linear Light. This is an excellent method for building up surface texture to help unify the composition. However, the downfall of this method is that there might be regions where the texture appears too prominent. The best way to remedy this is to target each solid color layer's mask separately and introduce some Black to Transparent gradients into the existing masks, hiding regions that appear too strong.

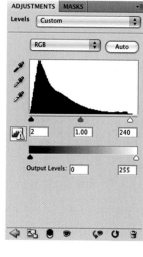

60 Now that we've added some texture, it is time to enhance the overall color and contrast. Create a new Hue/Saturation adjustment layer. In the Adjustments panel, simply increase the saturation by 12. Then create a Levels adjustment layer by choosing the levels option from the Create New Fill or Adjustment Layer menu as well. Simply drag the left and right input levels sliders inward a little, in the Adjustments panel, to increase the overall contrast slightly.

Where to go from here

Embellish the image further, employing the methods you've learned thus far.

a The raised regions could use some lighter areas at the highest points, to define them better. Try loading the glass channel as a selection again and then painting in within the selection in these areas on a new layer, using a very light color.

b Recessed regions could use a little more definition as well to enhance the volume of the creature. Try painting dark colors, at a low opacity on a new layer using a Linear Burn or Multiply blending mode. Gently build up darkness by overlaying strokes. Try working within a channel-based selection at times as well.

c Duplicate some of the texture layers and then mask out regions that cover the face. This will enhance the distress around the edges and, again, assist in unifying the composition.

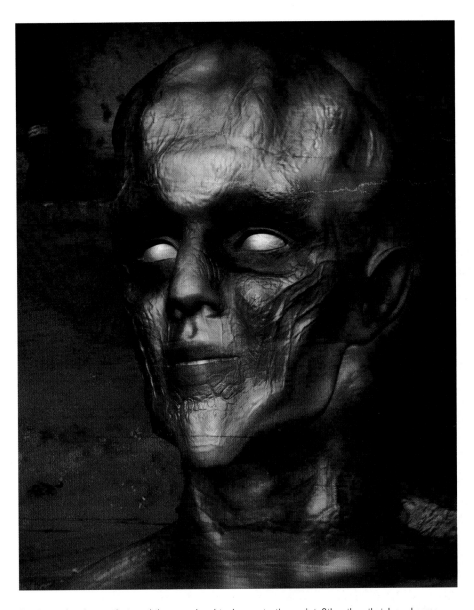

Here's another image that used the same head tool as a starting point. Other than that, I used some different alphas and a different approach to the sculpting process. After that, the same procedure was used in Photoshop to put it all together. The main difference here, apart from the figure itself, is the textures.